Better Homes and Gardens®

1988 BEST-RECIPES
YEARBOOK

ISSN: 8755-3090
ISBN: 0-696-02185-4

Better Homes and Gardens.

Our seal assures you that every recipe in the *1988 Best-Recipes Yearbook* has been tested in the Better Homes and Gardens® Test Kitchen. This means that each recipe is practical and reliable, and meets our high standards of taste appeal.

CONTENTS

JANUARY
Put Some Spice in Your Cooking ——— 6
What Makes Chili Chili? ——— 14

FEBRUARY
After-Work Cooking ——— 18

MARCH
Fast Family Favorites: Pasta! ——— 32
Fast Family Favorites: Quick-Cooking ——— 34
New Recipes that Will Change Your Life! ——— 35

APRIL
Fast Family Favorites: No-Chop Stir-Frys ——— 48
Microwave! Home-Style Cooking Now Faster, Easier ——— 50

MAY
Fast Family Favorites: Supper Salads ——— 64
The New Home Cooking! ——— 66

JUNE
Fast Family Favorites: Sandwiches! ——— 74
All-Out Cookouts ——— 76

JULY
Fast Family Favorites: Barbecue! ——— 88
Summer Cooking ——— 90
Fresh Fruit Desserts ——— 96

AUGUST
Fast Family Favorites: Microwave One-Dish Meals ——— 102
Summer Foods to Go! ——— 104

SEPTEMBER
Prize Tested Recipes®: 50 Winners from 50 Years ——— 114

OCTOBER
Fast Family Favorites: Pizza! ——— 138
Make-Ahead Cooking: 3 Breads and 3 Soups in 3 Hours ——— 140

NOVEMBER
Best of Season: Cranberries! ——— 148
An Elegant Thanksgiving Made Easy ——— 150
Picture-Perfect Pastry ——— 156

DECEMBER
Holiday Food for Busy, Busy Families ——— 164
Happy Hanukkah ——— 181
Mexican Fiesta! ——— 186
Super Sandwiches ——— 187

Every month, *Better Homes and Gardens®* magazine publishes hundreds of appetizing recipes and helpful ideas to satisfy your cooking needs. We have it all— quick and easy recipes if you're too busy to cook, nutritious recipes if you're thinking about your health, and creative new recipes if you're in the mood for something different. Rediscover our best recipes of 1987 through this exciting volume, our sixth annual recipe yearbook.

JANUARY

The Idea Magazine for American Families

January 1987 • $1.50

• SPECIAL REPORT •
WHAT'S NEW FOR FAMILIES IN '87–

Better Homes
and Gardens.

- DECORATING
- GARDENING
- HOUSING
- HEALTH
- MONEY
- FOOD
- CARS
- AND MORE

MASTER BEDROOM SUITES
3 Of The Best Designs
Plus **New Products
You Can Use
To Create Your
Own Suite**

AMISH DESIGN
COUNTRY QUILT
LESS THAN $50
MAKE IN A WEEKEND
See Page 33

FOOD•
**PUT SOME SPICE
IN YOUR COOKING!**
Plus Classic Regional
Chili Recipes

GARDENS•
SPRING PREVIEW
Our Picks For What
To Plant In '87

REMODELING•
**3 GREAT PLANS FOR
CORRIDOR KITCHENS**

DECORATING•
**WHERE TO PUT
YOUR TV/VIDEO
GEAR**

CRAFTS•
- **CREATIVE MACHINE-
STITCHERY PROJECTS**
- **QUICK-TO-KNIT
SWEATERS**

PUT SOME *SPICE* IN YOUR COOKING

By Terri Pauser Wolf

PEPPERS: Add the sweet peppers, banana peppers, and onions to the roux (a cooked flour-oil mixture) and simmer.

CAJUN-STYLE SEAFOOD STEW

Down in the bayou they love boldly seasoned food—

One pepper won't do the job! For gusto, this gumbo-like stew requires several pepper varieties—sweet peppers, banana peppers, black and red pepper, and hot pepper sauce. Don't forget the French bread to cool the fire and soak up the tasty broth.

JALAPEÑO PEPPERS: Wear gloves when seeding the peppers—they contain an oil that may irritate your skin.

GREEN CHILI ROUNDUPS

Stuffed peppers get a new twist as one-bite appetizers—

Looking for a unique nibble for your next party? Stuff jalapeño or serrano peppers with a creamy filling that'll keep your guests craving more. The peppery tingle comes from capsaicin (cap SAY uh sun) oil, found in the membranes of hot peppers.

A pinch here, a few dashes there and you're on your way to great-tasting, tongue-tingling food. Just follow our recipes and tips for using spices and seasonings to achieve the right zip for you.

MUSTARD-GLAZED PORK CHOPS

Mustard isn't just for hot dogs!

Not all mustards are created equal. The spice level depends on the plant from which the seed came. The brown mustard seed in this main dish has a bite similar to horseradish. For a fire-breathing hotness, use hot oriental dry mustard.

MUSTARD SEED: Crush the brown mustard seed before adding it to the cooked apricot mixture.

CUMIN-SPIKED ACORN SQUASH

Use nutty-flavored cumin for a side dish with flair—

The popular spice in southwestern cooking, cumin has a hot and pungent flavor. You've probably tasted it in many dishes because cumin is the main ingredient in chili powder. Try it American-style in this savory, stuffed acorn squash.

CUMIN: To release the flavor in cumin seeds, grind them using a mortar and pestle. Or, purchase ground cumin.

PUT SOME SPICE IN YOUR COOKING

GINGERROOT: No need to peel gingerroot before slicing. For matchstick pieces cut the slices into thin strips.

GINGERED TURKEY STIR-FRY

A Chinese cook without fresh gingerroot? Never!

Try more than a few tea-spoons of shredded ginger-root in your stir-fry. Go all out and use tablespoons of matchstick-size pieces for a sweet, fresh ginger taste. Choose the freshest pieces of gingerroot; they'll be firm with a thin, tight skin.

PEPPERCORNS: Heating the Szechwan peppercorns be-fore grinding releases even more of their essence.

SZECHWAN PORK ROAST

Wow your guests with this company-special entrée—

The Szechwan region of southwestern China is known for its kicky food, but Szechwan peppercorn is a surprise with an aromatic rather than a biting spice level. It was so prized centu-ries ago that it was given as tokens of affection in China.

RED-PEPPER
TWO-GRAIN SALAD

Pair this piquant salad with grilled meat or chicken—

For foods with pizzazz reach for the chili oil (sesame oil infused with red pepper). This couscous-bulgur salad relies on the oil and extra crushed red pepper for its lively character. You can purchase chili oil or make your own.

CHILI OIL: A snap to make! Just heat crushed red pepper and sesame oil and let stand overnight, then strain the oil.

GARLIC-SPINACH DIP

A few cloves of garlic may be fine but 10 are even better!

Ten cloves of garlic! Yes, for a real garlic dip. Go ahead, put a scoop of this cheese-topped dip on home-baked crackers for a zesty appetizer treat. Too peppy? Cut back on the number of cloves or use elephant garlic (it has a milder taste).
Buying information, page 94.

GARLIC: The finer you chop garlic, the stronger the flavor. Let the food processor or blender do the work for you.

ONE RECIPE—*FOUR* INTERNATIONAL FLAVOR CHOICES

GARAM MASALA | CHILI | CURRY | CAJUN

STUFFED MANICOTTI

Top with extra cheese—
- 12 manicotti shells
- 1 pound ground beef *or* pork
- 1 cup frozen peas
- 1 cup chopped walnuts
- 1 2-ounce jar sliced pimiento, drained and chopped
- 1 recipe Spiced Cheese Sauce (see recipe at right)

Cook manicotti following package directions. Drain. Rinse in cold water; drain. In skillet brown meat. Drain off fat. Stir in peas, nuts, pimiento, and *1 cup* of the sauce. Stuff *each* manicotti with about ¼ *cup* meat mixture. Arrange manicotti in a 13x9x2-inch baking dish. Pour remaining sauce over all. Bake, covered, in a 350° oven 30 minutes or till heated through. Serves 6.

Nutrition information per serving: 635 cal., 30 g pro., 43 g carbo., 38 g fat, 81 mg chol., 323 mg sodium.

— FLAVOR CHOICES —

Choose one of four international spice blends to make Stuffed Manicotti. Use a homemade or purchased spice blend.

▶ **Garam Masala:** A staple in Indian cooking made from coriander, cinnamon, pepper, cloves, cumin, and cardamom.

▶ **Chili Powder:** The homemade blend of hot peppers, cumin, garlic, coriander, oregano, and cloves is more potent than purchased.

▶ **Curry Powder:** A mixture of turmeric, black peppercorns, ginger, cumin, crushed red pepper, cardamom seed, cinnamon, and cloves.

▶ **Cajun Seasoning:** Cajuns use a pepper trio for seasoning because the black pepper gives the aromatic flavor, the white gives the bite, and the red gives the burn.

SPICED CHEESE SAUCE

Try a different spice blend each time—
- ½ cup chopped onion
- 1 clove garlic, minced
- 4 to 5 teaspoons desired spice blend: cajun seasoning, curry powder, garam masala, *or* chili powder
- 3 tablespoons margarine *or* butter
- 3 tablespoons all-purpose flour
- 2¼ cups milk
- 1½ teaspoons instant chicken bouillon granules
- 1 cup shredded Swiss cheese

In a small saucepan cook the onion, garlic, and desired spice blend in margarine or butter till onion is tender. Blend in flour; add milk and bouillon granules. Cook and stir till mixture is thickened and bubbly. Cook 1 minute more. Add cheese, stirring till melted. Remove from heat. Makes 2⅔ cups.

HOMEMADE CURRY POWDER

Homemade curry powder has its own unique flavor. Make some for a gift—

4½ teaspoons ground coriander
2 teaspoons ground turmeric
1¼ teaspoons cumin seed
½ to 1 teaspoon whole black peppercorns
½ to 1 teaspoon crushed red pepper
½ teaspoon whole cardamom seed (without pods)
½ inch stick cinnamon
¼ teaspoon whole cloves
¼ teaspoon ground ginger

In a blender container place coriander, turmeric, cumin seed, peppercorns, red pepper, cardamom seed, cinnamon, cloves, and ginger. Cover and blend for 1 to 2 minutes or till a fine powder.

Store spice mixture in an airtight container in a cool, dry place. Makes about ¼ cup curry powder.

HOMEMADE GARAM MASALA

A versatile roasted seasoning in northern Indian cooking—

2 tablespoons whole black peppercorns
4 teaspoons cumin seed
1 tablespoon coriander seed
2 teaspoons whole cloves
1 teaspoon whole cardamom seed (without pods)
3 inches stick cinnamon, broken in half

To roast the spices, place peppercorns, cumin seed, coriander seed, cloves, cardamom seed, and cinnamon in an 8x8x2-inch baking pan. Heat in a 300° oven for 15 minutes. Cool.

In a blender container place roasted spices; cover and blend to a fine powder. Store in an airtight container in a cool, dry place. Makes about ⅓ cup.

Note: To make *Homemade Garam Masala* from ground spices, mix 1 tablespoon ground *cumin,* 1 tablespoon ground *coriander,* 2 teaspoons black *pepper,* 2 teaspoons ground *cardamom,* 1 teaspoon ground *cinnamon,* and 1 teaspoon ground *cloves.* Makes about ¼ cup garam masala.

HOMEMADE CHILI POWDER

4 dried hot chili peppers
3 dried ancho peppers
4 teaspoons cumin seed
1 teaspoon garlic powder
1 teaspoon ground coriander
1 teaspoon dried oregano
½ teaspoon whole cloves

See instructions on *page 16* for handling chili peppers. Wearing gloves, remove the stems and seeds from chili peppers. Cut peppers into small pieces.

In a blender container combine cut-up peppers, cumin seed, garlic powder, coriander, oregano, and cloves. Cover and blend to a fine powder.

Store in an airtight container in a cool, dry place. Makes about ⅓ cup.

HOMEMADE CAJUN SEASONING

1 teaspoon white pepper
1 teaspoon garlic powder
1 teaspoon onion powder
1 teaspoon ground red pepper
1 teaspoon paprika
1 teaspoon black pepper

In a small mixing bowl combine white pepper, garlic powder, onion powder, red pepper, paprika, and black pepper.

Store in an airtight container in a cool, dry place. Makes 2 tablespoons.

CAJUN-STYLE SEAFOOD STEW

1 pound fresh *or* frozen fish fillets (cod, cusk, *or* monkfish)
½ pound fresh *or* frozen peeled and deveined shrimp
⅓ cup all-purpose flour
⅓ cup cooking oil
2 large onions, sliced and separated into rings
2 large red *or* green sweet peppers, coarsely chopped
3 banana peppers, seeded and sliced crosswise
2 cloves garlic, minced
½ teaspoon salt
½ teaspoon ground red pepper
¼ teaspoon black pepper
Several dashes hot pepper sauce
2½ cups fish stock *or* chicken broth
2 sweet potatoes, peeled and sliced (about 1 pound)
1 teaspoon filé powder
Hot cooked rice (optional)

Thaw fish and shrimp if frozen. In a Dutch oven stir together flour and cooking oil. Cook over medium-high heat for 5 minutes, stirring constantly. Reduce heat to medium. Cook and stir constantly for 15 to 20 minutes more or till a reddish-brown roux is formed.

Stir in onions, peppers, garlic, salt, red pepper, black pepper, and pepper sauce. Slowly stir stock into roux. Bring to boiling; reduce heat. Cover and simmer for 10 minutes. Add potatoes; simmer, covered, for 10 minutes more. Add the fish and shrimp. Simmer, covered, about 5 minutes or till shrimp turn pink and fish flakes easily. Remove from heat. Stir in filé. Ladle over rice. Makes 6 servings.

Nutrition information per serving: 340 cal., 25 g pro., 28 g carbo., 14 g fat, 75 mg chol., 608 mg sodium. U.S. RDA: 292% vit. A, 157% vit. C, 13% thiamine, 13% riboflavin, 20% niacin, 15% iron, 29% phosphorus.

GREEN CHILI ROUNDUPS

20 fresh green chili peppers
1 3-ounce package cream cheese with chives, softened
¼ cup finely chopped, thinly sliced smoked beef
2 tablespoons chopped pecans, toasted
¼ teaspoon dried basil, crushed
1 red sweet pepper (optional)
Fresh basil leaves (optional)

See information on *page 16* for handling chili peppers. Wearing gloves, remove tops and hollow out seeds from chili peppers. Cook peppers in enough boiling water to cover for 3 to 5 minutes or till tender; drain. Let peppers cool.

Combine cream cheese, smoked beef, pecans, and the ¼ teaspoon basil. Wearing gloves, fill each pepper with *1 to 2 teaspoons* of the cheese mixture. Cut each stuffed pepper crosswise into ½-inch pieces. Cover and chill.

Remove top, seeds, and veins from red pepper; slice crosswise into rings. Serve chili roundups over pepper rings. Garnish with basil. Makes about 64.

Nutrition information per roundup: 8 cal., 0 g pro., 0 g carbo., 1 g fat, 2 mg chol., 96 mg sodium.

MUSTARD-GLAZED PORK CHOPS

If you want a hot, spicy mustard flavor, use the oriental mustard option—

  4 pork loin chops, cut ¾ inch thick
  1 pound whole tiny new potatoes, sliced ¼ inch thick
  ¼ cup snipped dried apricots
  2 tablespoons brown sugar
  2 tablespoons vinegar
  1 green onion, sliced
  1 teaspoon instant chicken bouillon granules
  ¼ teaspoon ground turmeric
  2 tablespoons brown mustard seed, coarsely crushed, *or* 1 teaspoon hot oriental dry mustard
  1 tablespoon cornstarch

Preheat broiler. Trim excess fat from chops. Place chops on unheated rack of a broiler pan. Broil chops 3 to 4 inches from heat for 20 to 25 minutes or till no pink remains, turning once halfway through cooking time.

Meanwhile, place sliced potatoes in a steamer basket; season to taste with salt and pepper. Place over boiling water. Cover and steam for 10 to 12 minutes or till tender.

For mustard glaze, in a 1-quart saucepan combine apricots, brown sugar, vinegar, green onion, bouillon granules, turmeric and ½ cup *water*. Bring to boiling; reduce heat. Cover and simmer for 5 to 10 minutes or till apricots are tender.

If using oriental dry mustard, in a small bowl stir together mustard and 1 teaspoon *water;* set aside.

In a small mixing bowl stir together cornstarch and ½ cup *cold water*. Stir in crushed brown mustard seed or oriental mustard mixture. Stir cornstarch mixture into apricot mixture. Cook and stir till thickened and bubbly. Cook and stir for 2 minutes more.

To serve, arrange sliced cooked potatoes on individual serving plates; top each with a pork chop. Spoon mustard glaze over each chop. Makes 4 servings.

Nutrition information per serving: 388 cal., 29 g pro., 36 g carbo., 14 g fat, 80 mg chol., 160 mg sodium. U.S. RDA: 12% vit. A, 26% vit. C, 59% thiamine, 20% riboflavin, 34% niacin, 15% iron, 33% phosphorus.

CUMIN-SPIKED ACORN SQUASH

  2 medium-large acorn squash (1¼ to 1½ pounds each)
  1½ cups sliced celery
  ¼ cup chopped onion
  1 4-ounce can diced green chili peppers, drained
  1 tablespoon cumin seed, ground, *or* 1 tablespoon ground cumin
  ½ teaspoon garlic salt
  ⅛ teaspoon pepper
  2 tablespoons margarine *or* butter
  1 10-ounce package frozen whole kernel corn, thawed
  2 tablespoons sunflower nuts
Whole pimiento, cut into diamonds (optional)

Halve and seed squash. Place squash, cut side down, in a shallow baking pan. Bake in a 350° oven for 30 minutes. Turn and sprinkle with salt. Bake 20 to 30 minutes more or till tender. Cool slightly. Scoop out squash pulp, leaving a ¼- to ½-inch-thick shell. Place pulp in a medium mixing bowl; mash.

Meanwhile, in a saucepan cook celery, onion, chili peppers, cumin, garlic salt, and pepper in hot margarine till onion is tender but not brown; set aside.

Stir celery mixture, corn, and sunflower nuts into the mashed pulp. Fill shells and return to the baking pan. Bake for 25 to 30 minutes more or till heated through. Garnish with pimiento, if desired. Makes 4 servings.

Microwave directions: *Do not* halve squash. Prick in several places with a long-tined fork. Place squash in a 12x7½x2-inch microwave-safe baking dish. Micro-cook, uncovered, on 100% power (high) for 9 to 12 minutes or till tender, rearranging after 3 and 7 minutes. Let stand 5 minutes. Cut in half; remove seeds. Sprinkle with salt. Cool slightly. Scoop out cooked pulp, leaving a ¼- to ½-inch-thick shell. Place pulp in a mixing bowl and mash.

Meanwhile, in a 1-quart microwave-safe casserole cook celery, onion, chili peppers, cumin, garlic salt, and pepper in margarine, covered, on high for 3 to 4 minutes or till vegetables are tender. Prepare stuffing as directed. Bake conventionally as above.

Nutrition information per serving: 232 cal., 5 g pro., 42 g carbo., 8 g fat, 0 mg chol., 384 mg sodium. U.S. RDA: 27% vit. A, 93% vit. C, 30% thiamine, 15% niacin, 11% calcium, 19% iron, 16% phosphorus.

GINGERED TURKEY STIR-FRY

  1 pound boneless turkey breast tenderloin steaks
  4 teaspoons cornstarch
  1 tablespoon sugar
  ¼ teaspoon dry mustard
  ⅔ cup chicken broth
  3 tablespoons soy sauce
  2 tablespoons dry sherry
  2 cups small cauliflower flowerets
  1 tablespoon cooking oil
  6 green onions, bias sliced
  ¼ cup gingerroot (1½ ounces) cut into julienne pieces
  1 apple, cored and cut into thin wedges
  3 medium zucchini, shredded

Cut turkey steaks into bite-size strips. For sauce, combine cornstarch, sugar, and dry mustard. Stir in broth, soy sauce, and dry sherry; set aside.

In a large skillet with a bamboo steamer (or a steamer basket in a large saucepan), steam cauliflower for 8 to 10 minutes or till crisp-tender.

Meanwhile, preheat a wok or large skillet over high heat; add cooking oil. (Add more oil as necessary during cooking.) Stir-fry onions and gingerroot for 1 minute. Remove from wok.

Add *half* of the turkey to the hot wok. Stir-fry for 3 to 4 minutes or till turkey is no longer pink. Remove turkey. Stir-fry remaining turkey. Return all turkey to wok. Push from center.

Stir sherry mixture; add to center of wok. Cook and stir till thickened and bubbly. Stir in cauliflower, onion mixture, and apple; heat through.

Place zucchini in the steamer and steam for 1 minute. Serve turkey mixture over zucchini. Makes 4 servings.

Microwave directions: In a 1-quart microwave-safe casserole combine the cauliflower and 2 tablespoons *water*. Micro-cook, covered, on 100% power (high) for 4 to 5 minutes or till crisp-tender, stirring once. Drain. Use as directed above.

In a 1-quart microwave-safe casserole combine the zucchini and 2 tablespoons *water*. Cook, covered, on high for 3½ minutes or till tender. Drain. Use as directed above.

Nutrition information per serving: 309 cal., 33 g pro., 21 g carbo., 11 g fat, 60 mg chol., 1,950 mg sodium. U.S. RDA: 56% vit. C, 11% thiamine, 14% riboflavin, 61% niacin, 11% iron, and 40% phosphorus.

SZECHWAN PORK ROAST

1   3- to 3½-pound boneless pork
    top loin roast (double loin, tied)
2   to 3 tablespoons Szechwan
    peppercorns
1   teaspoon coriander seed
¼   cup dry sherry
¼   cup soy sauce
1   cup brown rice
1   tablespoon cooking oil
½   to 1 teaspoon chili paste *or* hot
    chili sauce
2   4-ounce cans sliced mushrooms,
    drained
2   tablespoons snipped parsley
½   cup chicken broth
Cooked pea pods (optional)

Untie roast. Trim excess fat. Pierce in several places with a long-tined fork. Place in a plastic bag in a shallow dish.

For marinade, cook and stir peppercorns over low heat for 4 to 5 minutes or till toasted. Cool slightly. In a blender container blend peppercorns and coriander till coarsely ground. Using a fine sieve, remove peppercorn husks and coriander hulls. Combine peppercorn mixture, sherry, and soy. Pour over roast in bag. Close bag. Marinate in refrigerator 6 hours or overnight, turning several times.

Meanwhile, for stuffing, in a 2-quart saucepan cook and stir rice in hot oil over medium heat for 4 to 6 minutes or till just brown. Cool slightly. Stir in 2 cups *water* and chili paste. Bring to boiling; reduce heat. Cover; simmer 30 to 40 minutes or till water is absorbed. Cool to room temperature. Stir in the mushrooms and parsley.

Drain roast, reserving marinade. Pat with paper towels. Spoon about *2 cups* of the stuffing into the center of roast. Retie roast. Place roast, fat side up, on a rack in a roasting pan. Insert a meat thermometer in the center. Place remaining stuffing in a 1-quart casserole; stir in chicken broth.

Roast meat, uncovered, in a 325° oven 2½ to 3 hours or till thermometer registers 170°. Brush occasionally with reserved marinade. Bake remaining stuffing, covered, the last 30 to 40 minutes. To serve, slice ¼ inch thick. Serve on pea pods, if desired. Serves 10 to 12.

Nutrition information per serving: 281 cal., 24 g pro., 16 g carbo., 13 g fat, 70 mg chol., 261 mg sodium. U.S. RDA: 49% thiamine, 15% riboflavin, 26% niacin, 26% phosphorus.

RED-PEPPER TWO-GRAIN SALAD

2   cups water
½   cup bulgur
½   cup couscous
1   medium carrot, shredded
½   cup sliced pitted ripe olives
4   green onions, sliced
¼   cup olive *or* salad oil
½   teaspoon finely shredded lime
    peel
¼   cup lime juice
2   teaspoons sugar
2   teaspoons crushed red pepper
1   teaspoon Red Chili Oil (see
    recipe below) *or* purchased
    chili oil
¼   teaspoon salt
Lettuce leaves (optional)
Lime wedges (optional)
Breadsticks (optional)

In a medium saucepan combine water and bulgur. Bring to boiling; reduce heat. Cover and simmer for 10 to 15 minutes or till bulgur is almost tender. Remove from heat; stir in the couscous. Let mixture stand, covered, for 5 minutes. Drain in a sieve. Rinse with cold water. Drain again. In a 1½-quart bowl stir together bulgur mixture, carrot, olives, and green onions; set aside.

For dressing, in a screw-top jar combine olive or salad oil, lime peel, lime juice, sugar, red pepper, Red Chili Oil, and salt. Cover and shake well. Pour over bulgur mixture; toss to coat. Cover and chill at least 2 hours.

To serve, spoon mixture onto individual lettuce-lined plates. Serve with lime wedges and breadsticks, if desired. Makes 4 to 6 side-dish servings.

Nutrition information per serving: 296 cal., 4 g pro., 32 g carbo., 18 g fat, 0 mg chol., 279 mg sodium. U.S. RDA: 109% vit. A, 10% vit. C.

RED CHILI OIL

½   cup sesame *or* cooking oil
⅓   cup crushed red pepper

In a saucepan heat oil till warm (200°). Remove from heat. Stir in crushed red pepper. Cover and let stand several hours or overnight. In a cheesecloth-lined strainer, strain mixture, pressing out oil with back of a spoon. Store, covered, up to 1 month in the refrigerator. Makes about ⅓ cup oil.

GARLIC-SPINACH DIP

10   cloves garlic *or* 1 large clove
    elephant garlic *or* 2 tablespoons
    purchased minced garlic
1   10¾-ounce can condensed
    creamy spinach soup
1   8-ounce carton dairy sour cream
2   tablespoons all-purpose flour
1   cup shredded Monterey Jack
    cheese (4 ounces)
1   recipe Festive Onion Crackers
    (see recipe, below)
Radish slices (optional)
Lettuce leaves (optional)

For garlic cloves, place in a food processor or blender container; cover and process 5 seconds or till minced. Blend or stir together minced garlic, soup, sour cream, and flour. Spoon into an 9-inch pie plate. Bake in a 375° oven about 15 minutes or till heated through. Top with cheese. Heat 3 to 5 minutes more or till cheese is melted. Serve with Festive Onion Crackers. Garnish with radish slices and lettuce. Makes 2¼ cups.

Nutrition information per tablespoon: 35 cal., 1 g pro., 2 g carbo., 3 g fat, 6 mg chol., 71 mg sodium.

FESTIVE ONION CRACKERS

1   cup all-purpose flour
¾   cup whole wheat flour
¼   teaspoon baking soda
2   tablespoons very finely chopped
    onion
½   cup plain yogurt
¼   cup mayonnaise *or* salad
    dressing
1   tablespoon honey

In a mixing bowl combine flours, baking soda, and a dash *salt*. Stir in onion. Combine yogurt, mayonnaise, and honey. Add yogurt mixture to flour mixture; stir till coarse crumbs form. Knead in bowl, if necessary, to mix.

Shape dough into 10 balls. On one end of a lightly greased baking sheet roll 1 ball of dough into a 6-inch circle (about 1/16 inch thick). Prick with fork. Repeat with a second ball of dough. Bake in a 350° oven for 10 to 12 minutes. Cool on a wire rack. Repeat with remaining dough. Makes 10 crackers.

Nutrition information per cracker: 130 cal., 3 g pro., 19 g carbo., 5 g fat, 4 mg chol., 81 mg sodium.

WHAT MAKES CHILI
CHILI?
IT DEPENDS...

By Joy Taylor and Terri Pauser Wolf

Visit any diner and you'll find chili listed on the menu. But just as the landscape and folklore change across the country, so goes the chili. With beans? Over noodles? No matter what the ingredients, all chili tastes delicious!

IDAHO CHILI

HAWAIIAN CHILI

NO MEAT! Here's the newest chili to hit the scene. Folks in the lentil-growing region of Idaho first created this meatless dish to show off their tasty legume. Now, they often combine lentils with another prized crop, potatoes. Top off this spoon chili with sour cream—a delicious way to top off *any* chili, in fact.

OVER RICE! Islanders prefer their chili on the mild side. Spoon the ground meat and kidney bean combo over generous mounds of hot cooked rice. Sprinkle crunchy chow mein noodles over and serve with chilled fresh fruit.

Ready to dig in? Challenge yourself to chopstick chili eating!

TEXAS CHILI

EXTRA HOT! A bowl of red, a scoop of beans, and never the twain shall meet! Texans insist on keeping the beans (pinto beans in this case) out of the chili pot, and ALWAYS serve them separately. Eat with caution—the meat is seasoned with hot peppers. Pass Texas toast to cut the burn.

CINCINNATI CHILI

FIVE LAYERS! Top noodles with the unique tomato sauce that has a hint of semisweet chocolate and sweet spices. Now add three more layers: kidney beans, chopped onions, and shredded cheese—lots of cheese. Stay in step with Cincinnatians and serve this famous chili on an oval dish.

Tips for Handling Chili Peppers: Because chili peppers contain volatile oils that can burn the skin and eyes, avoid direct skin contact with the peppers. Wear plastic or rubber gloves or work under cold running water. If your bare hands touch the chili peppers, wash your hands and nails with soap and water, and do not touch your eyes.

CINCINNATI CHILI

    2 pounds ground beef
    3 large onions, chopped (3 cups)
    3 cloves garlic, minced
    1 15-ounce can tomato sauce
    1 cup beef broth
    2 tablespoons chili powder
    2 tablespoons semisweet
       chocolate pieces
    2 tablespoons vinegar
    2 tablespoons honey
    1 tablespoon pumpkin pie spice
    1 teaspoon salt
    1 teaspoon ground cumin
    ½ teaspoon ground cardamom
    ¼ teaspoon ground cloves
   16 ounces fettuccine, broken into
       4-inch lengths
    2 15½-ounce cans kidney beans
    4 cups shredded American cheese
       (1 pound)

In 4½-quart Dutch oven cook beef, *2 cups* of the onion, and garlic till beef is brown and onion is tender. Drain fat. Stir in remaining ingredients *except* fettuccine, beans, and cheese. Bring to boiling; reduce heat. Cover; simmer over low heat for 1 hour. Skim off fat.

Cook fettuccine according to package directions. Drain and keep warm. In a 2-quart saucepan heat kidney beans; drain and keep warm.

To serve, divide fettuccine among 8 plates. Make indentations in centers. Top with meat sauce, beans, remaining chopped onion, and shredded cheese. Makes 8 main-dish servings.

Nutrition information per serving: 833 cal., 48 g pro., 78 g carbo., 37 g fat, 130 mg chol., 1,562 mg sodium. U.S. RDA: 32% vit. A, 16% vit. C, 48% thiamine, 40% riboflavin, 48% niacin, 45% calcium, 43% iron, 84% phosphorus.

IDAHO CHILI

    1 32-ounce can tomato juice
    2 cups water
    2 medium potatoes, peeled and
       chopped (2 cups)
    1 15-ounce can garbanzo beans,
       undrained
    1 cup lentils, rinsed and drained
    1 large onion, chopped (1 cup)
    2 carrots, cut into 1-inch julienne
       strips (1 cup)
    2 tablespoons chili powder
    2 teaspoons instant beef bouillon
       granules
    1 teaspoon dried basil, crushed
    ½ teaspoon garlic powder
   Dairy sour cream

In a Dutch oven combine all ingredients *except* sour cream. Bring to boiling; reduce heat. Simmer, covered, 30 minutes. Top with sour cream. Sprinkle with sliced *green onion* and serve with *tortilla chips,* if desired. Serves 6 to 8.

Nutrition information per serving with 2 tablespoons sour cream: 341 cal., 15 g pro., 55 g carbo., 9 g fat, 13 mg chol., 1,045 mg sodium. U.S. RDA: 177% vit. A, 58% vit. C, 20% thiamine, 14% riboflavin, 16% niacin, 33% iron, 27% phosphorus.

HAWAIIAN CHILI

    1 pound ground pork *or* beef
    1 15½-ounce can red kidney
       beans, drained
    1 14½-ounce can tomatoes, cut up
       and undrained
    1 8-ounce can tomato sauce
    2 tablespoons soy sauce
    1 tablespoon chili powder
    1 teaspoon dried minced onion
    ¼ teaspoon garlic powder
   Several dashes hot pepper sauce
   Hot cooked rice

In a 3-quart saucepan cook meat till brown. Drain fat. Stir in remaining ingredients *except* rice. Bring to boiling; reduce heat. Cover; simmer 20 minutes. Spoon over rice. If desired, serve with *chow mein noodles, pineapple,* and/or *grapes.* Makes 4 main-dish servings.

Nutrition information per serving: 466 cal., 35 g pro., 51 g carbo., 14 g fat, 80 mg chol., 1,104 mg sodium. U.S. RDA: 36% vit. A, 41% vit. C, 69% thiamine, 24% riboflavin, 39% niacin, 27% iron, 42% phosphorus.

TEXAS CHILI

    4 dried ancho peppers
   2½ pounds beef chuck steak, cut
       into ¼-inch cubes
    3 tablespoons cooking oil
    1 large onion, chopped
    1 tablespoon crushed red pepper
    2 cloves garlic, minced
   1½ teaspoons ground cumin
    1 14½-ounce can beef broth
    1 12-ounce can beer
    ¼ teaspoon salt
    1 recipe Texas Pinto Beans
   Texas toast (optional)
   Cilantro (optional)
   Fresh red and yellow chili peppers
       (optional)

Wearing gloves, remove stems and seeds from ancho peppers; cut into 1-inch pieces. In a blender container or food processor bowl, cover and blend or process peppers till ground. Set aside.

In a 4½-quart Dutch oven brown *half* of the meat in hot cooking oil. With a slotted spoon, remove meat; set aside. Add ancho peppers, remaining meat, onion, red pepper, garlic, and cumin. Cook till meat is brown.

Return all meat to Dutch oven. Stir in beef broth, beer, and salt. Bring to boiling; reduce heat. Simmer, uncovered, for 1 to 1¼ hours or till meat is tender, stirring occasionally.

Serve chili in bowls with Texas Pinto Beans and Texas toast. If desired, garnish with cilantro and fresh chili peppers. Makes 6 to 8 servings.

Texas Pinto Beans: Rinse 2 cups *dry pinto beans.* In 4½-quart Dutch oven combine beans and 6 cups *water.* Cover and soak overnight. (Or, bring to boiling; reduce heat and simmer 2 minutes. Remove from heat. Cover; let stand 1 hour.) Drain beans.

In the same Dutch oven combine beans; 4⅔ cups *water;* 1 teaspoon *salt;* 2 cloves *garlic,* minced; and ¼ teaspoon ground *red pepper.* Bring to boiling; reduce heat. Cover and simmer for 1½ to 2 hours or till beans are tender.

Nutrition information per serving of chili with ½ cup beans: 527 cal., 38 g pro., 49 g carbo., 19 g fat, 67 mg chol., 742 mg sodium. U.S. RDA: 111% vit. A, 40% thiamine, 25% riboflavin, 32% niacin, 13% calcium, 44% iron, 45% phosphorus.

FEBRUARY

The Idea Magazine for American Families

Better Homes and Gardens

$1.50
February 1987

MONEY! WHAT THE NEW TAX LAW MEANS TO HOMEOWNERS PAGE 27

AFTER-WORK COOKING
6 Families' Strategies For Delicious Meals In Minutes

REDECORATING WITH COLOR
It's Easy To Give Your Home A FRESH LOOK!

8 PRIZEWINNING NEW HOUSES
NEW TRENDS, NEW STYLES, NEW IDEAS

OBJECTS OF AFFECTION
5 Loving Gifts To CRAFT For Your Valentine

HEALTH:
Early Warning Signs Of Serious Childhood Ailments

EDUCATION:
Why Smart Kids Fail

PARENTING:
TEENS AND FREEDOM How Much Is Enough? How Much Is Too Much?

AFTER-WORK COOKING

BEAT-THE-CLOCK MEALS FROM SIX FAMILIES ACROSS THE COUNTRY

By Barbara Greenwood

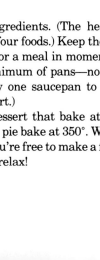

EXTRA-EASY OVEN DINNER

Alex and Susie Zera and their three children in their Northbrook, Illinois home.

- Sausage-Spinach Loaf
- Fudge Brownie Pie

THE ZERAS:

Alex and Susie's home is always open to foster babies. And because the infants arrive on short notice, the Zeras never know when their family might expand, making their active lives even busier. Consequently, Susie stocks specific convenience ingredients that allow her to instantly whip up a simple family meal—even on the days that the Zeras fill their nursery.

STRATEGIES:

- Latch on to recipes with few ingredients. (The hearty meat-filled loaf at right uses a mere four foods.) Keep the ingredients for those recipes on hand for a meal in moments.
- Watch for recipes requiring a minimum of pans—no one likes the cleanup job! (It takes only one saucepan to mix together the heavenly brownie dessert.)
- Pair an oven main dish and a dessert that bake at the same temperature. Both the loaf and pie bake at 350°. While they're in the oven for 30 minutes, you're free to make a fruit salad, set the table, and better yet—relax!

THREE MEALS IN 1½ HOURS

Dick and Sandy Wagner of Des Moines, with son and daughter.

PERRY STRUSE

- ●Reuben Submarine
- ●Home-Style Ham 'n' Bean Soup
- ●Pork Chop and Vegetable Skillet

STRATEGIES: Cook on the weekends for weekdays ahead. By interweaving preparation steps, you can turn out this main-dish trio in 1½ hours. Freeze the soup and chill the chops for later; eat the giant sandwich tonight.
- ●Simplify cooking wherever possible without sacrificing taste. Use canned beans and broth in the soup rather than soaking dry beans or making stock. Slice *unpeeled* potatoes for chop dish; it saves minutes *and* adds fiber to your meal.

THE WAGNERS: If teachers Dick and Sandy aren't in the classroom, they're planning lessons, grading papers, gardening, or going to church functions. That doesn't leave much time to cook! When Dick does get into the kitchen, he takes advantage of it by making several meals at once.

20

Phil and Barbara Metzger and family of San Rafael, California.

TWO FIX-AND-FORGET MEALS

- **Skirt Steak with Cream Gravy**
- **Crockery Beef Stew**

THE METZGERS: When Barbara went back to work, she and Phil agreed: He shops and cooks on weekdays; she handles weekends. Phil is challenged because he commutes an hour to his job. To create great meals without much kitchen time, Phil often uses a crockery cooker.

STRATEGIES: Simmer dinner in a crockery cooker. Start the meal before leaving in the morning. By the time you walk in the door at night, your family's dinner is ready. A crockery meal lets people eat in shifts, too.

● Speed up your early-morning preparation by using canned sliced mushrooms in the steak and bottled minced garlic in both dishes. Create the stew's flavor base with packaged soup mix. Then, cook frozen potato wedges and mixed vegetables (no chopping!), and serve the stew over them.

21

KID-PLEASING SUPPER IN 20 MINUTES

Sally Wagner
and sons of
Seattle.

ALAN ABRAMOWITZ FIELD EDITOR: TRISH MAHARAM

THE WAGNERS: A bustling single parent of two active boys, teacher Sally also participates in parent/child groups after hours. Max and Alec help Sally out by cooking alongside her one night a week. Even so, with two growing boys to feed, Sally needs meals that are ready fast.

● **Super Salmon Burgers**

STRATEGIES: Burgers always make a quick meal. Put these northwestern-style salmon patties together even faster by starting with canned salmon that already has the skin and bones removed.

● To slash time at the chopping board, make use of dried minced onion.

● Keep soft bread crumbs at your fingertips by putting day-old bread through the blender or food processor, then store the crumbs in the freezer.

● Pick up a salad and carrot sticks from your deli to round out the meal.

25-MINUTE CELEBRATION DINNER

Mardi Hudson and daughter of Northampton, Massachusetts.

- Orange-Sauced Chicken
- Bulgur-Raisin Pilaf

STRATEGIES: Search out ready-to-use products like boneless chicken breasts used for this speedy version of Chicken à l'Orange. Boneless chicken eliminates time spent boning *and* cooks faster than bone-in chicken.

● Check out your store's spice rack for timesaving seasonings. Dried parsley flakes save snipping time *and* avoid the waste of wilted parsley that small families often face. Dried grated orange peel is a handy option to grating fresh peel.

● Cut the time you spend wielding the knife by using frozen chopped onion.

THE HUDSONS: Teaching and attending classes, along with studying for a master's degree *and* being Mom to Katie, leaves Mardi with little time to spare. But, special occasions still get the attention they deserve, thanks to Mardi's quick-cooking recipes.

23

WM. HOPKINS

HOME-STYLE MEAL IN HALF THE TIME

Bill and
Joanne Geist
and family of
suburban
Chicago.

- **Mozzarella-Stuffed Meat Loaf**
- **Blueberry-Apple Crisp**

THE GEISTS: Professional demands (Joanne holds two part-time feature-writing jobs; Bill is a high school teacher and varsity coach) and six active children put time at a premium in the Geist household. Joanne uses her microwave oven constantly to prepare meals quickly.

STRATEGIES: Rely on your microwave
oven for more than reheating and defrosting! Use it to cook a whole meal on the double. This hearty meat loaf and old-fashioned dessert cook in the microwave in less than half the time both dishes would take to bake conventionally.
- Shave time off the meat loaf's preparation by purchasing cheese that's already shredded.
- Eliminate peeling and slicing! Start with a handy can of peeled and sliced apples to make this home-style fruit crisp super quick to put together.
- Round out your meal with a glass of milk and Italian-cut frozen green beans (no cleaning or cutting!). Sprinkle the beans with sliced almonds for an easy, yet special touch.

After-Work Extra-Easy Oven Dinner

Sausage-Spinach Loaf
Fudge Brownie Pie
Mixed fruit salad

What you'll need:
1 16-ounce loaf frozen bread dough
1 10-ounce package frozen chopped spinach
Margarine *or* butter
   2 ounces (2 squares) unsweetened chocolate
   3 eggs
Sugar
All-purpose flour
Vanilla
   ¾ pound bulk pork sausage
   1 8-ounce package shredded mozzarella cheese
Caraway seed
Desired fruit for salad
Fudge ice-cream topping
Mint chocolate-chip ice cream

How to do it in 60 minutes:
Night before
   Place the frozen bread dough and spinach in the refrigerator to thaw.

60 minutes before dinner
   Mix together the ingredients for the brownie pie. Bake.
   For the bread loaf, cook and drain the sausage. Roll out the thawed dough. Fill and seal.

30 minutes before dinner
   While the loaf bakes, prepare the fruit salad and set the table.
   Relax!
   Eat and enjoy!
   Before serving, top the brownie pie.

SAUSAGE-SPINACH LOAF

   ¾ **pound bulk pork sausage**
   1 **16-ounce loaf frozen bread dough, thawed***
   1 **8-ounce package shredded mozzarella cheese (2 cups)**
   1 **10-ounce package frozen chopped spinach, thawed and well drained***
   1 **slightly beaten egg white**
   1 **tablespoon water**
Caraway seed

In a medium skillet cook the sausage till no pink remains. Drain well. [Or, crumble the sausage into a 1½-quart microwave-safe casserole. Micro-cook, covered, on 100% power (high) for 4 to 6 minutes or till no pink remains, stirring once. Drain well.]
   On a lightly floured surface roll thawed dough into a 15x8-inch rectangle. Sprinkle the shredded cheese over dough, leaving a 1-inch border around all edges. Top with sausage and spinach. Bring the long sides of the dough together. Pinch to seal edges and ends. Place the loaf, seam-side down, on a greased baking sheet.
   In a small bowl stir together egg white and water; brush over loaf. Sprinkle with caraway seed.
   Bake in a 350° oven for 30 to 35 minutes or till golden brown. Let stand for 8 to 10 minutes. Cut into slices to serve. Makes 6 servings.
   ***Microwave thawing directions:** Place frozen loaf in a lightly greased 8x4x2-inch microwave-safe loaf dish. Cover with waxed paper. Micro-cook on 30% power (medium-low) for 4 minutes or till just slightly icy, turning loaf once. Let stand for 10 to 15 minutes.
   Place frozen spinach in a 1-quart microwave-safe casserole. Micro-cook, covered, on 100% power (high) for 3 to 4 minutes or till thawed. Drain well, pressing out excess liquid.
   Nutrition information per serving: 415 cal., 22 g pro., 39 g carbo., 19 g fat, 46 mg chol., 935 mg sodium. U.S. RDA: 65% vit. A, 35% thiamine, 29% riboflavin, 19% niacin, 36% calcium, 21% iron, 33% phosphorus.

FUDGE BROWNIE PIE

   ½ **cup margarine *or* butter**
   2 **squares (2 ounces) unsweetened chocolate**
   2 **eggs**
   1 **cup sugar**
   ¾ **cup all-purpose flour**
   1 **teaspoon vanilla**
Dash salt
Fudge ice-cream topping
Mint chocolate-chip ice cream *or* other desired flavor ice cream

In a medium saucepan melt the margarine or butter and unsweetened chocolate over low heat, stirring constantly. Remove from heat. [Or, in a large microwave-safe mixing bowl micro-cook margarine or butter and chocolate, uncovered, on 100% power (high) for 3 to 4 minutes or till melted, stirring once.] Cool slightly.
   Stir in eggs, sugar, flour, vanilla, and salt. Mix well. Pour mixture into a greased and floured 9-inch pie plate. Bake in a 350° oven about 30 minutes or till a slight imprint remains when touched in center. Cool on a wire rack for 30 minutes.
   To serve, warm the ice-cream topping according to package directions. Top pie with desired ice cream and drizzle with warmed topping. Serve at once. Makes 6 servings.
   Nutrition information per serving (with 2 tablespoons topping and ½ cup ice cream): 656 cal., 9 g pro., 85 g carbo., 35 g fat, 122 mg chol., and 317 mg sodium. U.S. RDA: 21% vit. A, 11% thiamine, 23% riboflavin, 16% calcium, 13% iron, and 21% phosphorus.

Three Meals in 1½ Hours

Reuben Submarine
Home-Style Ham 'n' Bean Soup
Pork Chop and Vegetable Skillet

What you'll need:
2 medium onions
1 small green pepper
½ pound fully cooked ham
½ pound thinly sliced corned beef *or*
    pastrami
1 8-ounce can sauerkraut
4 pork chops, cut ½ inch thick
Cooking oil
3 medium potatoes
1 7½-ounce can tomatoes
Paprika
Garlic salt
Caraway seed
2 15-ounce cans great northern *or*
    navy beans
1 16-ounce can sliced potatoes
1 16-ounce can diced carrots
2 14½-ounce cans chicken broth
½ cup frozen chopped onion
Dried parsley flakes
Bay leaf
Pepper
1 16-ounce loaf French bread
Margarine *or* butter
Dijon-style mustard
1 4-ounce package shredded Swiss
    cheese
Baby sweet pickles
Cherry tomatoes

How to do it in 1½ hours:
Getting started—first 30 minutes
For the pork-chop dish, slice onions and cut up green pepper.
For soup, cut up ham.
For submarine sandwich, cut up the corned beef. Rinse the sauerkraut and drain well.

Second 30 minutes
Start preparing the pork-chop dish. While chops simmer, slice potatoes.
For the soup, drain beans, canned potatoes, and carrots. Combine all ingredients in a large kettle or Dutch oven. Bring to boiling.

Finishing up—last 30 minutes
Simmer the soup. Transfer to a freezer container and cool.
Finish the pork-chop dish. Transfer to a baking dish and cool.
Prepare and broil the submarine sandwich. (Or, if you want to eat dinner later, save this step for just before you eat. It takes only 10 minutes!)
Seal, label, and freeze the soup.
Cover and chill the pork-chop dish.

PORK CHOP AND VEGETABLE SKILLET

The tomatoes, paprika, and caraway reflect Dick's fascination with Hungarian cooking triggered by overseas travels. Pictured on page 17—

4 **pork chops, cut ½ inch thick**
    (about 1¼ pounds total)
1 **tablespoon cooking oil**
2 **medium onions, thinly sliced and**
    separated into rings
1 **7½-ounce can tomatoes, cut up**
¾ **cup water**
2 **teaspoons paprika**
½ **teaspoon garlic salt**
½ **teaspoon caraway seed**
3 **medium potatoes, sliced**
1 **small green pepper, cut into**
    strips

Trim excess fat from pork chops. In a large skillet cook chops over medium-high heat in hot oil for 4 to 5 minutes on each side or till brown.

Remove the chops from the skillet. Add onions. Cook for 3 to 5 minutes or till tender. Drain off fat, if necessary.

Add *undrained* tomatoes, water, paprika, garlic salt, and caraway seed to skillet. Return chops to skillet. Bring to boiling. Reduce heat and simmer, covered, for 10 minutes.

Add sliced potatoes and green pepper strips. Cover and simmer for 15 to 20 minutes or till pork chops and potatoes are tender and no pink remains in the pork chops.

Serve immediately. (Or, transfer the pork-chop-vegetable mixture to a 12x7½x2-inch baking dish. Cool. Cover and chill up to 48 hours.)

To reheat in the oven: Bake the pork-chop-vegetable mixture, covered, in a 350° oven about 70 minutes or till heated through. Makes 4 servings.

To reheat in the microwave oven: Transfer the mixture to a microwave-safe baking dish. Cover with vented microwave-safe plastic wrap. Micro-cook on 70% power (medium-high) for 18 to 22 minutes or till heated through, stirring potatoes, rearranging pork chops, and spooning sauce over chops twice.

Nutrition information per serving: 316 cal., 22 g pro., 28 g carbo., 13 g fat, 52 mg chol., 361 mg sodium. U.S. RDA: 21% vit. A, 69% vit. C, 39% thiamine, 17% riboflavin, 30% niacin, 14% iron, 25% phosphorus.

HOME-STYLE HAM 'N' BEAN SOUP

When Dick has a little extra time, he'll use fresh potatoes, carrots, and onions. Pictured on page 17—

- 2 **15-ounce cans great northern** *or* **navy beans, drained**
- 2 **14½-ounce cans chicken broth**
- 1 **16-ounce can sliced potatoes, drained**
- 1 **16-ounce can diced carrots, drained**
- ½ **pound fully cooked ham, cut into bite-size pieces (1½ cups)**
- ½ **cup frozen chopped onion**
- ¼ **cup dried parsley flakes**
- 1 **bay leaf**
- ¼ **to ½ teaspoon pepper**

In a large kettle or Dutch oven combine beans, chicken broth, potatoes, carrots, ham, onion, parsley flakes, bay leaf, and pepper. Bring to boiling. Reduce heat. Simmer, covered, for 20 minutes.

Skim off fat, if necessary. Remove bay leaf. Serve at once. (Or, transfer to a 2½-quart moisture- and vaporproof freezer container. Cool. Seal, label, and freeze up to 6 months.)

To reheat on the stove top: Place frozen mixture in a 4½-quart Dutch oven. Cook, covered, over medium-low heat about 50 minutes or till heated through, breaking up gently after 30 and 40 minutes. Makes 6 servings.

To reheat in the microwave oven: Place frozen mixture in a 3-quart microwave-safe casserole. Micro-cook, covered, on 70% power (medium-high) for 30 to 35 minutes or till heated through, stirring and breaking up gently after 20 and 25 minutes.

Nutrition information per serving: 236 cal., 19 g pro., 32 g carbo., 4 g fat, 20 mg chol., 1,142 mg sodium. U.S. RDA: 119% vit. A, 19% vit. C, 31% thiamine, 13% riboflavin, 25% niacin, 11% calcium, 38% iron, 29% phosphorus.

REUBEN SUBMARINE

This simple sandwich deserves simple accompaniments. Try teaming it with baby sweet pickles and cherry tomatoes. Pictured on page 17—

- 1 **16-ounce loaf unsliced French bread, halved horizontally**
- ¼ **cup margarine** *or* **butter**
- ½ **pound thinly sliced corned beef** *or* **pastrami, cut into bite-size strips**
- 1 **8-ounce can sauerkraut, rinsed and well drained**

  Dijon-style mustard
- 1 **4-ounce package shredded Swiss cheese (1 cup)**

  Baby sweet pickles (optional)

  Cherry tomatoes (optional)

Spread cut sides of French bread with margarine or butter. Broil, spread side up, 3 to 4 inches from heat for 3 to 4 minutes or till toasted.

Meanwhile, in a medium mixing bowl combine corned beef or pastrami and sauerkraut.

Spread toasted bread halves with mustard. Divide meat mixture evenly between bread halves. Top each half with cheese. Broil about 1 minute more or till cheese is melted. If desired, serve with sweet pickles and cherry tomatoes. Makes 6 servings.

Nutrition information per serving: 447 cal., 22 g pro., 44 g carbo., 20 g fat, 55 mg chol., 1,147 mg sodium. U.S. RDA: 10% vit. A, 21% thiamine, 21% riboflavin, 19% niacin, 24% calcium, 22% iron, 23% phosphorus.

Two Fix-and-Forget Meals

Skirt Steak with Cream Gravy
Crockery Beef Stew

How to do it:
Night before

Put together one of these no-fuss crockery cooker meals, then cover and chill overnight.

In the morning

Plug in your electric crockery cooker.

Before serving

Prepare the vegetables or gravy.

CROCKERY BEEF STEW

- 1½ **pounds beef stew meat, cut into bite-size cubes**
- 1 **8-ounce can tomato sauce**
- ¾ **cup water**
- ¾ **cup dry red wine**
- 1 **1¼-ounce envelope** *regular* **onion soup mix**
- 1 **teaspoon bottled chopped garlic** *or* ¼ **teaspoon garlic powder**
- 1 **16-ounce package loose-pack frozen mixed broccoli, cauliflower, and carrots (4 cups)**
- ¼ **of a 24-ounce package (2 cups) thinly sliced potato wedges with peel**

For stew, in a 3½- to 4-quart electric slow cooker combine the stew meat, tomato sauce, water, wine, onion soup mix, and garlic.

Cook on the low-heat setting for 8 to 10 hours or on the high-heat setting for 4 to 5 hours or till meat is tender. Skim fat off stew.

Just before serving, cook mixed vegetables and potatoes, uncovered, in a large amount of gently boiling water about 5 minutes or till just tender. Spoon stew over vegetables in soup bowls. Makes 6 servings.

Nutrition information per serving: 288 cal., 26 g pro., 19 g carbo., 10 g fat, 69 mg chol., 825 mg sodium. U.S. RDA: 62% vit. A, 58% vit. C, 10% thiamine, 17% riboflavin, 26% niacin, 23% iron, 21% phosphorus.

SKIRT STEAK WITH CREAM GRAVY

Accompany this crockery cooker beef dish with your favorite vegetables. We chose zucchini and yellow summer squash for the photo on page 21—

- 2 **1-pound boneless beef plate skirt steaks** *or* **one 1½-pound boneless beef round steak (about ½ inch thick), rolled and tied**
- 1 **14½-ounce can beef broth**
- 1 **4-ounce can sliced mushrooms, drained**
- 1½ **teaspoons bottled minced garlic** *or* **¼ teaspoon garlic powder**
- ⅓ **cup light cream** *or* **milk**
- 2 **tablespoons all-purpose flour**
- 2 **tablespoons snipped fresh parsley** *or* **2 teaspoons dried parsley flakes**
- **Cooked vegetables (optional)**

Sprinkle beef with pepper. Place in a 3½- to 4-quart electric slow cooker. (Cut beef to fit, if necessary.) Add broth, mushrooms, and garlic. Cover and cook on the low-heat setting for 8 to 10 hours or on the high-heat setting for 4 to 5 hours or till beef is tender.

With a slotted spoon, transfer beef and mushrooms to a serving platter. Cover to keep warm. Skim fat from cooking liquid and discard.

For gravy, pour ⅔ cup of the cooking liquid into a small saucepan (reserve any remaining cooking liquid for another use such as soup or gravy). In a screw-top jar combine cream or milk and flour. Cover and shake well to mix. Add to liquid in saucepan. Cook and stir till thickened and bubbly, then cook and stir for 1 minute more. Stir parsley into gravy.

To serve, slice the beef. Spoon gravy over beef and mushrooms. Serve with vegetables, if desired. Makes 4 servings.

Microwave directions: Pour ⅔ cup of the cooking liquid into a 4-cup glass measure (reserve any remaining cooking liquid for another use). In a screw-top jar combine cream or milk and flour. Cover and shake well. Add to liquid in measure. Micro-cook, uncovered, on 100% power (high) for 3 to 5 minutes or till thickened and bubbly, stirring every 30 seconds. Cook, uncovered, on high 30 seconds more.

Nutrition information per serving: 274 cal., 30 g pro., 6 g carbo., 14 g fat, 97 mg chol., 498 mg sodium. U.S. RDA: 16% riboflavin, 28% niacin, 23% iron, 19% phosphorus.

Kid-Pleasing Supper In 20 Minutes

Super Salmon Burgers
Deli cucumber salad
Carrot sticks

How to do it:
Let the kids help you shape the salmon mixture and set the table.

SUPER SALMON BURGERS

Sally uses leftover cooked salmon to make these mildly flavored fish burgers for sons Max and Alec—

- 1 **12½-ounce can boneless skinless pink salmon** *or* **1½ cups cooked and flaked salmon**
- 1 **beaten egg**
- ½ **cup soft bread crumbs**
- ¼ **cup shredded cheddar cheese (1 ounce)**
- 1 **teaspoon dried minced onion**
- ½ **teaspoon dried thyme, crushed**
- 1 **tablespoon cooking oil**
- **Lettuce leaves**
- **Tomato slices**
- 2 **small pita bread rounds, halved crosswise**
- **Tartar sauce** *or* **cocktail sauce (optional)**

Drain canned salmon, reserving *2 tablespoons* of the liquid.

In a medium mixing bowl stir together the reserved liquid or 2 tablespoons water, beaten egg, soft bread crumbs, cheddar cheese, minced onion, and thyme. Add the drained salmon. Mix well. Shape the salmon mixture into four ½-inch-thick patties.

In a large skillet cook salmon patties in hot oil over medium heat for 2 to 3 minutes or till the first side is brown. Carefully turn the patties over and cook about 2 minutes more or till the remaining side is brown.

Serve the salmon patties in lettuce- and tomato-lined pita halves. Top with tartar sauce or cocktail sauce, if desired. Makes 4 servings.

Nutrition information per serving: 262 cal., 20 g pro., 12 g carbo., 15 g fat, 105 mg chol., 188 mg sodium. U.S. RDA: 11% vit. A, 12% thiamine, 28% niacin, 17% calcium, 10% iron, 24% phosphorus.

25-Minute Celebration Dinner

Orange-Sauced Chicken
Bulgur-Raisin Pilaf
Salad greens

What you'll need:
- ⅔ cup bulgur
- ¼ cup raisins
- Salt
- 4 skinless boneless chicken breast halves (about ¾ pound total)
- ⅓ cup frozen chopped onion
- Margarine *or* butter
- ½ cup orange juice
- ¼ cup dry sherry *or* dry white wine
- Brown sugar
- Dried parsley flakes
- Dried grated orange peel
- Dried savory
- Ground mace
- Cornstarch
- Fresh tarragon (optional)
- Orange (optional)
- Desired salad greens

ORANGE-SAUCED CHICKEN

Sometimes Mardi and Katie sauté sliced mushrooms with the chicken and onion. They also like the chicken served over rice with raisins—

Bulgur-Raisin Pilaf (see
    recipe, below)
4 skinless boneless chicken
    breast halves (about ¾ pound
    total)
⅓ cup frozen chopped onion
2 tablespoons margarine *or* butter
½ cup orange juice
¼ cup dry sherry *or* dry white wine
3 tablespoons brown sugar
2 teaspoons dried parsley flakes
1 teaspoon dried grated orange
    peel
¼ teaspoon dried savory, crushed
¼ teaspoon ground mace
1 tablespoon cold water
1 tablespoon cornstarch
Fresh tarragon (optional)
Orange slices, halved (optional)

Prepare Bulgur-Raisin Pilaf. Meanwhile, in a 10-inch skillet cook chicken and onion in hot margarine or butter over medium-high heat for 8 minutes, turning chicken to brown evenly.

In a small mixing bowl stir together orange juice, sherry or wine, brown sugar, parsley, orange peel, savory, and mace. Pour orange juice mixture over chicken in skillet.

Bring to boiling. Reduce heat and simmer, covered, for 3 to 5 minutes or till chicken is tender. Use a slotted spoon to transfer chicken to a warm serving platter. Cover and keep warm.

Stir water into cornstarch. Stir into liquid in skillet. Cook and stir till thickened and bubbly, then cook and stir for 2 minutes more. Spoon over chicken. If desired, garnish with tarragon and orange slices. Serve with Bulgur-Raisin Pilaf. Makes 4 servings.

Microwave directions: Prepare Bulgur-Raisin Pilaf. Meanwhile, in a 1½-quart microwave-safe casserole arrange chicken with meatiest portions toward outside of dish. Add onion. *Do not* add margarine or butter.

Stir together orange juice, sherry or wine, brown sugar, parsley, orange peel, savory, and mace. Pour orange juice mixture over chicken in casserole. Cover and micro-cook on 100% power (high) for 8 to 10 minutes or till chicken is tender, turning chicken after 4 minutes. Use a slotted spoon to transfer chicken to a warm serving platter. Cover to keep warm.

Stir water into cornstarch. Stir into liquid in casserole. Cook, uncovered, on high for 1½ to 2½ minutes or till thickened and bubbly, stirring each minute. Cook, uncovered, on high for 30 seconds more. Serve as above.

To reheat 2 servings in the oven: In a 10x6x2-inch baking dish cover and chill *half* of the cooked chicken, sauce, and pilaf up to 2 days. To reheat, bake, covered, in a 350° oven about 30 minutes or till heated through.

To reheat 2 servings in the microwave oven: Transfer to a microwave-safe baking dish. Micro-cook on 100% power (high) for 4 to 6 minutes or till heated through, giving the dish a half-turn once during cooking.

Nutrition information per serving with pilaf: 388 cal., 29 g pro., 43 g carbo., 9 g fat, 72 mg chol., and 203 mg sodium. U.S. RDA: 19% vit. C, 11% thiamine, 64% niacin, 15% iron, and 29% phosphorus.

BULGUR-RAISIN PILAF

1½ cups water
⅔ cup bulgur
¼ cup raisins
⅛ teaspoon salt

In a medium saucepan bring water to boiling. Stir in the bulgur, raisins, and salt. Simmer, covered, for 12 to 15 minutes or till the bulgur is tender. Makes 4 servings.

Home-Style Meal In Half the Time

Mozzarella-Stuffed Meat Loaf
Blueberry-Apple Crisp
Italian green beans with almonds

What you'll need:

1 egg
1 8-ounce can pizza sauce
¼ cup fine dry bread crumbs
¼ cup toasted wheat germ
1½ pounds ground beef
¾ cup shredded mozzarella cheese
¼ cup grated Parmesan cheese
Dried parsley flakes
1 20-ounce can sliced apples
2 cups frozen blueberries
½ cup quick-cooking rolled oats
Brown sugar
All-purpose flour
Ground cinnamon
Ground nutmeg
Margarine *or* butter
Light cream or milk
Frozen Italian-style green beans
Sliced almonds

How to do it in 40 minutes:
Night before
    Prepare meat loaf. Chill.

40 minutes before dinner
    Micro-cook meat loaf.
    Prepare dessert.
    Micro-cook dessert and vegetables while meat loaf stands.
    Finish cooking meat loaf.
    Eat!

MOZZARELLA-STUFFED MEAT LOAF

Joanne helps fill up her growing family by serving crusty garlic bread and a salad with this hearty loaf—

- 1 beaten egg
- 1 8-ounce can pizza sauce
- ¼ cup fine dry bread crumbs
- ¼ cup toasted wheat germ
- 1½ pounds ground beef
- ½ cup shredded mozzarella cheese (2 ounces)
- ¼ cup grated Parmesan cheese (1 ounce)
- 2 tablespoons dried parsley flakes
- ¼ cup shredded mozzarella cheese (1 ounce)

In a large mixing bowl stir together egg, ⅓ cup of the pizza sauce, bread crumbs, and wheat germ. (If making meat loaf the night before, cover and chill the remaining pizza sauce.)

Add the ground beef. Mix well. On a piece of foil pat the beef mixture into a 9x8x¾-inch rectangle.

For filling, in a small mixing bowl stir together the ½ cup mozzarella cheese, Parmesan cheese, and parsley.

Spoon the cheese mixture down the center third of the beef rectangle parallel to the 8-inch sides and to within ½ inch of the two 9-inch edges (see photo, above right).

Use the foil to bring the short ends of the beef together. Seal edges and ends of roll. Roll meat loaf from the foil onto a microwave-safe meat rack, seam-side down, in a 12x7½x2-inch microwave-safe baking dish. Cook immediately. (Or, cover and chill overnight.)

To cook, cover loaf with waxed paper. Micro-cook on 100% power (high) for 5 minutes. Give the dish a half-turn. Cook, uncovered, on 70% power (medium-high) for 12 to 16 minutes or till no pink remains, giving the dish a half-turn every 5 minutes and shielding ends with foil as necessary to prevent overcooking. Cover with foil. Let stand for 10 to 15 minutes.

Before serving, cook remaining pizza sauce on 100% power (high) for 1 minute or till heated through. Spoon pizza sauce over meat loaf. Sprinkle with the ¼ cup mozzarella cheese.

Return the meat loaf to the microwave oven. Cook, uncovered, on high for 1 minute or till the cheese is melted. Makes 6 servings.

Nutrition information per serving: 358 cal., 28 g pro., 9 g carbo., 22 g fat, 133 mg chol., 454 mg sodium. U.S. RDA: 10% vit. A, 13% thiamine, 19% riboflavin, 26% niacin, 19% calcium, 21% iron, 33% phosphorus.

BLUEBERRY-APPLE CRISP

Just like the prized fruit crisp your mom used to make, this homey dessert virtually begs for a generous dousing of light cream or milk—

- 1 20-ounce can sliced apples, drained
- 2 cups frozen blueberries
- ½ cup quick-cooking rolled oats
- ⅓ cup packed brown sugar
- ¼ cup all-purpose flour
- 1 teaspoon ground cinnamon
- ¼ teaspoon ground nutmeg
- 3 tablespoons margarine *or* butter
- Light cream *or* milk (optional)

In a 1½-quart microwave-safe casserole combine sliced apples and frozen blueberries. Micro-cook, covered, on 100% power (high) for 5 minutes, stirring the fruit mixture twice.

Meanwhile, for topping, in a medium mixing bowl stir together oats, brown sugar, flour, cinnamon, and nutmeg. Cut in the margarine or butter till the mixture resembles coarse crumbs.

Sprinkle the crumb topping over the apples and blueberries. Cook, uncovered, on high for 4 to 5 minutes or till heated through. Serve the hot fruit crisp with light cream or milk, if desired. Makes 6 servings.

Nutrition information per serving: 229 cal., 2 g pro., 42 g carbo., 7 g fat, 0 mg chol., 74 mg sodium.

MARCH

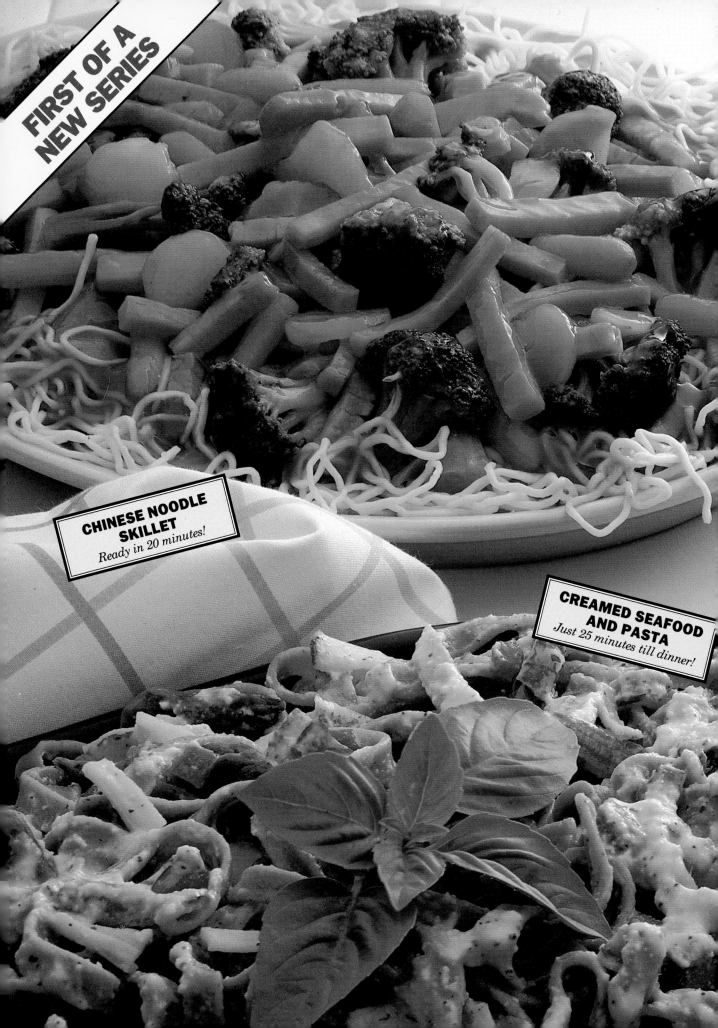

CHINESE NOODLE SKILLET
Ready in 20 minutes!

CREAMED SEAFOOD AND PASTA
Just 25 minutes till dinner!

PASTA!

MAIN DISHES FROM WHAT YOU HAVE ON HAND

By Barbara Greenwood

QUICK PASTA TIPS

- Next time you cook a ham, cut some thick slices; freeze for *Chinese Noodle Skillet.* To use, thaw slices, stack, then cut into strips at once.
- Gradually add the pasta to the boiling water so the water continues to boil.

- Go beyond macaroni and spaghetti! Start stocking your kitchen with the growing variety of fresh, frozen, and dried pastas that cook quickly. Check out our shopping guide on page 34 for some new types of pasta now available.

CHINESE NOODLE SKILLET

- 6 **ounces fresh, frozen, *or* dried Chinese egg noodles *or* fine noodles**
- 1 **16-ounce package frozen mixed broccoli, baby carrots, and water chestnuts**
- 3 **tablespoons dry sherry**
- 2 **tablespoons soy sauce**
- 2 **teaspoons cornstarch**
- ¼ **teaspoon ground ginger**
- ¼ **teaspoon garlic powder**
- 1 **tablespoon cooking oil**
- 8 **ounces fully cooked ham, cut into julienne strips (2 cups)**

Cook noodles according to package directions (fresh or frozen: about 4 minutes; dried: about 6 minutes); drain well. Return to pan; toss with a little *margarine* or *butter.* Cover; set aside.

Thaw vegetables under warm water. For sauce, combine sherry, soy sauce, cornstarch, ginger, garlic powder, and 3 tablespoons *water.*

Preheat a wok or large skillet over high heat. Add oil. (Add more oil as needed during cooking.) Stir-fry vegetables 1 to 2 minutes or till crisp-tender. Add ham; stir-fry 1 minute. Push vegetables and ham from center of wok. Stir sauce; add to wok or skillet. Cook and stir till bubbly. Cook and stir 2 minutes more. Serve over noodles on a warm platter. Makes 4 servings.

Nutrition information per serving: 353 cal., 20 g pro., 43 g carbo., 10 g fat, 70 mg chol., 1,239 mg sodium. U.S. RDA: 84% vit. A, 87% vit. C, 57% thiamine, 22% riboflavin, 29% niacin, 16% iron, 26% phosphorus.

CREAMED SEAFOOD AND PASTA

Divvy up the menu: one family member cuts crisp apple wedges, while another slices crusty French bread and pours dinner beverages—

- 10 **ounces linguine *or* thin spaghetti, broken in half**
- 1 **10-ounce package frozen cut asparagus**
- 1 **8-ounce package frozen salad-style crab-flavored fish**
- 2 **eggs**
- ½ **cup milk**
- 1 **3-ounce package cream cheese with chives, cut up**
- ½ **teaspoon dried basil, crushed**
- 1 **2-ounce jar diced pimiento, drained**

In a large saucepan bring 7 cups *water* to boiling. Add pasta. Boil, stirring occasionally, 4 minutes. Add asparagus and fish; boil 5 to 7 minutes more or till pasta and asparagus are tender, breaking up fish with a fork during cooking.

Meanwhile, in a blender container or food processor bowl combine eggs, milk, cream cheese, basil, and ¼ teaspoon *salt.* Cover; blend or process till smooth. Drain pasta mixture in a large colander. Give a firm shake to remove excess water. Immediately return pasta mixture to hot pan; place over low heat. Add cream cheese mixture and pimiento. Heat 1 to 2 minutes or till slightly thickened, tossing to coat. Serve at once. Top with fresh cracked *black pepper.* Serves 4.

Nutrition information per serving: 459 cal., 24 g pro., 64 g carbo., 12 g fat, 163 mg chol., 871 mg sodium. U.S. RDA: 28% vit. A, 36% vit. C, 52% thiamine, 32% riboflavin, 27% niacin, 13% calcium, 20% iron, 26% phosphorus.

PHOTOGRAPH: TIM SCHULTZ. FOOD STYLIST: KATHY GERMAN

QUICK-COOKING

VACUUM-PACKED TORTELLINI

NO-BOIL LASAGNA

EGG CAPELLINI

TOMATO AND EGG RAVIOLI

SPINACH FETTUCCINE

LASAGNA SHEETS

PASTAS

PASTA PRODUCTS JUST KEEP GETTING MORE CONVENIENT FOR YOU. These items cook fast and are easy to store.

The availability of specialty pastas varies by region and supermarket. If you don't find the products at your store, ask the manager to look into stocking them for you.

SHELF-STABLE TORTELLINI
● Even though it's filled with meat or cheese, you can store this tortellini right on the shelf, saving valuable refrigerator or freezer space. Both dried and vacuum-packed tortellini are available; but, the latter cooks about twice as fast.

NO-BOIL LASAGNA
● That's right—no boiling before layering this noodle.

For De Rosa's lasagna shown here (available in 30 states), simply wet it, layer with cheese and sauce, then bake or micro-cook.

Another lasagna sheet (available in six midwestern states) is precooked and frozen. Use it from the package as you would a cooked lasagna noodle.

FRESH AND FRESH-FROZEN PASTA
● These pastas cook four to five times faster than dried pasta. Spinach fettuccine, egg capellini, tomato and egg ravioli, and lasagna sheets (shown here) are just a start. Check out the variety at your market. The smaller and thinner the pasta, the quicker it cooks.

SAUCES

WHEN IT'S MEALTIME AND YOU'RE IN A PINCH, WHIP UP A FAST HOME-COOKED SIDE DISH. Toss one of these simple sauces with 4 ounces of your favorite pasta that's been cooked and drained. Serve as a fast and fancy companion to broiled poultry, fish, beef, or pork. Better yet, toss some cut-up cooked meat in with the pasta for a lickety-split main dish.

● Cook 1 teaspoon *bottled minced garlic* in a little *oil* till tender. Stir in ¼ teaspoon crushed *dried tarragon* and a little *salt* and *pepper*. Toss with 2 cups hot cooked *veggies* and desired *pasta*.

● In warm pan used to cook desired *pasta*, pour ¼ cup *light cream*, ¼ cup grated *Parmesan cheese*, and 1 tablespoon *margarine* or *butter* over pasta. Toss gently till well coated. Sprinkle with fresh-cracked *black pepper* and snipped *parsley*.

● Heat ½ of an 8-ounce container *soft-style cream cheese with chives and onion*, 3 tablespoons *milk*, 1 tablespoon *margarine* or *butter*, and 1 teaspoon *dried parsley flakes* over medium-low heat till cheese melts and mixture is warm, stirring occasionally. Stir in ¼ cup grated *Romano cheese*. Toss with *pasta*.

● In warm pan used to cook desired *pasta*, toss ½ cup shredded *Monterey Jack cheese with jalapeño peppers* or *caraway;* one 2-ounce jar *diced pimiento*, drained; ⅓ cup *whipping cream;* and a little *salt* with pasta. Cook and stir over medium heat 3 to 4 minutes or till cheese melts and sauce thickens.

● Toss ¼ cup *sour cream dip* (any flavor) with desired *pasta*. Sprinkle with grated *Parmesan cheese*.

SCOTT LITTLE

NEW RECIPES

THAT WILL

CHANGE YOUR LIFE!

YOU'LL BE HEALTHIER! YOU'LL BE HAPPIER!

By Lynn Hoppe

You can have it all—food that tastes sensational, looks great, and is good for you! A few simple changes in your cooking make the difference.

● **LOW FAT/CHOLESTEROL.** Cut back on egg yolks; choose low-fat dairy foods and lean meats (and trim fat); skimp on oil.

● **HIGH FIBER.** Add whole grains to your diet; use plenty of vegetables and fruits, and don't remove their edible peels.

● **LOW SODIUM.** Limit your use of salt, cheese, and processed foods including condiments (such as catsup, mustard, pickles).

● **VITAMIN PACKED.** A heavy-handed helping of dark green and yellow vegetables does the trick.

● **LOW CALORIE.** Fill up on complex carbohydrates; fry in the oven; sweeten with fruit and fruit juice instead of sugar.

Photographs: Tim Schultz. Food stylist: Kathy German

FAT-FIGHTER PIZZA

NO-SUGAR PIE

VITAMIN-PACKED STIR-FRY

LOW-FAT FAJITAS

LEAN AND LIGHT LASAGNA

VITAMIN-RICH CHICKEN

HIGH-FIBER STEW

LOW-CALORIE TORTE

LOW-FAT FISH

LOW-CHOLESTEROL CHOPS

NO-SUGAR PIE

PEAR-DATE PIE

Per serving

Calories 327

Sodium 76 mg	**Fiber** 6 g
Cholesterol 2 mg	**Protein** 5 g
Carbohydrate 60 g	**Fat** 9 g

Truly a pared-down pie! Snipped dates sweeten the filling without sugar; the oil crust has just enough fat to make it tender. The result: 100 fewer calories per serving than most fruit pies and half the fat.

BEEF STIR-FRY WITH BLUE CHEESE

Per serving

Calories 167

Sodium 185 mg	**Fiber** 2 g
Cholesterol 46 mg	**Protein** 18 g
Carbohydrate 12 g	**Fat** 5 g

Most of us get too much protein. Satisfy the protein requirements of six adults at one meal with just 1 pound of lean meat. Fill up on vitamin-rich veggies.

VITAMIN-PACKED STIR-FRY

NUMBERS TO REMEMBER

The dietary "rules of thumb" below are what most women 23 to 50 years old should strive to consume daily. In general, teens, pregnant women, and men need more calories. Older men and women need fewer calories. These are approximate figures. There's no harm in going over or under these figures in any single day, but aim for a balanced diet overall.

Calories 2,000	**Protein** 45–65 grams
Fat 67 grams	**Cholesterol** 300 milligrams
Sodium 1,100–3,300 milligrams	**Fiber** 25–35 grams

FAT-FIGHTER PIZZA

SHRIMP-ZUCCHINI
PIZZA

Per serving

Calories 238

Sodium 233 mg	**Fiber** 3 g
Cholesterol 51 mg	**Protein** 16 g
Carbohydrate 35 g	**Fat** 4 g

This razzmatazz pizza delivers fat-fighting tactics from the bottom to the top.

First, there's the crispy whole wheat crust with a mere 1 teaspoon oil. Next comes "skinny" vegetables—zucchini and mushrooms. Then add the cholesterol-fighting shrimp. (Some studies show that shrimp along with oysters, scallops, and salmon have health benefits. These seafoods are rich in omega-3 fatty acids which may reduce cholesterol levels in your blood.) Last, top with low-fat farmer cheese.

VITAMIN-RICH CHICKEN

CHICKEN
WITH SWEET POTATO PILAF

Per serving

Calories 243

Sodium 319 mg	**Fiber** 2 g
Cholesterol 72 mg	**Protein** 30 g
Carbohydrate 22 g	**Fat** 3 g

Make the most of naturally lean chicken—poach skinless breasts in broth. Serve the chicken with high-fiber pilaf pumped up with sweet potato.

LEAN AND LIGHT LASAGNA

LASAGNA PIE

Per serving

Calories 338

Sodium 251 mg	**Fiber** 3 g
Cholesterol 68 mg	**Protein** 29 g
Carbohydrate 37 g	**Fat** 8 g

A square meal in the round! We reworked a traditionally high-fat, high-sodium lasagna and punched it up, nutritionally speaking, without losing the Italian flavor you love.

NUMBERS TO REMEMBER

Your age, sex, body size, and level of activity determine your nutritional needs, which may deviate from the guidelines listed here. The best advice: Eat a variety of foods, aiming for a balanced diet overall.

Calories 2,000	**Protein** 45–65 grams
Fat 67 grams	**Cholesterol** 300 milligrams
Sodium 1,100–3,300 milligrams	**Fiber** 25–35 grams

LOW-FAT
FAJITAS

TURKEY FAJITAS
WITH
GREEN PEA GUACAMOLE
Per serving

Calories 321

Sodium 217 mg	**Fiber** 6 g
Cholesterol 60 mg	**Protein** 30 g
Carbohydrate 45 g	**Fat** 3 g

A couple of slick tricks make traditional fajitas—grilled strips of meat served in a tortilla—even better. Low-fat turkey steps in for beef. With the kicky green pea guacamole you can slather on flavor with a heavy hand. It has 0 g fat per tablespoon compared to 5 g fat in the avocado version. To assemble each fajita, pile on the good stuff: sweet peppers, onions, and shredded lettuce.

HIGH-FIBER STEW

HEARTY BEAN STEW

Per serving

Calories 229

Sodium 306 mg	**Fiber** 8 g
Cholesterol 0 mg	**Protein** 11 g
Carbohydrate 45 g	**Fat** 2 g

Enjoy a meatless meal once a week. Beans and grains supply the right combination of proteins in this snappy stew.

SESAME FISH
WITH BOK CHOY RELISH

Per serving

Calories 180

Sodium 128 mg	**Fiber** 1 g
Cholesterol 65 mg	**Protein** 22 g
Carbohydrate 9 g	**Fat** 6 g

Love fried fish? You'll love this oven-fried version even more; you get a crispy coating using half the fat! Top it with low-fat bok choy relish.

LOW-FAT FISH

PORK CHOPS
WITH SWEET-SOUR CABBAGE

Per serving

Calories 214

Sodium 219 mg	**Fiber** 4 g
Cholesterol 50 mg	**Protein** 17 g
Carbohydrate 20 g	**Fat** 8 g

You don't have to swear off meat—just limit cooked portions to 3 ounces per serving and opt for lean meat cuts and cooking methods.

NUMBERS TO REMEMBER

You needn't be a mathematical genius to maintain a healthful diet. But understanding what's good and what's bad for you will help you to make smart choices that add up to these daily guidelines.

Calories 2,000	**Protein** 45–65 grams
Fat 67 grams	**Cholesterol** 300 milligrams
Sodium 1,100–3,300 milligrams	**Fiber** 25–35 grams

LOW-CHOLESTERO[L] CHOPS

LOW-CALORIE TORTE

BROWNIE FRUIT TORTE

Per serving

Calories 210

Sodium 204 mg	**Fiber** 1 g
Cholesterol 7 mg	**Protein** 5 g
Carbohydrate 33 g	**Fat** 8 g

Indulgence minus decadence. A series of clever cooking tricks makes this luscious dessert a healthful choice. We substituted egg whites for whole eggs and cocoa powder (chocolate without cocoa butter) for baking chocolate. The best trick of all is in the filling: reduced-calorie cream cheese mixed with tofu. The fresh fruit topping makes it all the more enticing.

The best advice for any dessert: portion control. Don't pig out!

41

PEAR-DATE PIE

Use oats, which may lower blood cholesterol, in the crust. Also, use unsaturated vegetable oil instead of shortening—

- **1 recipe Oat Pastry**
- **6 cups peeled, sliced pears (6 to 7 medium pears)**
- **¼ cup raisins**
- **¾ cup pitted whole dates, snipped (4 ounces)***
- **¾ cup unsweetened pineapple *or* orange juice**
- **1 tablespoon cornstarch**
- **½ teaspoon ground cinnamon**
- **Dash ground nutmeg**
- **Skim milk**
- **Vanilla yogurt (optional)**

Prepare pastry. In a large mixing bowl combine pears and raisins. In a small saucepan combine dates, pineapple or orange juice, cornstarch, cinnamon, and nutmeg. Cook and stir till thickened and bubbly; stir into pears.

Fill the pastry-lined pie plate with pear mixture. Adjust top crust. Cut slits in top crust to allow for escape of steam. Trim top crust ½ inch beyond edge of pie plate. Fold extra pastry under bottom crust; flute edge. Brush with milk. Cover edge with foil.

Bake in a 375° oven for 25 minutes. Remove the foil. Bake for 30 to 35 minutes more or till crust is golden. Dollop each serving with yogurt, if desired. Makes 8 servings.

Oat Pastry: In a blender container or food processor bowl place 1¼ cups *rolled oats.* Cover and blend or process about 1 minute or till evenly ground (should have about 1 cup ground oats).

In a medium mixing bowl stir together ground oats, 1 cup *all-purpose flour,* and ¼ teaspoon *salt.* Pour ½ cup cold *milk* and ¼ cup *cooking oil* into measuring cup; add all at once to flour mixture. Stir lightly with a fork till moistened. (If necessary, add 1 to 2 tablespoons additional milk.) Form into 2 balls; flatten slightly with hands.

Cut waxed paper into four 12-inch squares. Dampen work surface with a little water to prevent sticking. Place each ball of dough between 2 squares of paper. Roll each ball into a 12-inch circle. Peel off top paper and fit dough, paper side up, into a 9-inch pie plate. Remove paper. Save remaining dough circle for top crust.

*Note: Use whole pitted dates, not chopped pitted dates, which are coated with sugar.

Nutrition information per serving: 327 cal., 5 g pro., 60 g carbo., 9 g fat, 2 mg chol., 6 g fiber, 76 mg sodium. U.S. RDA: 13% vit. C, 17% thiamine, 10% riboflavin, 11% iron, 11% phosphorus.

BEEF STIR-FRY WITH BLUE CHEESE

Want to know the secrets to low-fat stir-frying? Start by spraying a cool wok with nonstick spray coating and keep the oil you add later to a minimum. (Never spray the coating on a hot surface.) Or, simulate the stir-fry technique in your microwave oven using a microwave browning dish—

- **1 pound boneless beef top round steak, trimmed of fat**
- **1 8-ounce container plain low-fat yogurt**
- **¼ cup crumbled blue cheese**
- **2 tablespoons cornstarch**
- **½ teaspoon instant beef bouillon granules**
- **Nonstick spray coating**
- **2 cups broccoli flowerets**
- **2 medium carrots, thinly bias sliced**
- **2 medium onions, cut into thin wedges**
- **1 teaspoon cooking oil**
- **¾ cup water**
- **1 medium tomato, peeled, seeded, and chopped**

Partially freeze beef; bias-slice into thin bite-size strips. Set aside. For sauce, in a small mixing bowl combine yogurt, blue cheese, cornstarch, and bouillon granules. Set aside.

Spray a wok or large skillet with nonstick spray coating. Preheat over high heat till a drop of water sizzles. Stir-fry broccoli and carrots for 1 minute. Add onions. Stir-fry for 2 to 3 minutes more or till vegetables are crisp-tender. Transfer vegetables to a serving platter. Cover and keep warm.

Add oil to the hot wok, if necessary. Stir-fry *half* of the beef for 2 to 3 minutes or till done. Remove beef. Stir-fry remaining beef for 2 to 3 minutes or till done. Remove beef.

Add water to the wok. Cook and stir to scrape up crusty bits on bottom of wok. Stir sauce; add to wok. Cook and stir till thickened and bubbly; cook and stir 2 minutes more. Return beef to wok. Cook and stir till heated through; stir in tomato. Spoon over vegetables. Makes 6 servings.

Microwave directions: Partially freeze beef; thinly bias-slice into bite-size strips. Set meat aside. In a 2-quart microwave-safe casserole micro-cook broccoli, carrots, onions, and 2 tablespoons *water,* covered, on 100% power (high) for 7 to 9 minutes or till crisp-tender. Drain; cover and keep warm.

Preheat a 10-inch microwave browning dish on 100% power (high) for 5 minutes. Add oil to dish; swirl to coat. Add beef. Micro-cook, uncovered, on high for 2½ to 3½ minutes or till done, stirring twice. Drain.

In a 4-cup glass measure combine ½ *cup* water, yogurt, blue cheese, cornstarch, and bouillon granules. Micro-cook, uncovered, on high for 2 to 3 minutes or till thickened and bubbly, stirring after every minute. Micro-cook, uncovered, on high for 30 seconds more. Stir into beef and tomato in browning dish. Micro-cook, uncovered, on high for 1 minute more. Spoon over the cooked vegetable mixture.

Nutrition information per serving: 167 cal., 18 g pro., 12 g carbo., 5 g fat, 46 mg chol., 2 g fiber, 185 mg sodium. U.S. RDA: 149% vit. A, 39% vit. C, 15% riboflavin, 16% niacin, 13% calcium, 12% iron, 23% phosphorus.

SHRIMP-ZUCCHINI PIZZA

- ⅔ to 1 cup all-purpose flour
- ½ cup whole wheat flour
- 2 tablespoons cornmeal
- 1 package active dry yeast
- ½ teaspoon dried basil, crushed
- ¼ teaspoon salt
- ¼ teaspoon garlic powder
- ½ cup warm water (115° to 120°)
- 1 teaspoon cooking oil

Nonstick spray coating

- 1½ cups sliced fresh mushrooms
- 1 cup sliced zucchini
- ½ cup chopped onion
- ¼ cup water
- ½ teaspoon dried basil, crushed
- ¼ teaspoon instant chicken bouillon granules
- 1 5- *or* 6-ounce package frozen cooked shrimp, thawed and drained
- ¾ cup shredded farmer cheese
- 1 tablespoon snipped parsley

For crust, in a medium mixing bowl combine ⅔ *cup* all-purpose flour, whole wheat flour, cornmeal, yeast, ½ teaspoon basil, salt, and garlic powder. In small bowl combine ½ cup warm water and oil; stir into flour mixture till mixture forms a ball.

On a floured surface knead in enough of the remaining all-purpose flour to make a moderately stiff dough that is smooth and elastic (6 to 8 minutes total). Cover; let rest 10 minutes.

Spray a 12-inch pizza pan with nonstick spray coating. On a lightly floured surface roll the dough into a 13-inch circle; transfer to the prepared pan. Build up dough edges. Cover and let rise in a warm place for 30 minutes. Bake in a 425° oven for 15 to 17 minutes or till light brown.

Meanwhile, in a medium saucepan combine mushrooms, zucchini, onion, ¼ cup water, ½ teaspoon basil, and bouillon granules. Bring to boiling.

Cover and simmer for 3 to 4 minutes or till vegetables are crisp-tender. Drain vegetables well.

Top the crust with the zucchini mixture, shrimp, and cheese. Bake in a 425° oven for 5 minutes or till cheese is melted and topping is heated through. Sprinkle parsley atop before serving. Makes 4 servings.

Nutrition information per serving: 238 cal., 16 g pro., 35 g carbo., 4 g fat, 51 mg chol., 3 g fiber, 233 mg sodium. U.S. RDA: 18% vit. C, 22% thiamine, 22% riboflavin, 24% niacin, 12% calcium, 18% iron, 27% phosphorus.

CHICKEN WITH SWEET POTATO PILAF

Instead of a pilaf with both wild rice and wheat berries, you can use ½ cup of only one of the grains—

- ¼ cup wild rice
- ¼ cup wheat berries
- ⅔ cup coarsely shredded sweet potato
- 2 whole medium chicken breasts (1½ pounds total), skinned, boned, and halved lengthwise
- ¾ cup water
- 2 tablespoons red wine vinegar *or* white vinegar
- 1 tablespoon sodium-reduced soy sauce
- 1 teaspoon instant chicken bouillon granules
- ¼ teaspoon whole black pepper, crushed
- 1 tablespoon cornstarch
- 1 tablespoon cold water

Add wild rice and wheat berries to 1 cup boiling *water.* Add ¼ teaspoon *salt,* if desired. Simmer, covered, for 50 to 60 minutes or till liquid is absorbed, adding sweet potato during the last 10 minutes of cooking; stir once.

Meanwhile, rinse chicken and pat dry with paper towels; set aside. In an 8-inch skillet stir together ¾ cup water, vinegar, soy sauce, chicken bouillon

granules, and pepper. Bring to boiling. Add chicken. Reduce heat; cover and simmer for 15 minutes. Turn chicken, then simmer, covered, for 5 minutes more or till tender. Transfer the chicken and pilaf to a serving platter. Cover and keep warm. Reserve cooking liquid in the skillet.

For sauce, stir cornstarch into 1 tablespoon water. Stir into reserved cooking liquid in skillet. Cook and stir over medium heat till thickened and bubbly; cook and stir for 2 minutes more. Serve the sauce over chicken and pilaf. Makes 4 servings.

Microwave directions: Prepare the sweet potato pilaf as directed. Rinse chicken and pat dry. In a 10x6x2-inch microwave-safe baking dish arrange chicken with meatiest portions toward outside of dish. Cover with clear plastic wrap; vent by leaving a small area unsealed at edge of dish. Micro-cook on 100% power (high) for 6 to 8 minutes or till tender, turning the chicken and giving the dish a half-turn once. Transfer chicken and pilaf to a serving platter. Cover and keep warm.

For sauce, in a 2-cup glass measure stir together ¾ cup water, vinegar, soy sauce, chicken bouillon granules, pepper, and cornstarch. Micro-cook, uncovered, on high for 2½ to 4 minutes or till mixture is thickened and bubbly, stirring every minute. Micro-cook on high for 30 seconds more. Serve sauce with chicken and sweet potato pilaf.

Nutrition information per serving: 243 cal., 30 g pro., 22 g carbo., 3 g fat, 72 mg chol., 2 g fiber, 319 mg sodium. U.S. RDA: 73% vit. A, 10% thiamine, 14% riboflavin, 65% niacin, 10% iron, and 27% phosphorus.

LASAGNA PIE

We found that by using the low-sodium tomato sauce and adding just ¼ teaspoon salt to give a fuller flavor, we saved 340 mg sodium per serving—

    9 or 10 lasagna noodles
 1½ cups part-skim ricotta cheese
    3 tablespoons skim milk
  ½ teaspoon dried basil, crushed
  ¼ teaspoon pepper
    1 pound ground raw turkey
 1½ cups coarsely shredded carrot
  ½ cup chopped onion
    1 clove garlic, minced
    1 15-ounce can low-sodium
       tomato sauce
  ½ teaspoon dried oregano,
       crushed
  ¼ teaspoon salt
    2 small tomatoes, thinly sliced
Snipped fresh basil (optional)

Cook noodles according to package directions, *except* omit salt; drain. In a small mixing bowl stir together ricotta cheese, milk, dried basil, and pepper. Set aside.

For filling, in a 10-inch skillet cook turkey, carrot, onion, and garlic till turkey is brown and carrot is tender. Drain off fat, if necessary. Stir in tomato sauce, oregano, and salt. Cook over medium heat till heated through.

To assemble, line a lightly greased 9-inch springform pan with noodles, extending noodles over sides of pan. Layer *half* of the turkey mixture (about 2 cups), *1 cup* of the ricotta mixture, and remaining turkey mixture. Trim noodles so 3 inches extend over top of turkey mixture. Discard trimmings. Fold noodle ends over turkey mixture.

Place the springform pan on a 15x10x1-inch baking pan. Bake, covered, in a 375° oven for 30 minutes. Spread remaining ricotta mixture over top. Place tomatoes around edges, overlapping slightly. Cover and bake for 20 minutes more or till heated through. Let stand 10 minutes. Sprinkle with fresh basil, if desired. Cut into wedges to serve. Makes 6 servings.

Microwave directions: Prepare noodles according to package directions, *except* omit salt. In a small mixing bowl stir together ricotta cheese, milk, dried basil, and pepper.

In a 1½-quart microwave-safe casserole stir together turkey, carrot, onion, and garlic. Micro-cook, covered, on 100% power (high) for 6 to 7 minutes or till no pink remains and carrot is tender. Drain. Stir in tomato sauce, oregano, and salt. Micro-cook on high 2 to 3 minutes or till heated through.

To assemble, line a lightly greased 8x1½-inch round microwave-safe dish with noodles, extending noodles over dish edge. Layer *half* of the turkey mixture (about 2 cups), *1 cup* of the ricotta mixture and remaining turkey. Trim noodles so 3 inches extend over top of turkey mixture. Discard trimmings. Fold noodle ends over turkey mixture.

Cover with waxed paper. Micro-cook on high about 8 minutes or till heated through. Spread remaining ricotta mixture over top. Place tomato slices around edges, overlapping slightly. Micro-cook, uncovered, on high for 2 to 3 minutes more or till top is heated through. Let stand 10 minutes.

Nutrition information per serving: 338 cal., 29 g pro., 37 g carbo., 8 g fat, 68 mg chol., 3 g fiber, and 251 mg sodium. U.S. RDA: 183% vit. A, 34% vit. C, 28% thiamine, 24% riboflavin, 33% niacin, 22% calcium, 25% iron, and 34% phosphorus.

HEARTY BEAN STEW

To make the protein you get from beans nutritionally complete, we added pasta and a grain to this lemony stew—

  ½ cup dry garbanzo beans
  ½ cup dry red kidney beans
    1 medium onion, sliced and
       separated into rings
    2 teaspoons curry powder
 1½ teaspoons instant chicken
       bouillon granules
  ½ teaspoon salt
    2 cloves garlic, minced
    2 medium parsnips, sliced
    2 medium carrots, cut into julienne
       strips
    1 small zucchini, halved lengthwise
       and sliced
  ½ cup tiny shell macaroni
  ¼ cup cracked wheat cereal
  ¼ cup lemon juice
    2 cups fresh spinach
Lemon slices (optional)

Rinse beans. In a 4½-quart kettle or Dutch oven combine garbanzo and kidney beans and 3 cups *water*. Bring to boiling; boil 2 minutes. Remove from heat. Cover and let stand for 1 hour. (Or, soak beans in water overnight in a covered pan.) Drain beans.

In the same kettle or Dutch oven combine beans, onion, curry powder, bouillon granules, salt, garlic, and 8 cups *water*. Bring to boiling; reduce heat. Cover and simmer for 1 hour.

Meanwhile, in a small saucepan cook parsnips in a small amount of boiling water about 10 minutes or till very tender. Cool. Transfer *undrained* parsnips to blender container or food processor. Cover and blend till smooth.

Stir pureed parsnips, carrots, zucchini, macaroni, and cracked wheat into bean mixture. Simmer for 10 to 15 minutes more or till vegetables and cracked wheat are tender. Stir in lemon juice. Top each serving with spinach leaves. Garnish with lemon slices, if desired. Makes 6 servings.

Nutrition information per serving: 229 cal., 11 g pro., 45 g carbo., 2 g fat, 0 mg chol., 8 g fiber, 306 mg sodium. U.S. RDA: 161% vit. A, 29% vit. C, 20% thiamine, 10% niacin, 20% iron, and 18% phosphorus.

TURKEY FAJITAS WITH GREEN PEA GUACAMOLE

Fajitas are traditionally grilled. Because of concerns about hydrocarbons being released during grilling (especially when cooking high-fat meats in a covered grill), we chose lean turkey and open-grilled it. You also have the option to broil your fajitas—

  1 recipe Green Pea Guacamole
    (see recipe, at right)
  4 turkey breast tenderloin steaks
    (1 pound)
  ½ teaspoon finely shredded lime
    peel
  ½ cup lime juice
  2 cloves garlic, minced
  ½ teaspoon salt
  ½ teaspoon dried oregano,
    crushed
  ½ teaspoon ground cumin
Few dashes bottled hot pepper sauce
  3 red, yellow, *and/or* green sweet
    peppers, cut into thin strips
  1 medium onion, sliced
 10 6- *or* 7-inch flour tortillas
Shredded lettuce
  ¼ cup sliced pitted ripe olives
Plain low-fat yogurt (optional)

Grilling directions: Prepare guacamole. Rinse turkey; pat dry. For marinade, stir together lime peel, lime juice, garlic, salt, oregano, cumin, and hot pepper sauce. Add turkey, peppers, and onion. Cover and chill for 2 hours, turning turkey once.

Remove turkey, reserving the marinade. With a slotted spoon, remove peppers and onion; wrap in an 18-inch-square piece of heavy-duty foil. Stack tortillas and wrap in an 18x12-inch piece of heavy-duty foil.

Grill pepper-onion packet and turkey directly over *medium* coals for 8 minutes. Add tortilla packet to grill. Turn turkey steaks; grill for 4 to 6 minutes or till turkey is tender, brushing turkey occasionally with reserved marinade during grilling.

Remove turkey; cover and keep warm. Grill foil packets for 4 to 6 minutes more or till vegetables are tender and tortillas are heated through.

To serve, cut turkey into thin bite-size strips. Arrange turkey and pepper-onion mixture on a heated serving platter. Assemble fajitas at table: Spread guacamole on tortilla. Place some turkey, pepper-onion mixture, lettuce, and olives in the center of each tortilla. Top with yogurt, if desired. Roll up tortilla. Makes 5 servings.

Broiling directions: Prepare guacamole and marinate turkey steaks, peppers, and onions as directed for grilling. Wrap tortillas in foil. Set aside.

Remove turkey from marinade, reserving marinade. Place turkey on the unheated rack of a broiler pan. Broil 3 inches from heat for 10 to 12 minutes or till tender, turning once and brushing with marinade.

During the last 5 to 6 minutes of broiling, place wrapped tortillas on broiler rack next to turkey. Broil till heated through, turning once.

Meanwhile, with a slotted spoon remove peppers and onion from marinade. Spray a large skillet with *non-stick spray coating.* Preheat skillet over medium-high heat till a drop of water sizzles. Stir-fry pepper and onion for 4 to 5 minutes or till crisp-tender. Serve as directed.

Green Pea Guacamole: In a blender container or food processor bowl combine 2 cups *cooked peas or cooked green beans,* drained and chilled; 2 tablespoons chopped *onion;* 2 tablespoons *lime juice;* one 4-ounce can *diced green chili peppers,* rinsed and seeded; 1 clove *garlic,* minced; ¼ teaspoon *pepper;* and few dashes *bottled hot pepper sauce.* Cover and blend or process till smooth. Cover and chill till serving time.

Nutrition information per serving: 321 cal., 30 g pro., 45 g carbo., 3 g fat, 60 mg chol., 6 g fiber, and 217 mg sodium. U.S. RDA: 20% vit. A, 170% vit. C, 25% thiamine, 14% riboflavin, 38% niacin, 17% calcium, 29% iron, and 35% phosphorus.

PORK CHOPS WITH SWEET-SOUR CABBAGE

  4 pork chops, cut ¾ inch thick
    (1 to 1¼ pounds)
  ½ cup water
  ½ of a small head red *or* green
    cabbage, shredded (3 cups)
  2 tablespoons vinegar
  1 tablespoon Dijon-style mustard
 1½ teaspoons sugar
  ⅛ teaspoon salt
  ⅛ teaspoon caraway seed
Dash pepper
  2 small green apples, cored and
    cut into thin wedges
  ⅓ cup light *or* dark raisins

Trim excess fat from chops. Place chops on rack of unheated broiler pan. Broil 5 inches from heat for 20 to 25 minutes or till no pink remains, turning once.

In a large saucepan bring water to boiling. Add cabbage. Cook, uncovered, about 3 minutes or till almost tender. Drain; return to saucepan.

In a bowl gradually combine vinegar and mustard. Stir in sugar, salt, caraway seed, and pepper. Add apples and raisins; toss to coat.

Add apple mixture to cabbage; toss to mix. Cover; cook for 2 to 3 minutes or till apples are crisp-tender and mixture is heated through. Serve chops over cabbage mixture. Makes 4 servings.

Microwave directions: Broil chops as directed. Meanwhile, in a 2-quart microwave-safe casserole combine cabbage and *2 tablespoons* water. Micro-cook, covered, on 100% power (high) for 5 to 7 minutes or till almost tender, stirring once. Drain.

In a mixing bowl gradually combine vinegar and mustard. Stir in sugar, salt, caraway seed, and pepper. Add apples and raisins; toss to coat.

Add to apple mixture to cabbage; toss. Micro-cook, covered, on high for 2 to 3 minutes or till apples are crisp-tender and mixture is heated through. Serve chops atop cabbage.

Nutrition information per serving: 214 cal., 17 g pro., 20 g carbo., 8 g fat, 50 mg chol., 4 g fiber, and 219 mg sodium. U.S. RDA: 54% vit. C, 33% thiamine, 13% riboflavin, 17% niacin, and 18% phosphorus.

SESAME FISH WITH BOK CHOY RELISH

The mustard-seasoned bok choy relish has no fat compared to 11 g fat per tablespoon in tartar sauce. Steamed cauliflower flowerets make another low-fat accompaniment—

 - 4 **fresh *or* frozen catfish *or* orange roughy fillets (1 pound)**
 - ¼ **cup skim milk**
 - ¼ **cup fine dry bread crumbs**
 - ¼ **cup yellow cornmeal**
 - 1 **tablespoon toasted sesame seed**
 - 1 **tablespoon snipped fresh cilantro *or* 1 teaspoon dried coriander, crushed**
 - ¼ **teaspoon dry mustard**
 - ⅛ **teaspoon garlic powder**
   Dash pepper
   Nonstick spray coating
 - 1 **recipe Bok Choy Relish**

Thaw fish, if frozen. Rinse fish and pat dry with paper towels. Pour milk into a shallow dish. In another shallow dish combine bread crumbs, cornmeal, sesame seed, cilantro, mustard, garlic powder, and pepper. Dip fish into milk, then coat with crumb mixture.

Spray a 13x9x2-inch baking pan with nonstick spray coating. Arrange fish in pan. Bake in a 450° oven till fish is golden and flakes easily when tested with a fork. Allow 4 to 6 minutes per ½ inch thickness. Transfer to a serving platter. Serve with Bok Choy Relish. Makes 4 servings.

Microwave directions: To thaw frozen fish fillets, in a 12x7½x2-inch microwave-safe baking dish micro-cook fillets, uncovered, on 30% power (low) for 6 to 8 minutes or till nearly thawed. Drain. Let stand for 10 minutes.

Rinse, dry, and coat fish as directed. Return to 12x7½x2-inch baking dish. Cover with clear plastic wrap; vent by leaving a small area unsealed at the edge of the dish. Micro-cook on 100% power (high) for 5 to 7 minutes or

till fish flakes easily when tested with a fork. Transfer to a serving platter. Serve as directed at left.

Bok Choy Relish: In a small bowl combine 2 tablespoons plain *low-fat yogurt,* ½ teaspoon *prepared mustard,* and ⅛ teaspoon *pepper.* Stir in 1 cup finely chopped *bok choy,* 2 tablespoons sliced *green onion,* and 1 tablespoon chopped *pimiento.* Serve immediately or cover and chill for up to 8 hours.

Nutrition information per serving: 180 cal., 22 g pro., 9 g carbo., 6 g fat, 65 mg chol., 1 g fiber, 128 mg sodium. U.S. RDA: 11% vit. A, 15% vit. C, 12% niacin, 34% phosphorus.

BROWNIE FRUIT TORTE

   Nonstick spray coating
 - 1 **cup all-purpose flour**
 - ¼ **cup unsweetened cocoa powder**
 - 1 **teaspoon baking powder**
 - ¼ **teaspoon baking soda**
 - ¼ **cup margarine**
 - ⅔ **cup sugar**
 - ¾ **teaspoon vanilla**
 - ⅔ **cup ice-cold water**
 - 2 **egg whites**
 - ½ **of an 8-ounce carton reduced-calorie soft-style cream cheese**
 - ½ **cup diced fresh tofu (bean curd) (3 ounces)**
 - 1 **tablespoon sugar**
 - 2 **tablespoons frozen pineapple juice concentrate**
 - 1 **11-ounce can mandarin orange sections, drained**
 - 2 **kiwi fruits, peeled and sliced**
 - ¼ **cup sliced strawberries**
 - 1 **slice carambola (star fruit) (optional)**

Spray an 8x1½-inch round baking pan with nonstick spray coating; set aside. In a medium mixing bowl stir together flour, cocoa powder, baking powder, and baking soda; set aside.

In a large mixer bowl beat margarine on medium speed for 30 seconds. Add ⅔ cup sugar and vanilla; beat on medium speed till combined. Add dry ingredients and cold water alternately, beating on low speed after each addition. Thoroughly wash beaters.

In a small bowl beat egg whites till stiff peaks form (tips stand straight). Fold egg whites into flour mixture. Turn into the prepared pan. Bake in a 375° oven for 25 to 30 minutes or till cake springs back and leaves no imprint when lightly touched. Cool for 10 minutes on a wire rack. Remove from the pan; cool completely.

For filling, in blender container or food processor combine cream cheese and tofu. Cover and blend or process till smooth. Add 1 tablespoon sugar and pineapple juice concentrate and blend or process till mixed.

To assemble torte, use a sharp knife with a long blade to carefully cut cake horizontally into 2 layers. Place bottom half on a serving plate. Spread *half* of the cream cheese mixture on bottom half. Top with mandarin orange sections, reserving 6 sections to garnish cake.

Replace remaining cake layer, cut side down. Spread remaining cream-cheese mixture on top. Cut kiwi slices in half. Arrange reserved mandarin oranges, kiwi-fruit slices, strawberries, and carambola (if desired) on top of torte. Makes 10 servings.

Microwave directions: Cut circle of waxed paper to fit an 8x1½-inch round microwave-safe dish. Spray with nonstick spray coating. Prepare cake batter as directed. Micro-cook, uncovered, on 50% power (medium) for 9 minutes, giving the dish a quarter-turn every 3 minutes.

If not done, increase the power to 100% (high). Micro-cook for 30 seconds to 2 minutes more or till cake tests done (scrape wet surface with wooden toothpick to look for a crumb texture). Let stand for 5 minutes. Remove from baking dish; remove waxed paper. Continue as directed.

Nutrition information per serving: 210 cal., 5 g pro., 33 g carbo., 8 g fat, 7 mg chol., 1 g fiber, 204 mg sodium. U.S. RDA: 36% vit. C.

APRIL

FAST FAMILY FAVORITES

NO-CHOP STIR-FRYS

FIX ONE TONIGHT!

By Barbara Greenwood

OUT OF THE PAN IN 16 MINUTES!

Five-Spice Beef In Oyster Sauce

Finish off this meal simply with banana slices or orange wedges and tea—

- ⅓ cup oyster sauce *or*
  2 tablespoons soy sauce
- ¼ cup dry sherry
- 1 teaspoon cornstarch
- 1 teaspoon bottled minced garlic
- ½ teaspoon five-spice powder *or*
  ¼ teaspoon ground ginger
- 1 tablespoon cooking oil
- 3 cups cut-up vegetables (sliced mushrooms *or* zucchini; thinly sliced carrots, celery, *or* onion; and green pepper strips)
- ¾ pound lean ground beef

Hot cooked rice

● For sauce, combine oyster or soy sauce, sherry, cornstarch, and ¼ cup *water;* stir in garlic and five-spice powder or ginger.

● Preheat a wok or large skillet over high heat; add oil. Stir-fry vegetables about 3 minutes or till crisp-tender. Remove from wok.

● Break beef into large chunks. Add to hot wok. Stir-fry, breaking up slightly, about 3 minutes or till brown. Drain beef in a colander; pat off fat with paper towels. Wipe fat from wok.

● Return beef to wok; push away from center. Stir sauce; add to center of wok. Cook and stir till bubbly. Cook and stir 1 minute more. Return vegetables to wok; mix well. Cook and stir 1 minute. Serve over rice. Makes 4 servings.

Nutrition information per serving with ½ cup rice: 379 cal., 20 g pro., 34 g carbo., 16 g fat, 58 mg chol., 1,430 mg sodium. U.S. RDA: 174% vit. A, 16% thiamine, 16% riboflavin, 31% niacin, 23% iron, 24% phosphorus.

Photograph: M. Jensen Photography, Inc.
Food stylist: Janet Pittman

Hawaiian Chicken Stir-Fry

Most stir-frys are a meal in one. Just add a whole grain roll—

- 1 16-ounce package loose-pack frozen cut broccoli
- 2 cups frozen diced cooked chicken
- 1 15¼-ounce can pineapple chunks (juice pack)
- ¼ cup water
- 2 tablespoons vinegar
- 2 tablespoons soy sauce
- 1 tablespoon cornstarch
- ½ teaspoon onion powder
- ¼ to ½ teaspoon crushed red pepper
- ¼ teaspoon ground ginger
- 1 tablespoon cooking oil
- 1 3-ounce can chow mein noodles

● Thaw broccoli and chicken as directed in tip below; drain well. Drain pineapple, reserving juice.

● For sauce, stir together reserved juice, water, vinegar, soy sauce, cornstarch, onion powder, red pepper, and ginger. Set aside.

● Preheat a wok or large skillet over high heat; add oil. (Add more oil as needed during cooking.) Stir-fry broccoli 2 minutes or till crisp-tender. Remove from wok. Add chicken to hot wok. Stir-fry for 1 to 2 minutes or till heated through. Push from center of wok.

● Stir sauce; add to center of the wok. Cook and stir till thickened and bubbly. Cook and stir 2 minutes more. Add broccoli; mix well. Reduce heat. Stir in pineapple. Cover and cook 1 minute or till heated through. Serve over noodles. Makes 4 servings.

Nutrition information per serving: 351 cal., 26 g pro., 38 g carbo., 12 g fat, 55 mg chol., 791 mg sodium. U.S. RDA: 49% vit. A, 87% vit. C, 15% thiamine, 13% riboflavin, 44% niacin, 10% calcium, 14% iron, 26% phosphorus.

OUT OF THE PAN IN 18 MINUTES!

QUICK STIR-FRY TIPS

● **SCOUT OUT CUT-UP VEGETABLES** from your supermarket's salad bar to use for stir-frying. They eliminate chopping board time *and* let you pick your favorites. Our Test Kitchen recommends choosing smaller, thinner cuts of broccoli, cauliflower, carrots, and celery so they'll cook quickly and evenly.

● **FOR HOT RICE,** mix up quick-cooking rice just before you start stir-frying. Its 5-minute standing will be done by the time you're finished cooking.

● **QUICK-THAW FROZEN VEGETABLES** by running water over them. Do the same for frozen cut-up chicken, using cool water.

■ HAM WITH ORANGE-RAISIN SAUCE

COOKING TIME **Microwave:** 12 minutes

■ CHICKEN AND CREAMY MUSHROOMS

COOKING TIME **Microwave:** 12 minutes

We zipped up the easy sauce by adding a touch of horseradish—

Turn often: Prevent dry, overcooked spots in large cuts of meat by turning the meat with tongs a few times.

Gather your clan; dinn will be ready before th kids set the table—

Vent: Keep steam pressure from building up; peel back or corner of the plastic wrap bef cooking.

MICROWAVE!
HOME-STYLE COOKING
NOW FASTER, EASIER

By Terri Pauser Wolf

SAUCY MEATBALL SANDWICH

COOKING TIME   **Microwave:** 14 minutes

■ POT ROAST WITH SPRING VEGETABLES

COOKING TIME   **Microwave:** 75 minutes

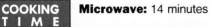

A quick-to-make, roll-up-your-sleeve, lick-your-finger sandwich—

Shape: Make meatballs of uniform shape and size for more even cooking, and more tender, juicier results.

As comforting as Grandma's pot roast, but super slick—

One-dish convenience: Keep the vegetables and roast warm in foil while you use the casserole to make the gravy.

MAIN DISHES
IDEAS THAT GO BEYOND REHEAT AND DEFROST

With the touch of a few buttons, homespun recipes are rejuvenated for today's cook—fast. Not just warmed-up leftovers, but fresh-tasting main dishes. When you say, "I'll have dinner in a minute," you'll mean it!

Micro-cook this sauce with confidence—

Whisk thoroughly: The egg-yolk-based sauce is very delicate, so whisk freqently to distribute the heat and prevent overcooking.

A speedy microwave rising, then into the ov for browning—

Fast rising time: A cup of water placed in the back of th microwave oven is needed to adequately raise yeast dough

MICROWAVE! SIDE DISHES
TIDBITS FOR ONE OR A POTLUCK FOR MANY

Want a warm, fresh-from-the-oven muffin right now?
Try our microwave muffin—it's ready in 1 to 3 minutes!
Need a crowd-pleasin' casserole in a jiff?
Micro-bake beans for 15 in less than 15 minutes!

■ BAKED BEANS SUPREME

Microwave: 14 minutes

■ APRICOT-BRAN MUFFINS

Microwave: 3 minutes

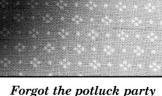

Forgot the potluck party tonight? Quick, make this baked bean recipe—

Simplify steps: Use just one dish and two easy steps to micro-cook this family-pleasing recipe.

You choose—cook 1 muffin in 1 minute or 6 muffins in 3 minutes—

Even placement: Position the six filled custard cups in a ring on a large microwave-safe plate so that the muffins cook evenly.

OVEN WATTAGE CAN MAKE A DIFFERENCE

■ Know your oven's wattage

Once you know the wattage of your microwave oven, you'll understand the variations in microwave cooking times. The higher the wattage, the faster a microwave oven cooks. The wattage may be listed on the back of your oven near the Underwriters Laboratories seal or in your owner's manual. If you can't find it, use this simple test to estimate the number of watts: In a 2-cup glass measure heat 1 cup tap water (about 70°), uncovered, on 100% power (high). If the water boils in less than 3 minutes, then your oven

RECIPES THAT BEGIN ON PAGE 57 INCLUDE TIMINGS FOR LOW-WATTAGE OVENS.

probably has 600 watts or more of output. If the water takes longer than 3 minutes to boil, your microwave oven probably has fewer than 600 watts.

Our microwave recipe timings are for the 600- to 700-watt ovens. *BH&G®* recipe timings usually include a range of cooking times; that's because microwave ovens will vary slightly from manufacturer to manufacturer.

■ Low-wattage ovens differ

Although a bargain in cost, compact 400- to 500-watt microwave ovens cook slower than the 600- to 700-watt ovens. Low-wattage ovens work best with smaller amounts of food. They're perfect for one-serving entrées. Most low-wattage microwaves have small cavities and use smaller cookware. A 12x7½x2-inch baking dish is too large for many low-wattage ovens.

We do not recommend cooking roasts that weigh more than 2 pounds, any pork cut, popcorn, or delicate egg mixtures in low-wattage ovens.

■ CARROT CAKE WITH PINEAPPLE

COOKING TIME **Microwave:** 15 minutes

Halve one tender layer to make a two-layer cake—

Line pan: Remove the cake from the pan with ease—use a waxed-paper liner that will also pull up the wet layer that forms on microwave cakes.

■ ICE CREAM WITH HOT-FUDGE SAUCE

COOKING TIME **Microwave:** 6 minutes

Home-style cooking at it. best; a warm, velvety, sti and-cook sauce—

Convenient serving: Measu and cook the four ingredients i the same bowl in which you pla to serve the tasty sauce.

MICROWAVE! DESSERTS
STEP-SAVING, STREAMLINED COOKING

One-dish cooking, oven-to-table cookware, less waiting, and light cleanup—they all add up to easier, quicker recipes. Now when it comes to desserts, you'll always have enough time to fix them.

■ OATMEAL CARAMEL BARS

■ RHUBARB PIE

COOKING TIME **Microwave:** 12 minutes

Crunchy oatmeal crust, oozy caramel middle, and chocolaty topping—

Streamline steps: Unwrap caramels while micro-cooking crust. Cool crust while making caramel-almond filling.

This recipe takes advantage of both the oven and the microwave—

Quick-thaw fruit: Use the microwave to thaw the frozen rhubarb for the filling before you mix it with the sugar.

MICROWAVE TIPS

FROM THE BH&G® FOOD STAFF WHO MICRO-COOK EVERY DAY

■ **Using lower powers for meat cooking:** In our testing, we've learned that most meats cook best on lower power levels. Ground meat and bacon are exceptions; cook them on high. Use medium-low or the defrost setting for thawing meat.

■ **Using metal:** Small amounts of foil can be used safely in the microwave. Never allow the metal to touch the sides of the microwave and never use silver- or gold-rimmed dishes. Consult your owner's manual before using metal in a microwave.

Placing baked products in a ring shape: Breads, muffins, and cakes are best micro-cooked in ring-shape or round pans because microwaves tend to concentrate in corners and cook there faster than in the center. If you don't have a microwave-safe ring-shape pan and are using a square or rectangular pan, try shielding the corners with foil.

■ **Cleaning your oven:** A clean microwave oven is not just for looks. Food spatters will absorb some of the microwaves, so the food will take longer to cook. Wipe out the inside of the oven while it is still moist and steamy rather than waiting till the spatters are cooked on. Don't forget to clean the door seal.

Dried food hard to remove? Test Kitchen home economist Marge Steenson recommends boiling some water in a glass bowl for a few minutes in the oven to allow the steam to soften the dried food.

Precook: Drain mushrooms on paper towels after precooking to remove excess water.

■ **SALMON-STUFFED MUSHROOM**

COOKING TIME   **Microwave:** 5 minutes

Cook and serve: Sprinkle with toppings; micro-cook a few seconds and take it to the table.

■ **BACON-CHEESE POTATO SLICE**

COOKING TIME   **Microwave:** 12 minutes

Easy preparation: Pull out the inner leaves and spoon out the choke from the artichoke.

■ **SHRIMP ARTICHOKE BITES**

COOKING TIME   **Microwave:** 7 minutes

Quick-cooking party fare: Shrimp Artichoke Bites, Bacon-Cheese Potato Slices, and Salmon-Stuffed Mushrooms.

MICROWAVE!

APPETIZERS
THE MICROWAVE IS THE GREAT ENTERTAINER!

When friends drop in, put the microwave to work heating up snacks and appetizers in minutes. Foods cool down as they sit out on the table? Use your microwave for a quick reheating.

HAM WITH ORANGE-RAISIN SAUCE

This orange-raisin sauce goes great with broiled pork chops, too—

- 1 2-pound fully cooked boneless ham slice, cut 1 inch thick
- ⅔ cup water
- 1 tablespoon cornstarch
- ¼ cup frozen orange juice concentrate, thawed
- ¼ cup raisins
- 1 tablespoon brown sugar
- 2 teaspoons prepared horseradish
- ½ teaspoon instant chicken bouillon granules

Place the ham in a 12x7½x2-inch microwave-safe baking dish. Cover baking dish with waxed paper. Micro-cook on 100% power (high) for 8 to 10 minutes (*low-wattage oven:* 11 to 13 minutes) or till heated through, turning meat over every 3 minutes (*low-wattage oven:* Turn meat over every 4 minutes). Cover baking dish to keep ham warm.

For sauce, in a 2-cup glass measure combine water and cornstarch. Stir in thawed orange juice concentrate, raisins, brown sugar, prepared horseradish, and chicken bouillon granules.

Cook mixture, uncovered, on high for 3 to 4 minutes or till the sauce is thickened and bubbly, stirring after every minute. Cook, uncovered, on high for 30 seconds more. To serve, pass sauce with ham. Makes 6 to 8 servings.

Nutrition information per serving with 2 tablespoons sauce: 268 cal., 32 g pro., 15 g carbo., 8 g fat, 80 mg chol., 1,855 mg sodium. U.S. RDA: 54% vit. C, 78% thiamine, 19% riboflavin, 31% niacin, 31% phosphorus, and 14% iron.

CHICKEN AND CREAMY MUSHROOMS

- 1 10-ounce package frozen long grain and wild rice
- 2 whole medium chicken breasts (1½ pounds total), skinned, boned, and halved lengthwise
- 2 thin slices fully cooked ham, halved crosswise
- ½ cup shredded Swiss cheese
- 1 cup sliced fresh mushrooms
- 1 tablespoon margarine *or* butter
- 2 tablespoons all-purpose flour
- 1 teaspoon instant chicken bouillon granules
- ¾ teaspoon dried tarragon, crushed
- 1 cup light cream *or* milk
- 2 tablespoons dry white wine

Prepare rice conventionally according to package directions. Meanwhile, rinse chicken; pat dry. Place 1 chicken piece, boned side up, between 2 pieces of clear plastic wrap. Working from center to the edges, pound lightly with a meat mallet to form a rectangle about ¼ inch thick. Remove plastic wrap. Repeat with remaining chicken.

Place 1 piece of ham and *2 tablespoons* of the cheese on each chicken piece. Fold in bottom edge and sides; roll as for jelly roll and secure with wooden toothpicks, if necessary.

Arrange rolls, seam side down, in an 8x8x2-inch microwave-safe baking dish. Cover with vented microwave-safe plastic wrap. Micro-cook on 100% power (high) for 5 to 7 minutes (*low-wattage oven:* 6 to 8 minutes) or till tender. After 3 minutes, give dish a half-turn and rotate rolls so center ends face outside. Cover to keep warm.

For sauce, in a 1-quart microwave-safe casserole cook mushrooms in margarine, covered, on high for 2 to 2½ minutes (*low-wattage oven:* 2½ to 3 minutes) or till tender. Stir in flour, bouillon, and tarragon. Add cream. Cook, uncovered, on high 3 to 4 minutes or till thickened and bubbly, stirring every minute. Cook on high for 30 seconds. Stir in wine. Serve sauce over chicken and rice. Makes 4 servings.

Nutrition information per serving with ¼ cup sauce: 464 cal., 51 g pro., 21 g carbo., 24 g fat, 133 mg chol., 766 mg sodium, 1 g fiber. U.S. RDA: 15% vit. A, 24% thiamine, 22% riboflavin, 70% niacin, 22% calcium, 14% iron, 41% phosphorus.

SAUCY MEATBALL SANDWICH

- 4 6-inch-long French-style rolls
- 1 beaten egg
- 1 pound bulk Italian sausage
- 1 small green pepper, finely chopped (½ cup)
- 1 small onion, finely chopped (¼ cup)
- 2 cloves garlic, minced
- 2 tablespoons margarine *or* butter
- 1 8-ounce can pizza sauce
- ½ teaspoon cornstarch
- ¼ cup shredded mozzarella cheese (2 ounces)

Using a sharp knife, cut a thin slice off the top of each roll and reserve. Hollow out roll bottoms, leaving ½-inch shells and reserving bread pieces. Tear tops and bread pieces into pea-size pieces (¾ cup soft bread crumbs).

Stir together bread crumbs and egg. Add sausage; mix well. Shape mixture into sixteen 1½-inch meatballs. (For evenly shaped balls, pat into a 1-inch-thick square. Then cut into 16 pieces. Roll each into a meatball.)

Arrange meatballs in an 8x8x2-inch microwave-safe baking dish. Cover with vented microwave-safe plastic wrap. Micro-cook meatballs on 100% power (high) for 5½ to 7½ minutes (*low-wattage oven:* 8 to 9 minutes) or till juices run clear, turning meatballs over and rotating dish once or twice. Drain.

For sauce, in a 1-quart microwave-safe casserole combine green pepper, onion, garlic, and margarine or butter. Cook, covered, on high for 2 to 2½ minutes (*low-wattage oven:* 3 minutes) or till tender. Stir together pizza sauce and cornstarch. Stir into vegetables. Cook, uncovered, on high for 1½ to 2½ minutes (*low-wattage oven:* 3 minutes) or till thickened and bubbly, stirring twice during cooking.

Place *four* meatballs in *each* roll. Place rolls in a 12x7½x2-inch microwave-safe baking dish or on a microwave-safe platter. Spoon sauce over each. Sprinkle each with cheese. Cook, uncovered, on high for 1½ to 2 minutes or till cheese melts. Makes 4 servings.

Nutrition information per sandwich: 575 cal., 25 g pro., 57 g carbo., 27 g fat, 120 mg chol., 1,462 mg sodium, 4 g fiber. U.S. RDA: 17% vit. A, 37% vit. C, 48% thiamine, 27% riboflavin, 29% niacin, 18% calcium, 23% iron, 27% phosphorus.

POT ROAST WITH SPRING VEGETABLES

This recipe is not recommended for low-wattage ovens because large cuts of meat do not cook evenly in these ovens—

- 1 2½- to 3-pound beef chuck arm pot roast (cut 1½ inches thick)
- 1 14½-ounce can beef broth
- 2 teaspoons Worcestershire sauce
- 2 cloves garlic, minced
- ½ teaspoon onion powder
- ½ teaspoon salt
- ½ teaspoon pepper
- 12 whole tiny new potatoes
- 2 cups brussels sprouts (12 to 14), halved
- 2 medium carrots, cut into strips
- 1 medium onion, sliced and separated into rings
- ¼ cup water
- 3 tablespoons all-purpose flour

Trim the fat from beef. In a 3-quart microwave-safe casserole combine beef broth, Worcestershire sauce, garlic, onion powder, salt, and pepper. Add beef; turn to coat. Micro-cook, covered, on 100% power (high) for 5 minutes. Cook, covered, on 50% power (medium) for 40 minutes. Turn beef over.

Meanwhile, peel the new potatoes, leaving a 1-inch band in the center of each. Add potatoes, brussels sprouts, carrots, and sliced onion to beef in casserole. Cook, covered, on medium for 20 to 30 minutes or till beef and vegetables are tender. Transfer beef and vegetables to a warm serving platter. Cover with foil to keep warm.

For gravy, pour juices into a 4-cup glass measure. Skim off fat. Measure juices; add water, if necessary, to equal 1½ cups. Pour juices into the casserole. Combine water and flour; stir into juices. Cook, uncovered, on 100% power (high) for 5 to 7 minutes or till thickened and bubbly, stirring every minute.

Slice beef. Serve with vegetables and gravy. Makes 6 to 8 servings.

Nutrition information per serving with 2 tablespoons gravy: 671 cal., 28 g pro., 18 g carbo., 54 g fat, 100 mg chol., 485 mg sodium, 3 g fiber. U.S. RDA: 142% vit. A, 73% vit. C, 13% thiamine, 16% riboflavin, 28% niacin, 25% iron, 19% phosphorus.

Linguine with White Clam Sauce

LINGUINE WITH WHITE CLAM SAUCE

To keep pasta warm, transfer the cooked pasta to a metal colander. Cover colander and place it over a pot of hot water—

- 4 ounces linguine
- ¼ cup thinly sliced green onion
- 1 clove garlic, minced
- 2 tablespoons margarine *or* butter
- 2 tablespoons all-purpose flour
- Dash white pepper
- ¾ cup milk
- 2 6½- *or* 7½-ounce cans minced clams
- ½ cup sliced pitted ripe olives
- 2 tablespoons snipped parsley

Cook linguine following package directions. Drain; keep warm.

In a 1-quart microwave-safe casserole micro-cook green onion, garlic, and margarine or butter, covered, on 100% power (high) for 1 to 2 minutes or till onion is tender. Stir in flour and pepper. Add milk. Cook, uncovered, on high for 3 to 5 minutes or till thickened and bubbly, stirring every minute.

Drain clams; reserve ¼ *cup* juice. Add clams, reserved juice, olives, and parsley to milk mixture. Cook, uncovered, on high for 1 to 2 minutes more or till mixture is heated through. Toss with linguine. Serve at once. Serves 2.

Nutrition information per serving: 535 cal., 27 g pro., 62 g carbo., 20 g fat, 70 mg chol., 1,509 mg sodium, and 3 g fiber. U.S. RDA: 22% vit. A, 40% thiamine, 35% riboflavin, 29% niacin, 28% calcium, 58% iron, 46% phosphorus.

VEGETABLES HOLLANDAISE

For even faster cooking, gather the sauce ingredients while the vegetables cook—

- 3 medium carrots, quartered lengthwise and cut into 2-inch sticks
- ¾ pound asparagus spears
- ¼ cup water
- 2 red sweet peppers, cut into strips
- ½ cup margarine *or* butter
- 2 tablespoons lemon juice
- ⅛ teaspoon salt
- Dash ground white pepper
- Dash ground red pepper
- 3 egg yolks
- 2 to 3 teaspoons hot water

Mound carrots at 1 end of an 8x8x2-inch microwave-safe baking dish. Wash asparagus; scrape off scales. Break off woody bases at point where spears snap easily. Mound asparagus in the center of the dish; add ¼ cup water. Cover with vented microwave-safe plastic wrap. Micro-cook on 100% power (high) for 5 minutes (*low-wattage oven:* 7 minutes), giving the dish a half-turn once.

Uncover and add sweet pepper to other end of dish. Cook, covered, on high for 3 to 4 minutes more (*low-wattage oven:* 5 to 6 minutes) or till vegetables are tender. Let vegetables stand, covered, in dish while preparing sauce.

For sauce, in a 2-cup glass measure combine margarine, lemon juice, salt, white pepper, and red pepper. Cook, uncovered, on high for 1 to 1½ minutes (*low-wattage oven:* about 2½ minutes) or till margarine is melted; stir.

In a 1-quart microwave-safe casserole beat egg yolks. Gradually add melted margarine mixture while beating constantly with a wire whisk. Beat till smooth. Cook, uncovered, on high for 30 to 45 seconds (*low-wattage oven:* 40 to 60 seconds) or till thickened, whisking every 10 seconds. Stir in hot water, *1 teaspoon* at a time, till sauce is of desired consistency.

Use a slotted spoon to transfer vegetables to a serving platter. Serve sauce over vegetables. Makes 4 servings.

Nutrition information per serving with ¼ cup sauce: 356 cal., 8 g pro., 13 g carbo., 32 fat, 397 mg chol., 370 mg sodium, 4 g fiber. U.S. RDA: 416% vit. A, 175% vit. C, 17% thiamine, 16% riboflavin, 17% iron, 21% phosphorus.

HOT CROSS BUNS

For fast yeast breads, try microwave proofing. Be sure to test your oven first (see proofing test below). If your lowest setting has too much power, it will kill the yeast before the bread can rise. Proofing is not recommended in low-wattage microwave ovens—

  2 to 2½ cups all-purpose flour
  1 package active dry yeast
  ½ teaspoon ground cinnamon
  ⅓ cup milk
  ¼ cup cooking oil
  3 tablespoons sugar
  ¼ teaspoon salt
  2 eggs
  ⅓ cup currants *or* raisins
  3 cups water
  1 slightly beaten egg white
  ½ cup sifted powdered sugar
  ¼ teaspoon vanilla
  1 to 2 teaspoons milk

Test your microwave oven for proofing bread (see test *below*).

In a small mixer bowl stir together ¾ cup of the flour, yeast, and cinnamon; set aside. In a 2-cup glass measure combine ⅓ cup milk, cooking oil, sugar, and salt. Micro-cook, uncovered, on 100% power (high) for 30 to 60 seconds or till warm (120° to 130°). Stir mixture to dissolve sugar.

Add to flour mixture. Add eggs. Beat with an electric mixer on low speed for 30 seconds, scraping sides of bowl constantly. Beat on high speed for 3 minutes. Stir in currants or raisins. Using a spoon, stir in as much of the remaining flour as you can.

Turn dough out onto a lightly floured surface. Knead in enough of the remaining flour to make a moderately soft dough that is smooth and elastic (3 to 5 minutes total). Shape dough into a ball. Place in a lightly greased microwave-safe bowl; turn once to grease surface. Cover with waxed paper; set aside.

Pour water into a 4-cup glass measure. Cook, uncovered, on 100% power (high) for 6½ to 8½ minutes or till boiling. Position hot water in the back of microwave oven. Add bowl of dough to microwave. Heat dough along with water on 10% power (low) for 10 to 12 minutes or till almost double. Punch dough down. Cover; let rest 10 minutes.

Divide dough into 9 pieces; form each piece into a smooth ball. Place balls on a greased 12-inch microwave-safe plate; cover loosely with waxed paper. Heat dough with water on low for 5 to 7 minutes or till nearly doubled.

With a sharp knife cut a shallow cross in the top of each bun. Brush tops with egg white. Bake in a 375° oven about 12 minutes or till brown. Transfer to a wire rack; cool slightly.

Meanwhile, for frosting, in a small mixing bowl stir together powdered sugar, vanilla, and enough of the 1 to 2 teaspoons milk to make a frosting of piping consistency. Using a pastry bag filled with frosting, pipe a cross on the top of *each* bun. Let frosting dry before storing buns. Makes 9 buns.

Proofing test: Place 2 tablespoons cold *stick margarine* in a 6-ounce glass custard cup. Cook, uncovered, on low (10% power) for 4 minutes. If margarine melts in *less* than 4 minutes, use a conventional proofing method.

Nutrition information per bun: 243 cal., 5 g pro., 38 g carbo., 8 g fat, 62 mg chol., 86 mg sodium, 1 g fiber. U.S. RDA: 11% vit. C, 14% thiamine, 12% riboflavin, 10% iron.

BAKED BEANS SUPREME

  1 large onion, chopped (1 cup)
  1 green pepper, cut into 1-inch pieces
  1 clove garlic, minced
  2 tablespoons water
  1 17-ounce can lima beans, drained
  1 15½-ounce can butter beans with molasses sauce and bacon
  1 15½-ounce can red kidney beans, drained
  1 15-ounce can garbanzo beans, drained
  1 8-ounce can sliced water chestnuts, drained
  ¾ cup catsup
  2 tablespoons brown sugar
  1 tablespoon Dijon-style mustard
  1 tablespoon Worcestershire sauce
  ¼ to ½ teaspoon pepper

If using a low-wattage oven, first check the oven cavity to be sure it will hold a 3-quart microwave-safe casserole.

In a 3-quart microwave-safe casserole combine onion, green pepper, garlic, and water. Micro-cook, covered, on 100% power (high) for 4 to 5 minutes or till onion and pepper are tender; drain.

Stir lima beans, *undrained* butter beans, kidney beans, garbanzo beans, water chestnuts, catsup, brown sugar, mustard, Worcestershire sauce, and pepper into vegetable mixture. Cook, covered, on high for 10 to 12 minutes (*low-wattage oven:* 20 to 22 minutes) or till hot, stirring every 5 minutes. Makes 15 servings.

Nutrition information per ½-cup serving: 136 cal., 6 g pro., 25 g carbo., 2 g fat, 1 mg chol., 359 mg sodium, 4 g fiber. U.S. RDA: 19% vit. C, 13% iron, 11% phosphorus.

APRICOT-BRAN MUFFINS

1 beaten egg
1 cup buttermilk *or* sour milk
¼ cup packed brown sugar
2 tablespoons cooking oil
½ cup whole bran cereal
1 cup all-purpose flour
1¼ teaspoons baking powder
¾ teaspoon ground cinnamon
½ teaspoon ground nutmeg
¼ teaspoon baking soda
⅛ teaspoon salt
½ cup snipped dried apricots
1 recipe Wheat Germ Topping

In a medium mixing bowl combine egg, buttermilk, sugar, and cooking oil. Stir in bran cereal. Let stand 5 minutes.

Meanwhile, in a medium mixing bowl combine flour, baking powder, cinnamon, nutmeg, baking soda, and salt. Add to bran mixture. Stir just till moistened. Fold in snipped apricots. Cover and chill batter in an airtight container up to 1 week.

To serve, line six 6-ounce glass custard cups or a microwave-safe muffin pan with paper bake cups. For *each* muffin, spoon about *3 tablespoons* batter into a lined cup. (If using custard cups, arrange in a ring on a microwave-safe plate.) Sprinkle *1 teaspoon* Wheat Germ Topping over *each* muffin.

Micro-cook, uncovered, on 100% power (high) for 30 to 60 seconds for 1 muffin, 1 to 2 minutes for 2 muffins, 1½ to 2½ minutes for 4 muffins, or 2½ to 3½ minutes for 6 muffins or till done, giving the plate or pan a half-turn every minute.

To test for doneness, scratch the slightly wet surface with a wooden toothpick. The muffin should be cooked underneath. If using custard cups, remove each cup as the muffin is done. Remove muffins from cups or pan. Let stand on a wire rack for 5 minutes. Serve warm. Makes about 12.

Wheat Germ Topping: In a small bowl combine 2 tablespoons *toasted wheat germ*, 2 tablespoons finely chopped *nuts*, and 1 tablespoon *brown sugar*. Store topping, covered, in an airtight container in refrigerator.

Nutrition information per muffin:
126 cal., 3 g pro., 21 g carbo., 4 g fat, 24 mg chol., 133 mg sodium, 2 g fiber. U.S. RDA: 11% vit. A.

CONFETTI CORN BREAD

To make plain corn bread, just omit the oregano, chili peppers, pimiento, and green onion. This recipe is not recommended for low-wattage ovens—

1 tablespoon yellow cornmeal
1 cup all-purpose flour
1 cup yellow cornmeal
2 to 4 tablespoons sugar
1 tablespoon baking powder
¼ teaspoon salt
¼ teaspoon dried oregano, crushed
2 slightly beaten eggs
1 cup milk
¼ cup cooking oil
1 4-ounce can chopped green chili peppers, drained
1 2-ounce jar sliced pimiento, diced and drained
2 tablespoons finely chopped green onion

Grease a 6½-cup microwave-safe ring mold. Coat with the 1 tablespoon cornmeal. Set aside.

In mixing bowl stir together flour, 1 cup cornmeal, sugar, baking powder, salt, and oregano. Add eggs, milk, and cooking oil. Beat with rotary beater just till combined (*do not* overbeat). Fold in green chili peppers, pimiento, and green onion. Pour evenly into mold.

Micro-cook, uncovered, on 50% power (medium) for 8 minutes, giving mold a quarter-turn after every 3 minutes. Cook, uncovered, on 100% power (high) for 1 to 1½ minutes or till done. To check doneness, scratch the slightly wet surface near the center with a wooden toothpick. There should be a crumb texture just beneath the surface.

Let stand for 10 minutes in mold on a wire rack. Using a knife or a narrow metal spatula, loosen edge. Invert onto a wire rack; remove mold. Serve warm. Makes 1 ring, 10 to 12 servings.

Nutrition information per serving:
185 cal., 5 g pro., 24 g carbo., 8 g fat, 57 mg chol., 203 mg sodium, and 3 g fiber. U.S. RDA: 10% thiamine, 12% calcium, 10% phosphorus.

CARROT CAKE WITH PINEAPPLE

1 cup all-purpose flour
1 cup packed brown sugar
1 teaspoon baking powder
½ teaspoon ground cinnamon
¼ teaspoon baking soda
1½ cups finely shredded carrots
⅓ cup cooking oil
⅓ cup milk
1 beaten egg
¼ cup finely chopped pecans
1 8-ounce can crushed pineapple
1 tablespoon cornstarch
1 recipe Pineapple Frosting

Grease the bottom of an 8x1½-inch microwave-safe round baking dish. Line bottom with waxed paper. Combine flour, sugar, baking powder, cinnamon, soda, and ⅛ teaspoon *salt*. Add carrots, oil, milk, and egg. Stir just till mixed. (Batter will be thin.) Stir in nuts.

Pour into dish. Micro-cook, uncovered, on 50% power (medium) 13 to 15 minutes. Give a quarter-turn every 5 minutes. (*Low-wattage oven:* Micro-cook on 100% power (high) 8½ to 9½ minutes, turning every 2 minutes.)

To test for doneness, scratch wet surface with a toothpick. Cake should be cooked underneath. If not, cook on 100% power (high) for 30 seconds to 2 minutes more. Cool on a rack for 5 minutes. Loosen edges and invert. Remove waxed paper. Cool cake.

For filling, drain pineapple, reserving juice. Set aside ¼ cup pineapple for frosting. In a 2-cup glass measure mix reserved juice and cornstarch. Stir in remaining pineapple. Cook, uncovered, on high for 2 to 3½ minutes or till bubbly, stirring every minute. Cook, uncovered, on high for 30 seconds more. Cover; cool. Cut cake in half crosswise. Spread half with filling. Top with remaining half. Frost with Pineapple Frosting. Makes 6 to 8 servings.

Pineapple Frosting: In a small mixer bowl beat 3 tablespoons *margarine* or *butter* and 2 cups sifted *powdered sugar* with an electric mixer on low speed till well mixed. Add reserved *pineapple* and beat till fluffy. Add ¼ to ½ cup additional powdered sugar to make frosting spreadable.

Nutrition information per serving:
609 cal., 5 g pro., 101 g carbo., 23 g fat, 47 mg chol., 248 mg sodium, 2 g fiber. U.S. RDA: 161% vit. A, 11% vit. C, 17% thiamine, 10% riboflavin, 11% calcium, 16% iron.

ICE CREAM WITH HOT-FUDGE SAUCE

This thick, rich sauce could become a household favorite—

½ cup sugar
3 squares (3 ounces) semisweet chocolate *or* ½ cup semisweet chocolate pieces
¼ cup margarine *or* butter
1 5-ounce can (⅔ cup) evaporated milk
1 teaspoon vanilla
Ice cream

In a 1-quart microwave-safe casserole or a 4-cup glass measure combine sugar, semisweet chocolate or chocolate pieces, and margarine or butter, and evaporated milk.

Micro-cook mixture, uncovered, on 100% power (high) for 2 to 3 minutes (*low-wattage oven: 3 to 4 minutes*) or till bubbly, stirring after every minute. Cook on high 3 minutes more (*low-wattage oven: 4 to 5 minutes*) or till sugar is dissolved and mixture is thickened, stirring once. Stir in vanilla.

Serve sauce warm over ice cream. Cover and store any remaining sauce in refrigerator. Makes 1⅓ cups sauce.

Microwave reheating directions: Spoon ½ *cup* sauce in a 1-cup glass measure. Cook, uncovered, on high about 1 minute (*low-wattage oven: 1½ to 2 minutes*) or till heated through, stirring once.

Nutrition information per 2 tablespoons sauce and ½ cup ice cream: 281 cal., 4 g pro., 33 g carbo., 16 g fat, 35 mg chol., 130 mg sodium, 0 g fiber. U.S. RDA: 10% vit. A, 13% riboflavin, 14% calcium, 12% phosphorus.

RHUBARB PIE

Bake your piecrust in the conventional oven while you prepare the filling—

1 recipe Baked 9-inch Pastry Shell
1½ pounds fresh rhubarb, cut into 1-inch pieces, *or* 6 cups frozen unsweetened sliced rhubarb (1½ 16-ounce packages)
1¼ cups sugar
¼ cup cornstarch
Whipped cream *or* ice cream (optional)

Prepare pastry shell and cool. To thaw frozen rhubarb, place in a 2-quart microwave-safe casserole and micro-cook, uncovered, on 100% power (high) about 5 minutes (*low-wattage oven: 7 minutes*) or till fruit is thawed; *do not* drain.

Combine sugar with cornstarch, then stir into fresh or thawed rhubarb in casserole. Let stand for 5 minutes.

Cook fruit mixture, uncovered, on high for 8 to 10 minutes (*low-wattage oven: 18 to 20 minutes*) or till thickened and bubbly, stirring every 2 minutes (*low-wattage oven: Stir every 5 minutes*) till fruit mixture begins to thicken, then every minute. Cook on high for 1 minute more.

Pour the fruit mixture into pastry shell. Cool completely. Cover and chill, if desired. Cut into wedges. Serve with dollops of whipped cream or scoops of ice cream, if desired. Makes 8 servings.

Baked 9-inch Pastry Shell: In a mixing bowl stir together 1¼ cups *all-purpose flour* and ½ teaspoon *salt*. Cut in ⅓ cup *shortening* till pieces are the size of small peas. Sprinkle 1 tablespoon of *cold water* over part of the mixture; gently toss with a fork. Push to side of bowl. Repeat with 2 to 3 more tablespoons *cold water* till all is moistened. Form dough into a ball.

On a lightly floured surface flatten dough with hands. Roll dough from center to edge, forming a circle about 12 inches in diameter. Wrap pastry around rolling pin. Unroll onto a 9-inch pie plate. Ease pastry into pie plate, being careful not to stretch. Trim to ½ inch beyond edge of pie plate; fold under extra pastry. Flute edge. Prick bottom and sides with a fork. Bake in a 450° oven for 10 to 12 minutes or till golden. Cool on a wire rack.

Nutrition information per serving: 274 cal., 1 g pro., 50 g carbo., 8 g fat, 0 mg chol., 167 mg sodium, 3 g fiber.

OATMEAL CARAMEL BARS

1½ cups quick-cooking rolled oats
¾ cup all-purpose flour
⅔ cup packed brown sugar
¼ teaspoon baking soda
⅔ cup margarine *or* butter
25 vanilla caramels
2 tablespoons margarine *or* butter
1 tablespoon milk
½ cup sliced almonds
⅓ cup miniature semisweet chocolate pieces

In a mixing bowl stir together quick-cooking oats, flour, brown sugar, and baking soda; set aside. In a 1-cup glass measure micro-cook ⅔ cup margarine or butter, uncovered, on 100% power (high) for 45 to 60 seconds (*low-wattage oven: 1 to 1½ minutes*) or till melted. Stir into oat mixture.

For topper, sprinkle *1 cup* of the oat mixture evenly in an ungreased 8x8x2-inch microwave-safe baking dish. Cook, uncovered, on high for 3 to 3½ minutes or till bubbly and mixture starts to look dry, stirring after 2 minutes. (Don't overcook. If the mixture turns dark brown, then it has burned.) Turn out onto foil and cool. (Mixture will crisp as it cools.) Crumble.

For crust, pat remaining oat mixture evenly onto the bottom of the same baking dish. Cook, uncovered, on 50% power (medium) for 3 to 5 minutes (*low-wattage oven: 4 to 5 minutes on high*) or till surface appears puffy and begins to look dry, giving the dish a half-turn after 2 minutes (*low-wattage oven: a quarter-turn twice*). (Mixture will firm upon cooling.) Cool on a rack for 10 minutes.

In a 1-quart microwave-safe casserole combine caramels, the 2 tablespoons margarine or butter, and milk. Cook, uncovered, on 100% power (high) for 1 to 2 minutes (*low-wattage oven: 2 to 3 minutes*) or till caramels are softened and can be stirred smooth. Stir in almonds. Spread over cooled crust.

Top with crumbled topper, pressing lightly into caramel mixture. Sprinkle with chocolate pieces. Cook, uncovered, on high for 30 to 60 seconds (*low-wattage oven: 1 to 1½ minutes*) or till chocolate is just softened. Cool. Cut into squares. Makes 16.

Nutrition information per bar: 258 cal., 3 g pro., 32 g carbo., 14 g fat, 0 mg chol., 159 mg sodium, 1 g fiber.

SALMON-STUFFED MUSHROOMS

Prepare the mushroom caps and filling ahead, then fill the caps just before your guests are scheduled to arrive—

- 20 large fresh mushrooms
- 1 3-ounce package cream cheese, softened
- ¼ cup finely chopped green onion
- 2 tablespoons finely chopped pecans
- ½ teaspoon dried dillweed
- ½ teaspoon Worcestershire sauce
- ¼ teaspoon salt
- Several dashes bottled hot pepper sauce
- 1 6½-ounce can boneless, skinless pink salmon, drained and flaked
- Caviar (optional)
- Parsley leaves (optional)

Clean mushrooms; remove stems. Place *half* of the mushroom caps, stem side up, around edge of a 10- or 12-inch round microwave-safe plate. Cover caps with waxed paper; micro-cook on 100% power (high) for 2 to 4 minutes or till almost tender and just starting to water out, giving the plate a half-turn once. Invert onto paper towels. Repeat with remaining mushroom caps.

Meanwhile, for filling, in a mixing bowl stir together cream cheese, onion, pecans, dillweed, Worcestershire sauce, salt, and hot pepper sauce. Stir in salmon. Spoon about *1 rounded teaspoon* of the filling into *each* mushroom cap.

Place *half* of the filled caps around the edge of the same plate. Cook, uncovered, on high for 1½ to 2½ minutes or till heated through, giving the dish a half-turn once.

Top each mushroom cap with caviar and a small parsley leaf, if desired. Serve immediately. Cook the remaining mushroom caps. Makes 20 caps.

Nutrition information per appetizer: 38 cal., 2 g pro., 1 g carbo., 3 g fat, 7 mg chol., 81 mg sodium, 1 g fiber.

BACON-CHEESE POTATO SLICES

When you're in a hurry, substitute precooked bacon pieces for the bacon and skip half the work—

- 3 slices bacon
- 2 medium baking potatoes
- 2 tablespoons finely chopped green onion
- 2 tablespoons sliced pitted ripe olives
- ¾ cup shredded sharp cheddar cheese (3 ounces)

Arrange bacon slices on 3 layers of microwave-safe paper towels on a microwave-safe plate. Top with a microwave-safe paper towel. Micro-cook on 100% power (high) for 2½ to 3 minutes or till done. Let slices stand 3 minutes to crisp. Crumble bacon and set aside.

Meanwhile, scrub baking potatoes; trim ends. Do not peel. Cut into ⅜-inch-thick slices. Evenly arrange slices on a 12-inch microwave-safe plate, putting smaller-diameter slices in the center.

Sprinkle each potato slice with some of the green onion. Cook potatoes and onion, covered with vented microwave-safe plastic wrap, on high for 7 to 10 minutes or till potato is tender, giving the dish a half-turn once.

Top each potato slice with some of the crumbled bacon, ripe olives, and shredded cheddar cheese. Cook, uncovered, on 50% power (medium) for 1 to 1½ minutes (*low-wattage oven:* Cook on *high*) till cheese just begins to melt. Serve immediately. Makes 4 servings.

Nutrition information per 4 slices: 273 cal., 10 g pro., 35 g carbo., 10 g fat, 27 mg chol., 271 mg sodium, and 2 g fiber. U.S. RDA: 15% vit. C, 10% riboflavin, 14% niacin, 18% calcium, 31% iron, 21% phosphorus.

SHRIMP ARTICHOKE BITES

- 2 medium artichokes
- Lemon juice
- ¼ cup water
- 1 8-ounce container soft-style cream cheese with chives and onion
- 2 tablespoons sunflower nuts
- 1 4½-ounce can shrimp, rinsed, drained, and chilled
- Assorted crackers

Rinse artichokes; trim stems. Remove loose outer leaves. Cut off 1 inch from tops; snip off sharp leaf tips. Brush cut edges with lemon juice. Remove and discard center leaves.

Place the artichokes upright in an 8x8x2-inch microwave-safe baking dish. Add water. Cover with vented microwave-safe plastic wrap. Micro-cook on 100% power (high) for 5 to 7 minutes (*low-wattage oven:* 8 to 10 minutes) or till tender and a leaf pulls out easily. Let stand, covered, for 4 minutes. Drain and chill thoroughly.

At serving time, in a small mixing bowl stir together cream cheese and sunflower nuts. Using a spoon, remove and discard chokes from artichokes. Pull the leaves off *one* artichoke. Reserve the leaves. Chop artichoke heart and stem; stir into cheese mixture.

Using a table knife, spread a small amount of the cheese mixture on the edible end of each reserved leaf. Top each with a shrimp. Fill the center of the whole artichoke with the remaining cheese mixture. Serve filled leaves and crackers with the whole artichoke. Makes 10 appetizer servings.

Nutrition information per 2 filled artichoke leaves: 114 cal., 6 g pro., 4 g carbo., 9 g fat, 43 mg chol., 127 mg sodium, 1 g fiber.

SUPPER SALADS

FRESH, ELEGANT, READY IN MINUTES!

By Barbara Greenwood

TOSSED TURKEY, GREENS, AND BERRIES

Strawberries and greens . . . an unlikely, yet elegant and tasty, duo—

- **1 pint fresh strawberries**
- **4 cups torn mixed greens (such as spinach and red leaf lettuce)**
- **¼ cup red wine vinegar and oil salad dressing**
- **½ of a sweet red onion, sliced, separated into rings, and halved**
- **¾ pound turkey breast tenderloin steaks *or* skinless, boneless chicken breasts, cut into bite-size strips**
- **2 tablespoons honey**
- **¼ teaspoon dried dillweed**

● Hull strawberries; discard hulls. Halve strawberries. In a large mixing bowl combine strawberries and mixed greens. Set aside.

● In a 12-inch skillet heat *half* of the dressing. Add the red onion. Stir-fry for 1½ to 2 minutes or till onion is tender. Remove from the skillet. Heat the remaining dressing in same skillet.

● Stir-fry turkey or chicken in hot dressing for 2 to 3 minutes or till done. Add onion, honey, and dillweed; heat through. Remove the skillet from heat. Immediately add greens mixture; lightly toss about 1 minute or till greens begin to wilt. Serve at once, passing additional dressing. Season with salt and pepper. Makes 4 servings.

Nutrition information per serving: 259 cal., 23 g pro., 18 g carbo., 10 g fat, 45 mg chol., and 997 mg sodium. U.S. RDA: 52% vit. A, 97% vit. C, 14% riboflavin, 42% niacin, 11% iron, and 27% phosphorus.

MOROCCAN SALAD EXPRESS

Irresistible and special enough to deserve your good china—

- **⅓ cup water**
- **1 teaspoon margarine *or* butter**
- **⅓ cup quick-cooking couscous**
- **½ pound fresh asparagus spears**
- **¼ cup mayonnaise *or* salad dressing**
- **1 teaspoon lemon juice**
- **½ teaspoon coarse-grain brown mustard**
- **¼ teaspoon dried tarragon, crushed**
- **3 lemon slices, halved**
- **6 ounces thinly sliced, fully cooked ham**
- **1 tablespoon pine nuts *or* almonds, toasted**

● In a small saucepan bring water and margarine or butter to boiling. Add couscous. Remove from heat. Cover; let stand 4 minutes or till liquid is absorbed. Transfer to a bowl. Chill in freezer 10 minutes, stirring once.

● Rinse asparagus spears; break off and discard woody bases. Place spears in a 10x6x2-inch microwave-safe baking dish. Add 2 tablespoons *water*. Cover with clear plastic wrap; vent by leaving a small area unsealed at the edge of the dish. Micro-cook on 100% power (high) for 3½ to 4½ minutes or till tender. Place spears in ice water.

● For dressing, in a small mixing bowl combine mayonnaise or salad dressing, lemon juice, mustard, and tarragon. Chill in the freezer.

● Divide couscous and lemon slices between 2 plates. Fold ham slices into quarters; place beside couscous. Drain asparagus; place atop couscous. Spoon on the dressing. Sprinkle with pine nuts. Garnish with a mint leaf, if desired. Makes 2 servings.

Nutrition information per serving: 476 cal., 25 g pro., 23 g carbo., 33 g fat, 63 mg chol., 1,235 mg sodium. U.S. RDA: 24% vit. A, 66% vit. C, 55% thiamine, 19% riboflavin, 26% niacin, 16% iron, 26% phosphorus.

THE NEW
HOME COOKING!
FABULOUS BEEF AND PORK RECIPES FOR TODAY'S LIGHTER TASTES

By Barbara Greenwood

Home cooking in the '80s—it's light, lean, and easy on meat. But, it's still full of taste and satisfaction. These meals show you the best ways to include meat in your home cooking. Read on for healthful hints you can use every day!

▲Peppered Meatballs In Tomato Sauce

Be smart; bake the meatballs on a rack in a pan. The fat drips away! So no one walks off hungry, pump the sauce full of vegetables and serve over spaghetti squash.

◄Light 'n' Spicy Tostada Cups

Savor this meal-in-a-shell without kissing sound nutrition good-bye. Brown naturally lean flank steak in a small amount of cooking oil. Bake, rather than deep-fry, the tortilla cup.

Sirloin with Apple-Yogurt Sauce ▶

When warm weather hits, celebrate by throwing a steak on the grill. But, just don't overdo a good thing. To keep up healthful eating habits, let a 1½-pound steak serve six people.

Photographs: Ron Crofoot
Food stylist: Judy Tills

HOME COOKING!
THE NEW

▲Vegetable and Pork Stir-Fry

Stir-frying is a healthful way to cook just as long as you use a light hand with the oil. Start by spraying your wok with nonstick spray coating. That way, you'll need to add only a smidgen of fat later.

Make the juicy meat strips (the protein) go farther, and up the carbohydrates you're eating by mixing in a heaping portion of crisp-cooked vegetables.

Better Burgers ▶

Here's the perfect recipe for big, juicy patties: Pick out 1 pound of 85- to 90-percent lean ground beef.

Next, add fiber by mixing in a bit of bulgur (precooked cracked wheat).

Finally, put your burgers under the broiler—the health-smart way to cook them. Bid the fat adieu as it cooks out and away from the meat!

Pork with Spring Rhubarb Sauce ▶

Pork loin roasts and loin chops head the "good pork cuts" list because they're so lean. When you're shopping for your meat, select the rib roast that has the least amount of fat on the outside. If you cook the roast bone side down, the ribs will act like a rack, letting the fat drip away.

Pork Tenderloin With Gingered Fruit Sauce ▶

Um-m-m-m, tenderloin. It may sound sinful, but it's not. Although tenderloin is inherently tender and juicy, it's still amazingly low in fat. That's why it's a great choice for people interested in a light-eating lifestyle.

For health's sake, serve each person three thin slices (about 3 ounces total of the cooked meat). Such a serving provides the needed protein for any one meal.

69

LIME BEEF AND VEGETABLES

HERB-TOMATO BEEF KABOBS

HOME COOKING!
THE NEW
20-MINUTE MEALS FROM PRECUT BEEF

Talk about more convenience! Many supermarkets now offer stir-fry meat and ready-to-cook kabobs in their fresh meat cases. (The butchers do the slicing or cutting and threading for you.) Try these handy meats in these lickety-split recipes.

Herb-Tomato Beef Kabobs

- 1 6-ounce can (⅔ cup) tomato juice
- ½ of a 0.7-ounce envelope Italian dry salad dressing mix (2½ teaspoons)
- 1 teaspoon cornstarch
- 4 fresh ready-to-cook beef kabobs

● In small saucepan combine juice, dressing mix, and cornstarch. Cook and stir till thickened and bubbly. Cook and stir 2 minutes more.

● Preheat broiler unit. Place kabobs on the unheated rack of a broiler pan. Broil 4 to 5 inches from heat to desired doneness (8 minutes for medium-rare to 12 minutes for well-done), turning and brushing with tomato mixture often.

● Or, grill kabobs, uncovered, directly over *hot* coals to desired doneness (8 minutes for medium-rare; 12 minutes for well-done); turn and brush with tomato mixture often. Serve with herb-buttered toasted French bread, if desired. Makes 4 servings.

Nutrition information per serving: 185 cal., 22 g pro., 13 g carbo., 5 g fat, 60 mg chol., 482 mg sodium. U.S. RDA: 10% vit. A, 24% vit. C, 20% riboflavin, 26% niacin, 20% iron, 17% phosphorus.

Lime Beef and Vegetables

- ½ teaspoon finely shredded lime peel
- 2 tablespoons lime juice
- 2 tablespoons Worcestershire sauce
- 2 teaspoons sugar
- 1½ teaspoons cornstarch

• • •

Nonstick spray coating
- 1 9-ounce package frozen French-style green beans with toasted almonds, thawed and drained
- 2 green onions, cut into ½-inch lengths
- 1 teaspoon bottled minced garlic
- ¾ pound precut stir-fry beef
- 1 4-ounce can sliced mushrooms, drained

Hot cooked couscous *or* rice (optional)

● For sauce, mix lime peel, lime juice, Worcestershire sauce, sugar, cornstarch, and 1 tablespoon *water*.

● Spray a 12-inch skillet or a wok with nonstick spray coating. Preheat skillet or wok over high heat. Add the beans and almonds, onions, and garlic. Cook and stir 2 to 3 minutes or till tender. Remove from skillet.

● Stir-fry beef 2 to 3 minutes or till done. Push beef from center of skillet. Stir sauce. Add to skillet. Cook and stir till thickened and bubbly. Cook and stir for 1 minute more. Add bean mixture and mushrooms; mix well. Heat through. Serve over couscous. Garnish with lime slices, if desired. Makes 4 servings.

Nutrition information per serving: 180 cal., 21 g pro., 12 g carbo., 6 g fat, 55 mg chol., 263 mg sodium. U.S. RDA: 11% vit. C, 14% riboflavin, 26% niacin, 20% iron, 24% phosphorus.

PEPPERED MEATBALLS IN TOMATO SAUCE

  1 **egg white**
  ¼ **cup milk**
  3 **tablespoons fine dry bread crumbs**
  2 **tablespoons chopped green onion**
  ¼ **teaspoon pepper**
  1 **pound lean ground pork**
  1 **3-pound spaghetti squash**
1½ **cups loose-pack frozen mixed cauliflower, broccoli, and carrots, cooked**
  1 **15½-ounce jar meatless chunky-style spaghetti sauce**
  3 **tablespoons dry red wine**
Grated Parmesan cheese (optional)

In a bowl mix egg white and milk. Stir in crumbs, onion, and pepper. Add pork; mix well. Shape into thirty-two 1-inch meatballs. Place on rack in shallow baking pan. Bake in a 375° oven 25 to 30 minutes or till no pink remains.

Meanwhile, halve squash lengthwise; discard seeds. Place in a Dutch oven. Add *water* to depth of 2 inches. Bring to boiling; reduce heat. Cover and simmer 25 to 30 minutes or till tender.

Drain mixed vegetables; halve any large pieces. In a saucepan mix spaghetti sauce and wine; heat through, stirring often. Gently stir in meatballs and mixed vegetables. Heat through.

Drain squash. Use a fork to shred pulp onto 4 plates. Top with sauce and cheese, if desired. Garnish with fresh herb, if desired. Makes 4 servings.

Nutrition information per serving: 373 cal., 29 g pro., 33 g carbo., 12 g fat, 61 mg chol., 845 mg sodium, 6 g dietary fiber. U.S. RDA: 54% vit. A, 61% vit. C, 163% thiamine, 138% riboflavin, 22% niacin, 18% iron, 20% phosphorus.

LIGHT 'N' SPICY TOSTADA CUPS

  1 **pound beef flank steak**
Nonstick spray coating
  6 **7-inch flour tortillas**
  1 **cup salsa**
  1 **teaspoon cornstarch**
  ½ **teaspoon instant beef bouillon granules**
  1 **medium zucchini, cut into julienne strips (about 2 cups)**
  4 **green onions, bias-sliced into 1-inch lengths**
  1 **tablespoon cooking oil**
Mustard greens *or* lettuce leaves
  ½ **cup shredded Monterey Jack cheese (2 ounces)**

Partially freeze beef. Slice across the grain into thin bite-size strips.

For tostada cups, spray six 10-ounce custard cups with nonstick spray coating. Brush tortillas lightly with warm water to soften. Gently press into cups. Bake in a 350° oven 12 to 15 minutes or till crisp. Remove from cups.

For sauce, combine salsa, cornstarch, and bouillon granules.

Spray a large skillet with nonstick spray coating. Preheat skillet over high heat. Cook and stir zucchini over high heat for 1½ minutes. Add onions; cook and stir 1½ minutes more or till crisp-tender. Remove vegetables from skillet.

Add oil to skillet. Cook and stir beef, *half* at a time, for 2 to 3 minutes or till done. Return all beef to skillet. Stir sauce. Add to skillet. Cook and stir till thickened and bubbly. Cook and stir for 2 minutes more. Stir in vegetables.

Place each tostada cup atop greens on a plate. Divide meat mixture among cups. Top with cheese. Garnish with cherry peppers, if desired. Serves 6.

Nutrition information per serving: 240 cal., 20 g pro., 18 g carbo., 9 g fat, 56 mg chol., 378 mg sodium, 3 g dietary fiber. U.S. RDA: 17% vit. A, 13% vit. C, 12% riboflavin, 14% niacin, 17% calcium, 19% iron, 24% phosphorus.

SIRLOIN WITH APPLE-YOGURT SAUCE

  1 **1½-pound boneless beef top sirloin steak, cut 1¼ to 1½ inches thick**
  ¾ **cup apple juice *or* apple cider**
  1 **small onion, chopped (¼ cup)**
  2 **cloves garlic, minced**
  ½ **teaspoon dried oregano, crushed**
  ¼ **teaspoon salt**
  2 **tablespoons cornstarch**
  1 **8-ounce carton plain yogurt**
  1 **tablespoon snipped chives**

Preheat broiler. Trim fat from beef. Place on unheated rack of broiler pan. Broil 3 inches from heat to desired doneness, turning once. (Or, grill, uncovered, directly over *medium-hot* coals, turning once.) Allow 14 to 16 minutes total for rare, 18 to 20 minutes for medium, 25 minutes for well-done.

For sauce, in a saucepan bring juice, onion, garlic, oregano, and salt to boiling. Cover and simmer about 3 minutes or till onion is just tender. Stir cornstarch into yogurt. Stir into onion mixture. Cook and stir till thickened and bubbly. Cook and stir for 2 minutes more. Top sauce with chives.

Serve sauce over beef along with steamed vegetables and poached apple slices sprinkled with ground nutmeg, if desired. Makes 6 servings.

Nutrition information per serving: 183 cal., 18 g pro., 9 g carbo., 7 g fat, 52 mg chol., 156 mg sodium. U.S. RDA: 12% riboflavin, 16% niacin, 12% iron, 19% phosphorus.

BETTER BURGERS

  1 **slightly beaten egg white**
  ⅓ **cup bulgur**
  ¼ **cup catsup**
  1 **tablespoon snipped fresh parsley *or* 1 teaspoon dried parsley flakes**
  1 **teaspoon Italian seasoning**
  ¼ **teaspoon garlic salt**
  ⅛ **teaspoon pepper**
  1 **pound lean ground beef**
  4 **whole wheat hamburger buns, split and toasted**
Lettuce leaves
  4 **tomato slices**
Alfalfa sprouts

In a medium mixing bowl combine egg white, bulgur, catsup, parsley, Italian seasoning, garlic salt, and pepper. Add beef; mix well. Shape mixture into four ½-inch-thick patties.

Place patties on the unheated rack of a broiler pan. Broil 3 inches from heat for 10 to 12 minutes or to desired doneness, turning once. (Or, grill patties, uncovered, directly over *medium-hot* coals for 12 to 15 minutes or to desired doneness, turning once.)

Place patties on hamburger buns with lettuce, tomato, and alfalfa sprouts. Serve with dill pickles and crisp crackers, if desired. Serves 4.

Nutrition information per serving: 353 cal., 30 g pro., 34 g carbo., 11 g fat, 81 mg chol., 576 mg sodium, 7 g dietary fiber. U.S. RDA: 10% vit. A, 10% vit. C, 16% thiamine, 17% riboflavin, 35% niacin, 29% iron, 34% phosphorus.

VEGETABLE AND PORK STIR-FRY

Some folks call hoisin sauce an Oriental barbecue sauce. Look for it in the Oriental section of your grocery store—

1 pound lean boneless pork (such as loin chops or roast)
⅔ cup dry sherry
¼ cup hoisin sauce
1 tablespoon grated fresh gingerroot
3 cloves garlic, minced
½ pound baby carrots *or* carrots, cut into 2-inch pieces
2 cups fresh pea pods *or* one 6-ounce package frozen pea pods, thawed
1 tablespoon cornstarch
Nonstick spray coating
1 tablespoon cooking oil
1 15-ounce can oyster, straw, *or* shiitake mushrooms, drained and cut into bite-size pieces
2 cups shredded bok choy leaves *or* cabbage

Partially freeze pork; bias-slice into thin bite-size strips. Place in a plastic bag set in a bowl. Combine sherry, hoisin sauce, gingerroot, garlic, and ⅓ cup *water;* pour over pork. Close bag. Marinate 15 minutes at room temperature or 1 to 2 hours in the refrigerator.

Meanwhile, cook carrots, covered, in a small amount of boiling salted water for 5 minutes; drain. Halve pea pods crosswise. Drain pork; reserve marinade. Stir cornstarch into marinade.

Spray a wok or 12-inch skillet with nonstick spray coating. Preheat wok over high heat. Stir-fry carrots for 2 minutes. Add pea pods; stir-fry 2 minutes more or till vegetables are crisp-tender. Remove vegetables from wok.

Add oil to wok. Stir-fry pork, half at a time, for 2 to 3 minutes or till no pink remains. Return all pork to wok. Push from center of wok.

Stir reserved marinade; add to center of wok. Cook and stir till thickened and bubbly. Cook and stir for 1 minute more. Return vegetables to wok. Add mushrooms. Cook and stir for 1 minute more. Serve over bok choy with melon slices, if desired. Makes 4 servings.

Nutrition information per serving: 394 cal., 24 g pro., 34 g carbo., 15 g fat, 63 mg chol., 225 mg sodium, 6 g dietary fiber. U.S. RDA: 366% vit. A, 40% vit. C, 52% thiamine, 28% riboflavin, 31% niacin, 12% iron, 27% phosphorus.

PORK WITH SPRING RHUBARB SAUCE

Our Test Kitchen created a beautiful sauce by using a red rhubarb variety such as strawberry rhubarb—

1 3-pound pork loin center rib roast (about 8 ribs)* *or* one 2½-pound boneless beef rump roast
¼ teaspoon salt
¼ teaspoon coarsely ground pepper
½ pound rhubarb, chopped (2 cups)
¼ cup frozen apple juice concentrate, thawed
2 tablespoons honey
Several dashes ground nutmeg
1 teaspoon cornstarch

Rub roast with salt and pepper. Place pork, bone side down, in a small shallow roasting pan. (Or, place beef on a rack in a shallow roasting pan.) Insert a meat thermometer in the thickest portion of the roast, making sure bulb doesn't touch fat, bone, or pan.

Roast pork, uncovered, in a 325° oven for 1¼ to 1½ hours or till thermometer registers 150°. (Or, roast beef, uncovered, in a 325° oven 1¼ hours or till thermometer registers 140°.)

For sauce, in a saucepan combine rhubarb, juice concentrate, honey, and nutmeg. Bring to boiling; reduce heat. Cover; simmer 10 minutes or till rhubarb is very tender. Stir 2 tablespoons *water* into cornstarch; stir into rhubarb. Cook and stir till thickened and bubbly. Cook and stir 2 minutes more.

When pork registers 150° (beef, 140°), spoon some of the sauce over roast. Continue roasting pork for 30 to 45 minutes more or till the thermometer registers 170°, spooning on additional sauce occasionally. (Roast beef for 15 to 40 minutes more or till thermometer registers 150° to 170°.)

Let roast stand 15 minutes before carving. Heat any remaining sauce and pass with roast. Serve roast with hot cooked fettuccine sprinkled with sesame seed and steamed squash slices, if desired. Makes 8 servings.

**Note:* To make carving easier, ask your butcher to loosen roast backbone.

Nutrition information per serving: 225 cal., 21 g pro., 9 g carbo., 11 g fat, 69 mg chol., 119 mg sodium, and 1 g dietary fiber. U.S. RDA: 44% thiamine, 15% riboflavin, 20% niacin, and 20% phosphorus.

PORK TENDERLOIN WITH GINGERED FRUIT SAUCE

1 pound pork tenderloin
1 8-ounce can pineapple tidbits (juice pack)
⅔ cup orange juice
1 tablespoon cornstarch
1 tablespoon soy sauce
½ teaspoon grated fresh gingerroot
Dash ground red pepper
4 green onions, bias-sliced into 1-inch pieces
1 medium carrot, cut into thin strips
1 clove garlic, minced
1 tablespoon margarine *or* butter

Place pork on rack in shallow roasting pan. Insert meat thermometer in thickest portion, making sure bulb doesn't touch pan. Roast, uncovered, in a 325° oven for 1 hour or till thermometer registers 170°. Cover to keep warm.

Meanwhile, for sauce, drain pineapple, reserving juice. Combine reserved pineapple juice, orange juice, cornstarch, soy sauce, gingerroot, and red pepper. Set aside.

In a medium saucepan cook onions, carrot, and garlic in hot margarine or butter for 3 to 4 minutes or till crisp-tender. Stir sauce; add to vegetables. Cook and stir till thickened and bubbly. Cook and stir 2 minutes more. Stir in pineapple; heat through.

Slice pork; spoon sauce atop. Serve with prepared lentil or rice pilaf mix on lettuce leaves, if desired. Serves 4.

Microwave directions: Roast pork as above. For sauce, drain pineapple, reserving juice. Mix reserved juice, orange juice, cornstarch, soy sauce, gingerroot, and red pepper. Set aside.

In a 1½-quart microwave-safe casserole micro-cook onions, carrot, garlic, and margarine or butter, covered, on 100% power (high) for 3 to 4 minutes or till crisp-tender, stirring once. Stir sauce; add to vegetables. Cook, uncovered, on high for 3 to 5 minutes or till thickened and bubbly, stirring after every minute. Stir in pineapple. Cook, uncovered, on high for 1 to 1½ minutes or till heated through. Serve as directed.

Nutrition information per serving: 203 cal., 19 g pro., 18 g carbo., 6 g fat, 57 mg chol., 340 mg sodium, 1 g dietary fiber. U.S. RDA: 105% vit. A, 29% vit. C, 46% thiamine, 16% riboflavin, 17% niacin, 21% phosphorus.

JUNE

SANDWICHES!

By Barbara Greenwood

DELICIOUSLY DIFFERENT, READY IN MINUTES

STUFFED-TO-THE-RIM VEGETABLE ROLL

Cut thin slice off top of a round *club roll.* Hollow out bottom; leave ½-inch shell. (Save inside for bread crumbs.) Pile very thin slices of *smoked ham* inside roll bottom. Fill roll with drained deli *marinated vegetable salad.* Top with *havarti cheese* slices. Broil a minute or two till cheese oozes. Recap with roll top. Ah, perfection! *About 400 calories—*

Photograph: Ron Crofoot. Food Stylist: Judy Tills

SOUTHERN-STYLE BEEF AND SLAW SPECIAL

Cut slices of *cooked beef* into bite-size strips. Toss with your favorite *barbecue sauce,* jazzed up with *prepared horseradish.* If you like, heat it up. Pile onto bottom of a split *hoagie roll.* Crown with *coleslaw* and roll top. It screams for a pickle! *About 450 calories—*

CURRIED CHICKEN CROISSANT

Whisk a dash of *sugar* and *curry powder* into some *plain yogurt.* Toss with shredded *cabbage,* chopped *cooked chicken, raisins* or *mixed dried fruit bits,* and a sprinkling of *peanuts.* Spoon onto a split *croissant.* Fancy chicken salad! *About 450 calories—*

PICK-A-CHEESE PITA POCKET

Line *pita bread* with *cheese* slices (*Colby, provolone,* and so forth). Combine *creamy buttermilk salad dressing* with *cottage* or *ricotta cheese;* spoon into pita. Now, stuff in torn *mixed greens* and cut-up *vegetables.* (Buy a variety—spinach, broccoli cuts, tomato wedges—from a salad bar.) Health-food enthusiasts, you'll love it! *About 650 calories—*

MEAT-LOAF BURRITO TO GO

Brush *tortilla* with *water* to soften. Top with a *lettuce* leaf and *dairy sour cream.* Stack on *cooked meat loaf* and *cheddar cheese* slices, *avocado* wedges, and *onion* slices. Add *sweet pepper* pieces and *salsa.* Roll up; fasten with *ripe-olive*-topped toothpick. Micro-warm on 100% power (high) ½ to 1 minute. Add a hot pepper, if you're brave! *About 490 calories—*

ALL-OUT COOKOUTS

SURE-FIRE TECHNIQUES FOR GREAT GRILLING!

By Lynn Hoppe

TENDER JUICY RIBS

PEANUT-SAUCED RIBS

A zesty, Indian-inspired dish—

A secret sauce—it's just as important to a barbecue master's success as time-tested technique. Claim this spicy-hot peanut sauce as your trademark and enjoy the accolades.

DIRECT OR INDIRECT

● **Direct grilling:** Use this method for smaller cuts of meat that are up to 2 inches thick, such as steaks, chops, and burgers. Spread the coals and grill the food, uncovered, directly over the coals.

● **Indirect grilling:** This works best for larger cuts, such as roasts, ribs, and whole chicken. Place a drip pan in the center and arrange the preheated coals around it. Test the heat above the pan. Place the food over the pan, not over the coals. Cover and grill.

RIB GLOSSARY

● **Pork loin back ribs:** Evenly covered with meat; premium ribs.

● **Pork country-style ribs:** Meatiest pork ribs; resemble small chops.

● **Pork spareribs:** A favorite, though less meaty; more fatty.

● **Beef chuck short ribs:** A less tender rib. (Choose leaner *chuck* instead of *plate* short ribs.)

● **Beef back ribs:** Also called dinosaur ribs; long bones from rib-eye roast; more tender meat.

● **Beef country-style ribs:** Mock ribs (chunks of pot roast with bone attached); meaty.

◄ PREP CROWN
Precooking the crown assures that it gets cooked throughout. Shape crown with meaty side of ribs facing the center; tie. Cook in a small amount of water till no pink remains.

◄ STUFFED CROWN OF RIBS

Showy, yet deceptively simple—

Shape two slabs of ribs into a circle and tie with string. The resulting ring of ribs corrals the stuffing that drinks up the flavorful meat juices.

RIB GRILLING TIPS
WHY PRECOOK?

For tender beef ribs, precooking is best. With pork ribs, you choose. Precooking makes them more tender, but you get less intense smoky flavor.

● **With precooking:** Cover ribs with boiling water; simmer, covered, till tender (45 to 60 minutes for pork spareribs/loin ribs; 50 to 60 minutes for beef chuck ribs). Grill, covered, indirectly over *medium-slow* heat for 15 minutes or till done.

● **Without precooking:** Grill pork spareribs/loin ribs, covered, indirectly over *medium* heat 60 minutes. Uncover; grill 15 to 30 minutes more or till done.

▲ TEXAS RIBS

Robust for big appetites—

Bring on the barbecue! Here's the kind of blue-ribbon recipe—lusty, yet all-American—that earned a name for barbecue. Of course, in Lone Star cattle country, meaty beef chuck short ribs are primo.

Photographs: Ron Crofoot
Food stylist: Judy Tills

COAL CONTROL

For perfectly done grilled food, you must maintain the coals at just the right temperature. Here's how:

● **Coals not hot enough?** Gently shake the grill or tap the coals with long-handled tongs to shake off excess ash.

● **Coals too hot?** Cover the grill and reduce the airflow to the coals for several minutes.

COOKOUTS

MOIST DELICIOUS SEAFOOD

BLACKENED FISH

Restaurant fare at home—

When the smoky haze clears, Louisianians will look with envy at your skilletful of moist fish fillets encased in a peppery crust. Try blackening the fish that best suits your family: catfish, redfish, cod, pollock, pompano, or haddock.

◄ POSITION SKILLET
Place a cast-iron skillet directly on hot coals. Heat the skillet for 5 minutes.

◄ DRIZZLE WITH MARGARINE
Add fish; drizzle with margarine. Grill till blackened. Turn fish; repeat.

GREAT GRILLING CHOICES

● **Halibut:** Delicate flavor. Best cut: steaks
● **Monkfish:** Poor man's lobster. Best cut: fillets
● **Salmon:** Favorite grilling fish in West. Best cuts: steaks, fillets.
● **Shark:** Usually mild flavored. Stronger flavored varieties benefit from a marinade. Best cut: steaks.
● **Swordfish:** Mild-flavored, firm-fleshed fish. Favorite grilling fish in the East. Best cut: steak.
● **Trout:** Moist fish. Best choices: dressed, pan-dressed.
● **Tuna:** Mild fish. Best choices: small pan-dressed, steaks, fillets.

◀ SPLIT THE
LOBSTER TAILS
To halve each
lobster tail
lengthwise, use
kitchen shears to
cut through the
underside shell and
meat. Turn the
lobster tail over
and cut through
the hard shell.

◀DEVILED CRAB LOBSTER TAILS

To make an occasion special—

For an assured four-star rating, serve classy lobster tails with a glorious crab stuffing. The bonus is that your lobster tail goes twice as far: one tail serves two people.

▲ FISH-GRILLING TIPS
COOKING TIMES ARE KEY

● **Fish steaks, fillets, or cubes—** Measure thickness. Place fish into a well-greased grill basket or pierced foil packet. Grill, on an uncovered grill, directly over *medium-hot* coals till fish flakes easily. (Allow 4 to 6 minutes per ½ inch of thickness. If more than 1 inch thick, turn during grilling.)

● **Dressed fish (3 to 4 pounds):** Place fish into a well-greased grill basket or pierced foil packet. Place on grill over drip pan but not over coals. Grill, on a covered grill, indirectly over *medium-hot* coals for 40 to 50 minutes or till fish flakes easily when tested with a fork.

▲ LIME-SEASONED SALMON

A light and easy salad—

The tangy sesame-lime marinade assumes a double identity. As a marinade, it moistens and prevents the salmon steaks from sticking to the grill. Heated as a sauce, it flavorfully dresses the salmon and wilts the salad greens.

▲ USE A GRILL BASKET
A grill basket, handy for grilling large pieces of fish, reduces sticking and allows for easy turning.

SUCCULENT SMOKED POULTRY

▲
HAZELNUT-PESTO TURKEY BREAST

Turkey with summery trimmings—

Whether you hobnob with beer drinkers or champagne sippers, your guests will relish this! A spinach-basil stuffing is pocketed between the skin and the smoke-seasoned turkey breast.

▲ STUFFING THE BREAST
Loosen the skin from the meat, leaving skin attached at one long edge. Spread pesto over the meat.

┌ SMOKE FLAVOR DIRECTORY ┐

Use woods from fruit or nut trees. Soft woods, such as pine, discolor the food and add a bitter taste. Choose your favorite wood or mix and match your own signature blend.

● **Hickory:** Always popular. Intense, sweet flavor.

● **Mesquite:** Light and clean, smoky flavor.

● **Osage orange, apple, or cherry:** Delicately sweet smoke.

So that the chips smolder rather than flame when added to hot coals, soak the wood in water at least one hour before smoking.

◀ **GRILL-SMOKING**
In a covered grill, arrange preheated coals around a foil drip pan. For steam, pour 1 inch of water in pan. Sprinkle soaked chips over hot coals.

◀ APPLE CHICKEN WITH PILAF

A white-linen meal from the grill—

After more than an hour of soaking up the smoke flavor, the chicken comes to your table bronzed and beautiful. The wheat-berry pilaf makes the perfect accompaniment.

▲ FIVE-SPICE GAME HENS

Big-flavored, little hens—

As the sweet perfume of burning hickory chips wafts from house to house, your neighbors will covet the smoky aroma of these crisp-skinned petite birds.

▲ **SMOKER METHOD**
Follow manufacturer's directions for arranging hot coals, wood, and water pan in water smoker.

— SMOKER TIPS —
A COVERED GRILL OR A WATER SMOKER?

Either a water smoker or a covered grill works well for smoking, though a smoker allows for slightly better circulation of heat and steam around food. The longer smoking time necessary in a water smoker also intensifies the smoke flavor.

One caution: Do *not* use a water smoker to cook large birds such as a turkey. Because the heat fluctuates, there's no way to guarantee that the bird reaches the temperature critical for safety within four hours. Water smokers work well for smaller birds and any size of other meats.

CREATE A KABOB!

4 EASY STEPS

1. PICK A MEAT

Allow 4 servings per pound of meat or fish (3 servings per pound of shrimp with shell or chicken with the bone).

- **Shrimp.** Thaw shrimp, if frozen. Shell and devein the shrimp.

- **Sea scallops.** Thaw the sea scallops, if frozen.

- **Fish.** Choose from tuna, swordfish, shark, catfish, *or* sea bass steaks or fillets. Thaw the fish, if frozen. Cut fish steaks or fillets into 1-inch pieces.

- **Chicken breasts.** Skin, bone, and cut chicken into 1-inch cubes.

- **Lamb, boneless.** Cut lamb into 1-inch pieces.

- **Beef sirloin, boneless.** Cut beef sirloin into 1-inch pieces.

- **Pork, lean boneless.** Cut into 1-inch cubes.

2. PICK A FRUIT OR VEGETABLE

Plan on 1 cup fruit or vegetables per person.

PRECOOK THESE
- **Summer squash.** Cut into ½-inch slices.
- **Broccoli or cauliflower flowerets.**
- **Baby scallopini squash.**
- **Fresh ears of corn.** Cut into 1-inch pieces.
- **Whole tiny new potatoes.** Halve potatoes.
- **Baby carrots.**
- **Green onions *or* leeks.** Cut into 1-inch pieces.

NO NEED TO PRECOOK
- **Red *or* green pepper.** Cut into 1-inch pieces.
- **Apple wedges.**
- **Papaya.** Peel, seed, and cut into 1-inch pieces.
- **Orange slices.**
- **Fresh pineapple.** Cut into 1-inch pieces.
- **Pea pods.** Thaw, if frozen.
- **Frozen artichoke hearts.** Thaw.
- **Jicama.** Peel and cut into 1-inch pieces.

3. PICK A MARINADE

Allow 1 recipe marinade per pound of meat.

- **APPLE MARINADE**

  Combine ¼ cup *water;* ¼ cup *frozen apple juice concentrate,* thawed; 2 tablespoons *white wine vinegar;* 2 tablespoons *olive oil* or *cooking oil;* 2 tablespoons *soy sauce;* and 1 teaspoon *dried savory,* crushed. Makes 1 cup.

- **LIME MARINADE**

  Combine ½ cup *chicken broth;* 1 teaspoon shredded *lime peel;* ⅓ cup *lime juice;* 2 tablespoons *cooking oil;* 1 tablespoon *brown sugar;* 2 cloves *garlic,* minced; and ⅛ teaspoon ground *red pepper.* Makes 1 cup.

- **WINE MARINADE**

  Combine ¼ cup *olive oil* or *cooking oil;* ¼ cup *dry white wine;* 1 tablespoon *minced dried onion;* ½ teaspoon *dried basil,* crushed; ½ teaspoon *dried rosemary,* crushed; and ¼ teaspoon *pepper.* Makes ⅔ cup.

4. PUT THEM ALL TOGETHER

Here's how!

- **MARINATE**

  Prepare marinade. Place seafood, fish, or meat in a plastic bag in shallow dish. Pour marinade over; close bag. Chill 2 to 4 hours for fish, seafood, or chicken (6 hours or overnight for lamb, beef, or pork), turning once. Remove meat; reserve marinade.

- **PRECOOK**

  Cook vegetables in a small amount of boiling water 1 to 2 minutes (4 to 5 minutes for carrots, onions, or leeks; 6 to 8 minutes for corn; 12 to 15 minutes for potatoes).

- **THREAD KABOBS**

  On skewers thread meat, vegetables, and fruits.

- **GRILL KABOBS**

  For fish or seafood, grease grill rack. Grill kabobs on an uncovered grill over *hot* coals 8 to 12 minutes or till done. Turn and brush often with marinade.

PEANUT-SAUCED RIBS

Chopped apple and peanuts make a crunchy complement to the spicy ribs—

- 3 to 4 pounds pork spareribs *or* loin back ribs
- ⅓ cup cooking oil
- ⅓ cup peanut butter
- 2 tablespoons soy sauce
- 1 tablespoon curry powder
- 2 cloves garlic, minced
- ⅛ to ¼ teaspoon ground red pepper
- ½ of a 6-ounce can (⅓ cup) frozen limeade concentrate, thawed

Cut ribs into 2- or 3-rib portions. For sauce, in a bowl combine cooking oil, peanut butter, soy sauce, curry powder, garlic, and red pepper. Stir in limeade concentrate. Brush sauce over ribs.

In a covered grill arrange preheated coals around a drip pan. Test for *medium* heat above pan (coals will be medium-hot). Place ribs on a rib rack, if desired. Place on grill rack over pan but not over coals. Lower grill hood.

Grill ribs for 60 minutes. Brush with sauce. Uncover; grill for 15 to 30 minutes more or till ribs are tender and no pink remains. Turn ribs once. Brush with sauce occasionally. Serves 4.

Nutrition information per serving: 620 cal., 41 g pro., 4 g carbo., 48 g fat, 163 mg chol., and 279 mg sodium. U.S. RDA: 37% thiamine, 31% riboflavin, 41% niacin, 15% iron, and 38% phosphorus.

STUFFED CROWN OF RIBS

Use two large spatulas to lift the crown of ribs from the grill to a serving platter. Once transferred, untie the crown—

- 4 pounds pork loin back ribs (2 slabs)
- 1¼ cups water
- ¾ cup finely chopped celery
- 1 6-ounce package mixed dried fruit bits
- ½ cup chopped onion
- ¼ cup millet
- 1½ teaspoons instant chicken bouillon granules
- 2 tablespoons margarine *or* butter
- ¼ cup snipped parsley
- 1 teaspoon dried basil, crushed
- 1 teaspoon dried marjoram, crushed
- ¼ teaspoon pepper
- 5 to 7 slices whole wheat bread, dried and cut into ½-inch cubes (4 cups)
- ¼ cup crab apple *or* currant jelly
- 1 tablespoon brown sugar
- 1 tablespoon lemon juice
- ¼ teaspoon dry mustard

To form a ring with the ribs, place slabs, end to end with edges overlapping slightly and the meaty side of ribs facing toward center. Tie string securely around ribs to form a crown (8 to 9 inches in diameter). Place crown in a large kettle or Dutch oven. Add about 2 inches of *water*. Bring to boiling; reduce heat. Cover and simmer 45 to 60 minutes or till no pink remains. Drain.

Meanwhile, for stuffing, in a medium saucepan combine 1¼ cups water, celery, dried fruit, onion, millet, and bouillon granules. Bring to boiling; reduce heat. Cover and simmer for 15 minutes. Stir in margarine or butter, parsley, basil, marjoram, and pepper. Let stand, covered, for 5 minutes. Add bread cubes to millet mixture. Toss to mix. If necessary, add additional *water* (about ¼ cup) to moisten.

For glaze, in a small saucepan mix jelly, brown sugar, lemon juice, and mustard. Cook and stir till jelly is melted and mixture is smooth. Brush ribs on all sides with some of the glaze.

In a covered grill arrange preheated coals around outer edge of grill, leaving a 9-inch circle in center without coals. Test for *medium* heat above area without coals. Place crown on grill on a double layer of greased heavy-duty foil over area without coals. Spoon stuffing into center of crown. Brush crown with some of the glaze. Lower grill hood.

Grill for 50 to 60 minutes or till crown is brown and stuffing is heated through, brushing with glaze occasionally. If necessary, cover stuffing with foil to prevent overbrowning. Brush ribs with glaze before serving. Serves 6.

Nutrition information per serving: 514 cal., 38 g pro., 44 g carbo., 21 g fat, 95 mg chol., 325 mg sodium, 3 g dietary fiber. U.S. RDA: 14% vit. A, 58% thiamine, 25% riboflavin, 36% niacin, 19% iron, 39% phosphorus.

TEXAS RIBS

Small grill? A rib rack increases the cooking space on your grill up to 50 percent by letting you stand the rib pieces up rather than laying them flat—

- 4 pounds meaty beef chuck short ribs
- 2 tablespoons Worcestershire sauce
- 1 tablespoon vinegar
- 1 tablespoon cooking oil
- ½ teaspoon instant beef bouillon granules
- 1 clove garlic, minced
- ¼ to ½ teaspoon ground red pepper
- ¼ teaspoon dry mustard
- ¼ teaspoon chili powder
- 1 tablespoon brown sugar
- 1 teaspoon cornstarch
- ¼ cup catsup

To precook the ribs, in a large kettle or Dutch oven cover the ribs with *water*. Bring to boiling; reduce heat. Simmer, covered, 50 to 60 minutes or till tender.

In a small bowl mix Worcestershire sauce, vinegar, cooking oil, beef bouillon granules, garlic, red pepper, mustard, chili powder, and ⅓ cup *water*. Set aside ¼ cup of garlic mixture.

In a covered grill arrange preheated coals around a drip pan; test for *medium-slow* heat above pan (coals will be medium). Place ribs on rib rack, if desired. Place ribs on grill rack over pan but not over coals. Lower grill hood.

Grill ribs 15 minutes, turning ribs halfway through grilling and brushing occasionally with garlic mixture.

Meanwhile, for sauce, in a small saucepan combine brown sugar and cornstarch. Stir in the reserved garlic mixture and catsup. Cook and stir till thickened and bubbly. Cook and stir for 2 minutes more. Serve sauce with ribs. Makes 5 or 6 servings.

Microwave directions: Precook and grill ribs as above. For sauce, in a 2-cup glass measure combine brown sugar and cornstarch. Stir in reserved garlic mixture and catsup. Micro-cook, uncovered, on 100% power (high) 2 to 3 minutes or till thickened and bubbly, stirring every minute. Serve as above.

Nutrition information per serving: 409 cal., 41 g pro., 8 g carbo., 22 g fat, 128 mg chol., 343 mg sodium. U.S. RDA: 19% riboflavin, 33% niacin, 30% iron, 21% phosphorus.

FRUITED SPARERIBS

Cantaloupe and grapes make this sweet-sour sauce a summer delight—

- 4 to 5 pounds pork spareribs *or* loin back ribs
- ¼ cup sliced green onion
- 1 teaspoon grated gingerroot *or* ¼ teaspoon ground ginger
- 2 tablespoons margarine *or* butter
- ½ of a 10-ounce jar (½ cup) pineapple preserves
- 2 cups finely chopped cantaloupe
- ¼ cup water
- 2 tablespoons vinegar
- 4 teaspoons cornstarch
- ½ cup seedless green *or* red grapes, halved

Cut ribs into 2- or 3-rib portions. In a medium saucepan cook green onion and gingerroot in margarine or butter about 2 minutes or till tender.

Cut up any large pineapple pieces in preserves. Stir preserves and cantaloupe into onion mixture. Cook and stir till preserves melt.

Stir water and vinegar into cornstarch. Stir into onion mixture. Cook and stir till thickened and bubbly. Cook and stir for 2 minutes more.

In a covered grill arrange preheated coals around a drip pan; test for *medium* heat above drip pan (coals will be medium-hot). Place ribs on a rib rack, if desired. Place grill rack over pan but not over coals. Lower grill hood.

Grill ribs for 60 minutes, brushing with sauce after 30 minutes. Uncover; grill 15 to 30 minutes more or till ribs are tender and no pink remains. Turn once. Brush occasionally with sauce. During the last 15 minutes of grilling, place pan with sauce on side of grill to warm sauce. Stir in grapes just before serving. Pass sauce with ribs. Makes 5 or 6 servings.

Nutrition information per serving: 650 cal., 47 g pro., 31 g carbo., 37 g fat, 175 mg chol., 189 mg sodium. U.S. RDA: 46% vit. A, 34% vit. C, 60% thiamine, 32% riboflavin, 46% niacin, 17% iron, 35% phosphorus.

BLACKENED FISH

Because fillets vary in thickness, you may need to remove the thinner ones from the skillet and cook the thicker fillets for just a minute or two longer—

- 4 fresh *or* frozen catfish, cod, pollock, pompano, *or* haddock fillets (1 pound)
- ½ teaspoon onion powder
- ½ teaspoon garlic salt
- ½ teaspoon ground red pepper
- ½ teaspoon dried basil, crushed
- ¼ teaspoon ground white pepper
- ¼ teaspoon dried thyme, crushed
- ¼ teaspoon pepper
- ⅛ teaspoon ground sage
- ¼ cup margarine *or* butter, melted
Lemon slices, halved (optional)

Thaw fish, if frozen. In a small mixing bowl combine onion powder, garlic salt, red pepper, basil, white pepper, thyme, pepper, and sage. Brush both sides of fish with some of the melted margarine or butter. Coat both sides of fish with seasoning mixture.

If using a charcoal grill, remove grill rack and place an unoiled 12-inch cast-iron skillet directly on *hot* coals. (If using a gas grill, turn to high and place skillet on the grill rack.)

Preheat the skillet for 5 minutes or till a drop of water sizzles. Add coated fillets to skillet. Carefully drizzle about *2 teaspoons* of the melted margarine or butter over the fish.

Grill fish for 2½ to 3 minutes or till blackened. Turn fish and drizzle with *2 teaspoons* of the melted margarine or butter. Grill for 2½ to 3 minutes more or till blackened and fish flakes easily when tested with a fork.

Transfer fish to a serving platter. Drizzle with remaining melted margarine or butter. Garnish each serving with a halved lemon slice, if desired. Makes 4 servings.

Nutrition information per serving: 198 cal., 20 g pro., 1 g carbo., 12 g fat, 42 mg chol., 442 mg sodium. U.S. RDA: 12% vit. A, 12% niacin, and 22% phosphorus.

DEVILED CRAB LOBSTER TAILS

When you can't turn food as it grills, use a covered grill to cook it more evenly—

- 2 8- to 10-ounce frozen lobster tails, thawed
- ½ teaspoon lemon-pepper seasoning
- 2 tablespoons sliced green onion
- 1 tablespoon sliced celery
- 1 tablespoon margarine *or* butter
- 1½ teaspoons all-purpose flour
- ⅛ teaspoon dry mustard
Dash ground red pepper
- ¼ cup light cream *or* milk
- ½ teaspoon Worcestershire sauce
- ½ of a 6-ounce package frozen crabmeat, thawed
- 2 tablespoons plain croutons, coarsely crushed

Use kitchen shears to halve lobster tails lengthwise. Cut a lengthwise slit in meat of *each* half; spread meat apart slightly. Use a sharp knife to cut between meat and shells. *Do not* remove meat from shells. Sprinkle slits with lemon-pepper seasoning. Set aside.

In a small saucepan cook green onion and celery in margarine or butter till tender but not brown. Stir in flour, mustard, and red pepper. Add cream and Worcestershire sauce. Cook and stir till thickened and bubbly. Cook and stir 1 minute more. Remove from heat. Gently stir in crab and croutons. Spoon mixture into slits in lobster meat.

Grill stuffed tails, shell side down, on a covered grill, directly over *medium-hot* coals about 12 minutes or till lobster is opaque. Makes 4 servings.

Nutrition information per serving: 184 cal., 21 g pro., 5 g carbo., 8 g fat, 108 mg chol., 324 mg sodium. U.S. RDA: 14% vit. A, 30% thiamine, 11% niacin, 24% phosphorus.

LIME-SEASONED SALMON

Not all sesame oil has the nutty, sesame flavor you'll want for this recipe. What works best is a dark-color sesame oil—

- **4 fresh *or* frozen salmon, tuna, whitefish, *or* sea bass steaks, cut 1 inch thick (about 1 pound)**
- **¼ cup salad oil**
- **¼ cup lime juice**
- **1 tablespoon water**
- **1 tablespoon soy sauce**
- **2 teaspoons sesame oil**
- **2 teaspoons honey**
- **4 cups shredded mixed greens**
- **½ cup shredded radishes**
- **½ cup alfalfa sprouts**
- **1 tablespoon toasted sesame seed**
- **1 canned green chili pepper, rinsed, seeded, and chopped**
- **Lime slices (optional)**
- **Alfalfa sprouts (optional)**

Thaw fish, if frozen. Place the fish in a plastic bag; set in a shallow pan.

For marinade, in a small mixing bowl stir together salad oil, lime juice, water, soy sauce, sesame oil, and honey; pour over the fish. Close bag; marinate in refrigerator for 6 hours, turning bag occasionally to distribute marinade.

In a large bowl toss together mixed greens, radishes, ½ cup alfalfa sprouts, sesame seed, and chili pepper. Place on a serving platter.

Drain the fish, reserving marinade. Place fish in a well-greased wire grill basket, if desired, or grease grill rack. Grill fish, on an uncovered grill, directly over *medium-hot* coals for 8 to 12 minutes or till fish flakes easily when tested with a fork, turning halfway through grilling.

Meanwhile, transfer the reserved marinade to a small saucepan. Place on side of grill; heat till bubbly.

Just before serving, pour hot marinade over greens mixture; toss to wilt greens slightly. Serve fish atop wilted greens mixture and garnish with lime slices and additional alfalfa sprouts, if desired. Makes 4 servings.

Nutrition information per serving: 425 cal., 26 g pro., 9 g carbo., 32 g fat, 40 mg chol., 328 mg sodium, 3 g dietary fiber. U.S. RDA: 41% vit. A, 30% vit. C, 16% thiamine, 13% riboflavin, 10% calcium, 16% iron, 34% phosphorus.

HORSERADISH-DILL TROUT

No grill basket? Tear a piece of heavy foil large enough to hold the fish in a single layer. With a fork, prick a few holes in foil. Wrap fish in foil—

- **3 12- to 14-ounce fresh *or* frozen pan-dressed rainbow trout, lake perch, *or* pike**
- **¼ cup whipping cream**
- **2 tablespoons mayonnaise *or* salad dressing**
- **1½ teaspoons snipped fresh dill *or* ½ teaspoon dried dillweed**
- **1½ teaspoons prepared horseradish**
- **6 sprigs dill *or* ¾ teaspoon dried dillweed (optional)**
- **2 tablespoons margarine *or* butter, melted**
- **¼ teaspoon seasoned salt**

Thaw fish, if frozen. For sauce, beat cream till soft peaks form. Fold in mayonnaise, snipped dill, and ½ *teaspoon* horseradish. Cover; chill up to 1 hour.

Spread insides of the fish with the remaining horseradish. Insert 2 dill sprigs into each fish cavity. (Or, sprinkle dried dillweed into each.) Wrap tails in greased foil.

Stir together margarine and salt; brush onto fish. Place fish in a well-greased wire grill basket or foil packet. Grill fish, on an uncovered grill, directly over *medium-hot* coals for 8 minutes. Brush with margarine mixture. Turn and brush again. Grill 5 to 8 minutes more or till fish flakes easily with a fork. Serve with chilled sauce. Serves 3.

Nutrition information per serving: 648 cal., 49 g pro, 1 g carbo., 48 g fat, 158 mg chol., 284 mg sodium. U.S. RDA: 13% vit. A, 12% thiamine, 28% riboflavin, 95% niacin.

HAZELNUT-PESTO TURKEY BREAST

- **4 cups apple *or* cherry wood chips**
- **¼ cup chopped hazelnuts, toasted**
- **1 egg yolk**
- **1 cup lightly packed fresh spinach leaves**
- **1 cup lightly packed fresh basil leaves**
- **1 tablespoon hazelnut *or* cooking oil**
- **1 clove garlic, minced**
- **¼ cup grated Parmesan *or* Romano cheese**
- **1 2½- to 3-pound fresh turkey breast half with bone**
- **Cooking oil**
- **Steamed carrot strips (optional)**
- **Steamed zucchini strips (optional)**

In a large bowl soak the wood chips in enough water to cover for 1 hour.

For pesto, in a blender container or food processor bowl blend or process hazelnuts till very finely chopped. Add egg yolk, spinach, basil, hazelnut or cooking oil, and garlic. Blend or process till smooth. If necessary, stop processor and scrape container sides. Stir in the Parmesan cheese. Set aside.

To loosen turkey skin, slip your fingers under the skin of the turkey breast to loosen it from the meat, leaving skin attached at one long edge.

Spread the pesto over the meat under the skin. Fold the skin over pesto. Insert a meat thermometer in the thickest portion of turkey breast, making sure it doesn't touch the bone.

Drain wood chips. In a covered grill arrange preheated coals around a drip pan; test for *medium* heat above pan (coals will be medium-hot). Pour 1 inch of water into pan. Sprinkle *half* of the drained wood chips on top of the preheated coals.

Place turkey breast, stuffed side up, on the grill rack over drip pan but not over coals. Brush skin with cooking oil. Lower grill hood.

Grill turkey breast till meat thermometer registers 170° (2 to 2¼ hours), adding remaining chips after 45 minutes. Add more water to the drip pan as necessary. To maintain *medium-hot* coals throughout the whole smoking time, add 6 to 8 new coals to the firebox every 20 or 30 minutes during cooking.

Place turkey on a serving platter. Let stand for 10 minutes before slicing. Serve with steamed carrot and zucchini strips,* and garnish with basil, if desired. Makes 6 to 8 servings.

Note: To get the "foot-long" pieces of shredded carrot and zucchini as shown on page 80, use a Japanese carrot shredder. Look for the nifty gadget at a gourmet kitchen shop.

Nutrition information per serving: 301 cal., 51 g pro., 2 g carbo., 9 g fat, 168 mg chol., 185 mg sodium, 2 g dietary fiber. U.S. RDA: 24% vit. A, 14% vit. C, 17% riboflavin, 61% niacin, 11% calcium, 19% iron, 47% phosphorus.

APPLE CHICKEN WITH PILAF

Stuff the bird loosely, allowing room for the stuffing to expand during cooking—

      4   **cups apple wood chips**
      1   **medium orange**
   2½   **cups chicken broth**
      ½   **cup wheat berries**
      1   **shallot, chopped**
      ½   **teaspoon ground ginger**
      ¼   **teaspoon pepper**
      ½   **cup regular brown rice**
      ½   **cup slivered almonds, toasted**
      1   **3- to 4-pound broiler-fryer chicken**
      ¼   **cup margarine *or* butter**
      1   **tablespoon honey**
Orange peel strips (optional)
Grape clusters (optional)
Fresh coriander leaves (optional)

In a large bowl soak the wood chips in enough water to cover for 1 hour.

Finely shred enough orange peel to make 2 teaspoons; set aside. Peel and section the orange over a small bowl, reserving the juice; set juice aside.

For stuffing, in a saucepan combine *half* the peel, chicken broth, wheat berries, shallot, ginger, and pepper. Bring to boiling; reduce heat. Cover and simmer for 15 minutes. Add rice. Return to boiling; reduce heat. Cover; simmer 45 minutes. Stir in orange sections, reserved juice, and almonds.

Rinse chicken; pat dry. Sprinkle cavity with salt. Spoon stuffing into neck cavity. Skewer neck skin to back. Loosely spoon stuffing into body cavity. Tie legs together with string. Twist wing tips under back. Insert a meat thermometer in the thigh, if desired, making sure it doesn't touch bone.

Place any remaining stuffing in center of a double thickness of heavy-duty foil. Bring up long edges of foil and seal tightly with a double fold, leaving a little space for expansion of steam. Fold in short ends to seal.

In a small mixing bowl stir together the remaining shredded orange peel, margarine, and honey. Set aside.

Drain wood chips. In a covered grill arrange the preheated coals around a drip pan; test for *medium* heat above drip pan (coals will be medium-hot). Pour 1 inch of water into the drip pan. Sprinkle *half* of the drained chips over preheated coals.

Place chicken, breast side up, on the grill rack over the drip pan but not over the coals. Lower grill hood.

Grill for 1¼ to 1½ hours or till a thermometer registers 180° to 185° or a drumstick moves easily in its socket. Add remaining chips and brush bird with margarine mixture after 30 minutes. Place packet of stuffing on grill rack with chicken during the last 20 to 25 minutes of grilling to heat through.

Spoon stuffing from the foil packet onto a platter. Add bird and top with orange peel strips, if desired. Garnish the platter with grapes and coriander leaves, if desired. Makes 6 servings.

Apple Turkey with Pilaf: Prepare bird, stuffing, and margarine mixture as directed above *except* use an 8- to 10-pound turkey and *double* the stuffing ingredients. *Do not* stuff the turkey.

Place the stuffing in center of a double thickness of 24x18-inch heavy-duty foil and fold as directed above.

Grill turkey as directed above for 2½ to 3 hours or till a thermometer registers 180° to 185° or a drumstick moves easily in its socket. Add new coals as necessary. Add the remaining chips and brush bird with margarine mixture during the last 30 minutes. Place packet of stuffing on the grill rack with turkey during last 30 to 45 minutes of grilling to heat through.

Cover the turkey with foil and let stand 15 minutes before carving. Serve as directed above. Makes 12 servings.

Nutrition information per serving: 467 cal., 39 g pro., 27 g carbo., 22 g fat, 101 mg chol., 504 mg sodium, 2 g dietary fiber. U.S. RDA: 14% vit. C, 15% thiamine, 20% riboflavin, 67% niacin, 14% iron, 38% phosphorus.

FIVE-SPICE GAME HENS

A platter of steamed vegetables colorfully complements the hens. We chose sweet peppers, pea pods, and baby turnips—

      4   **cups hickory wood chips**
      ¼   **cup thinly sliced green onion**
      ¼   **cup molasses**
      2   **tablespoons cooking oil**
      1   **tablespoon lemon juice**
   1¼   **teaspoons five-spice powder**
      ¼   **teaspoon garlic salt**
      2   *or* 3 **Cornish game hens**
Five-spice powder
Steamed vegetables (optional)

In a large bowl soak the wood chips in enough water to cover for 1 hour.

For glaze, in a small mixing bowl stir together green onion, molasses, cooking oil, lemon juice, 1¼ teaspoons five-spice powder, and garlic salt.

Rinse Cornish game hens; pat dry with paper towels. Sprinkle cavities with additional five-spice powder, salt, and pepper. If desired, tie legs to tail.

To grill, drain the wood chips. In a covered grill arrange the preheated coals around a drip pan; test for *medium* heat above pan (coals will be medium-hot). Pour 1 inch of water into the drip pan. Sprinkle *half* the drained chips on top of the preheated coals.

Place birds, breast side up, on the grill rack over drip pan but not over coals. Brush birds with some of the glaze. Lower grill hood.

Grill for 1 to 1¼ hours or till the juices run clear and a drumstick moves easily in its socket, brushing birds occasionally with more of the glaze. After 30 minutes, add remaining wood chips and more water, if necessary; cut the string, if legs are tied to tail.

To smoke-cook, drain wood chips. In a water smoker arrange the preheated coals, *half* of the drained wood chips, and the water pan in the smoker according to the manufacturer's directions; pour water into pan.

Place birds, breast side up, on grill rack over water pan. Brush with some of the glaze. Lower smoker hood.

Smoke for 3 hours or till juices run clear and drumstick moves easily in its socket, brushing occasionally with the glaze. After 2 hours, add remaining chips and more water, if necessary; cut string, if legs are tied to tail. Add new coals as necessary.

To serve, brush birds with remaining glaze and arrange on a serving platter with steamed vegetables. Makes 4 to 6 servings.

Nutrition information per serving: 330 cal., 33 g pro., 14 g carbo., 15 g fat, 101 mg chol., 222 mg sodium. U.S. RDA: 13% riboflavin, 53% niacin, 16% iron, 24% phosphorus.

JULY

TONIGHT'S HOT-OFF-THE-GRILL DINNER

- **SPEEDY SALMON FILLET**
- **PEPPER SALAD**
- **CROISSANTS WITH CHEESE**

READY IN 45 MINUTES.

BARBECUE!

FANCY ENOUGH FOR FRIENDS, FAST ENOUGH FOR FAMILY

By Barbara Greenwood

SPEEDY SALMON FILLET

- 1 1½-pound boneless skinless fresh salmon fillet
- 3 tablespoons lemon juice
- 1 tablespoon snipped fresh basil
- 1 tablespoon cooking oil
- 1 tablespoon soy sauce
- 1 teaspoon Worcestershire sauce
- ½ teaspoon bottled minced garlic
- ¼ teaspoon pepper

Rinse salmon; pat dry. For sauce, in a small mixing bowl combine remaining ingredients; brush some over salmon. Place salmon in a greased grill basket, turning thin ends of fillet under to make an even thickness. Measure fillet's thickness. Close basket. Place on uncovered grill directly over *medium-hot* coals. Grill 4 to 6 minutes per ½-inch thickness or till salmon flakes easily when tested with a fork, brushing often with sauce. (If salmon is 1 inch or more thick, turn halfway through grilling.) Serves 6.

Nutrition information per serving: 205 cal., 23 g pro., 1 g carbo., 11 g fat, 40 mg chol., 233 mg sodium. U.S. RDA: 11% thiamine and 27% phosphorus.

PEPPER SALAD

Add some color! Use half of both a red and yellow sweet pepper—

- 1 medium sweet pepper, sliced into rings
- ½ of a small red onion, sliced and separated into rings
- 1 cup bean sprouts
- 1 2¼-ounce can sliced pitted ripe olives, drained
- 1 medium plum tomato, cut into thin wedges

Lettuce leaves
- ¼ cup dairy sour cream
- 2 tablespoons green goddess *or* creamy buttermilk salad dressing
- 1 tablespoon snipped fresh basil *or* 1 teaspoon dried basil, crushed

For salad, on a platter arrange pepper, onion, sprouts, olives, and tomato atop lettuce. For dressing, combine sour cream, salad dressing, and basil. Cover each; chill till serving time. Pass dressing with salad. Makes 6 servings.

Nutrition information per serving: 77 cal., 2 g pro., 5 g carbo., 6 g fat, 4 mg chol., 119 mg sodium. U.S. RDA: 51% vit. C.

CROISSANTS WITH CHEESE

- ⅓ cup soft-style cream cheese with chives and onion
- ⅓ cup shredded Monterey Jack *or* mozzarella cheese
- 6 small croissants, split

Combine cheeses. Spread *1 rounded tablespoon* of mixture between halves of *each* croissant. Wrap tightly in foil. Place on uncovered grill directly over *medium-hot* coals. Grill 3 to 4 minutes or till heated through, turning at least every minute. Makes 6 servings.

Nutrition information per serving: 184 cal., 5 g pro., 13 g carbo., 12 g fat, 19 mg chol., 172 mg sodium. U.S. RDA: 10% thiamine and 10% riboflavin.

Photograph: George Selland. Food stylist: Stevie Bass

READY IN 45 MINUTES

6:00–6:05 *Mound briquettes in grill; ignite.*
6:05–6:15 *Fix salad and dressing; chill.*
6:15–6:20 *Stir up sauce for salmon. Place salmon in greased grill basket.*
6:20–6:25 *Fill croissants.*
6:25–6:30 *Spread out the coals; test them for medium-hot heat.* *
6:30–6:45 *Grill salmon; add foil-wrapped croissants the last few minutes.*
6:45 *Dinner's ready!*

*Hold the palm of your hand over the place the food will be cooked. Count seconds by saying "one 1,000, two 1,000 . . ." and so on. If you need to remove your hand after three seconds, the coals are medium-hot.

QUICK, LIGHT, AND LUSCIOUS!
SUMMER COOKING

MAIN DISHES READY IN 30 MINUTES OR LESS

By Joy Taylor

PHOTOGRAPHS: GEORGE SELLAND. FOOD STYLIST: STEVIE BASS

Quick, light, and luscious—your favorite style of cooking on hot summer nights, right? Then you'll enjoy these ultrafast, no-fuss suppers that we designed with you in mind.

●**SALADS.** *New, nutritious ideas that use the summer's best produce.*

●**SAUTÉS.** *Entrées featuring thin meat cuts that cook in a jiffy.*

●**SANDWICHES.** *The quintessential quickie meal goes haute.*

CRISP CUCUMBER SEAFOOD PLATE

Save time: Buy shelled shrimp—

- ¾ cup loose-pack frozen peas
- 1 small cantaloupe, chilled
- 1 small cucumber, chilled
- ⅓ cup Italian salad dressing
- 2 tablespoons lemon juice
- 1 teaspoon sugar
Bibb lettuce leaves
- 1 7-ounce can solid white tuna, chilled and drained
- 6 ounces cooked, shelled shrimp

Run cold water over peas to thaw. Halve cantaloupe crosswise; remove and discard seeds. Cut into 9 thin slices. Halve cucumber lengthwise. Scoop out and discard seeds; thinly slice cucumber. For dressing, combine salad dressing, lemon juice, and sugar. Line 3 dinner plates with lettuce. Top with cantaloupe and cucumber. Toss together peas, *half* of the dressing, tuna, and shrimp. Spoon onto plates; drizzle with remaining dressing. Makes 3 servings.

Per serving: 341 cal., 34 g pro., 20 g carbo., 14 g fat, 112 mg chol., 353 mg sodium, 4 g fiber. U.S. RDA: 67% vit. A, 93% vit. C, 13% thiamine, 60% niacin, 17% iron, 31% phosphorus.

PORK WITH PINEAPPLE

Serve with fresh pineapple, chopped pecans, and steamed red pepper for a colorful and classy look—

- 1 pound pork tenderloin
- ¼ cup margarine *or* butter
- 1 8-ounce can crushed pineapple (juice pack)
- 1 small zucchini, cut into julienne strips

Slice pork tenderloin crosswise into 1-inch-thick pieces. In a 12-inch skillet cook pork in hot margarine or butter 5 minutes per side or till no longer pink. Remove from skillet; cover and keep warm.

For sauce, add *undrained* pineapple and zucchini strips to skillet. Bring to boiling, scraping up brown bits in skillet with a wooden spoon. Boil 3 minutes. Season to taste with *salt* and *pepper*. To serve, arrange pork on 4 individual plates. Top with the sauce. Makes 4 servings.

Per serving: 268 cal., 25 g pro., 10 g carbo., 14 g fat, 74 mg chol., 192 mg sodium. U.S. RDA: 12% vit. A, 10% vit. C, 79% thiamine, 20% riboflavin, 27% niacin, 10% iron, and 29% phosphorus.

BEGGERS' POCKETS

Finger food for lazy summer evenings—

- 1 14-ounce package frozen thinly sliced beef
- ¼ cup chicken broth
- 1 tablespoon soy sauce
- 1 teaspoon cornstarch
- 1 tablespoon cooking oil
- 1 cup chopped broccoli
- 2 carrots, thinly bias sliced
- 4 large flour tortillas, halved

Alfalfa sprouts
Bottled plum sauce

Remove paper between frozen beef slices. Stack slices; cut into strips. Combine broth, soy, and cornstarch. In skillet stir-fry frozen beef in oil, *half* at a time, over medium-high heat 2 minutes or till brown. Remove from skillet. Stir-fry broccoli and carrots 3 to 4 minutes. Drain. Add beef to skillet. Stir broth; add to skillet. Cook till bubbly. Cover; cook 1 minute. Top each tortilla half with ⅓ cup meat mixture and sprouts; roll up. Pass sauce. Serves 4.

Per serving: 281 cal., 24 g pro., 20 g carbo., 12 g fat, 65 mg chol., 397 mg sodium, 3 g fiber. U.S. RDA: 210% vit. A, 28% vit. C, and 26% iron.

SOUTHERN TOSTADAS

Tortilla chips can replace the shells—

- 1 15-ounce can black-eyed peas
- 1 8-ounce can red kidney beans
- 1 15-ounce can Spanish rice*
- 1 4-ounce can diced green chili peppers, drained
- 1 stalk celery, thinly sliced
- 2 tablespoons tomato paste
- 1 to 2 teaspoons chili powder
- 2 cups shredded Monterey Jack *or* cheddar cheese (8 ounces)
- 10 tostada shells

Toppers: shredded lettuce, dairy sour cream, guacamole, chopped tomato, sunflower nuts (optional)

Drain peas and beans. In saucepan combine peas, beans, rice, peppers, celery, tomato paste, and chili powder. Bring to boiling; reduce heat. Simmer, covered, 5 minutes. Stir in *1 cup* cheese. Serve hot over tostadas with remaining cheese and toppers. Makes 5 servings.

*Or, use ¾ cup *quick-cooking rice* plus 1½ cups *vegetable juice cocktail.*

Per serving: 473 cal., 22 g pro., 54 g carbo., 20 g fat, 40 mg chol., 757 mg sodium, 9 g fiber. U.S. RDA: 36% vit. A, 75% vit. C, 43% calcium.

WILTED SAVOY SALAD

A 20-minute meal for a twosome—

- 1 6-ounce jar marinated artichoke hearts *or* two 4-ounce jars pickled mushrooms
- 1 yellow sweet pepper, cut into thin strips
- 6 ounces sliced Canadian-style bacon, halved
- 8 cups torn Savoy cabbage *or* Chinese cabbage

Tomato wedges
Coarsely cracked black pepper

Drain artichokes, reserving marinade; cut up any large pieces. In a 12-inch skillet heat ⅓ *cup* reserved marinade. Add sweet pepper; cook and stir 3 minutes. Add artichokes and bacon; toss to coat. Cook 2 minutes. Add cabbage. Cook over low heat about 1 minute, tossing just till cabbage wilts. Transfer to 2 plates. Top with tomato and pepper. Pass any remaining marinade. Makes 2 servings.

Per serving: 415 cal., 24 g pro., 27 g carbo., 26 g fat, 43 mg chol., 1,602 mg sodium, 11 g fiber. U.S. RDA: 63% vit. A, 203% vit. C, 59% thiamine, 19% riboflavin, 35% niacin, 14% iron.

CREAMY TURKEY SAUTÉ

Quick-cooking rice, corn-on-the-cob, and crunchy pea pods balance the rich-tasting poultry entrée——

- **2 turkey breast tenderloin steaks (8 ounces total)**
- **1 tablespoon olive *or* cooking oil**
- **8 ounces fresh mushrooms, sliced**
- **1 large green onion, sliced**
- **1 3-ounce package cream cheese, cut into cubes**
- **3 tablespoons milk**

In a 10-inch skillet cook turkey steaks in hot oil for 2 to 3 minutes per side or till light brown and tender. Remove turkey from skillet to platter; cover and keep warm. Add the sliced mushrooms and onion to drippings in skillet. Cook for 2 to 3 minutes or till tender. Stir in cream cheese and milk till well blended. Season sauce to taste with *salt* and *pepper*. To serve, spoon mushroom sauce over turkey. Makes 2 or 3 servings.

Per serving: 377 cal., 34 g pro., 8 g carbo., 23 g fat, 119 mg chol., 197 mg sodium, 3 g fiber. U.S. RDA: 13% vit. A, 12% thiamine, 44% riboflavin, 59% niacin, 18% iron, 42% phosphorus.

FOR MORE SUMMER-COOKING RECIPES see page 94.

ANTIPASTO-STYLE OMELET

Mound antipasto favorites onto your plate: salami, olives, cherry tomatoes, and pickled peppers—

- **4 beaten eggs**
- **½ teaspoon dried marjoram, crushed**
- **¾ cup cooked spaghetti, cut up**
- **1 green onion, thinly sliced**
- **2 tablespoons margarine *or* butter**
- **1 2.25-ounce can sliced pitted ripe olives (½ cup), drained**
- **¼ cup grated Parmesan cheese**

Snipped parsley

Combine eggs, marjoram, 2 tablespoons *water*, and ⅛ teaspoon *pepper*. Stir in spaghetti and onion. In a 10-inch skillet melt margarine. Add egg mixture. Cook over medium-low heat, running spatula around edge, lifting to allow uncooked portion to flow underneath. Top with olives and *half* the cheese. Fold omelet in half. Slide omelet onto plate. Top omelet with remaining cheese and parsley. Serves 2.

Per serving: 440 cal., 21 g pro., 19 g carbo., 31 g fat, 559 mg chol., 784 mg sodium. U.S. RDA: 30% vit. A, 24% riboflavin, 28% calcium, 22% iron.

INDIAN CHICKEN AND RICE

For a spicier sauce, add ¼ teaspoon ground red pepper—

- ½ cup long grain rice
- 8 ounces boneless, skinless chicken breasts
- 1 tablespoon margarine *or* butter
- ⅓ cup orange juice
- 1 teaspoon dried minced onion
- 1 teaspoon curry powder
- ½ teaspoon ground coriander
- ½ cup seedless grapes, halved
- 1 tablespoon apricot, pineapple, *or* peach preserves

Cook the rice according to the package directions.

Meanwhile, in a 10-inch skillet brown chicken in hot margarine or butter for 5 minutes, turning once. Add the orange juice, onion, curry powder, and coriander. Bring to boiling, then reduce heat. Cover and simmer for 5 minutes or till chicken is tender.

Transfer chicken to a serving platter. Cover to keep warm. Bring pan juices to boiling over medium-high heat. Stir in grapes and preserves. Serve juices over chicken with rice. Makes 3 servings.

Nutrition information per serving: 280 cal., 20 g pro., 38 g carbo., 5 g fat, 44 mg chol., 98 mg sodium, and 1 g dietary fiber. U.S. RDA: 5% vit. A, 16% vit. C, 15% thiamine, 5% riboflavin, 49% niacin, 3% calcium, 10% iron, and 19% phosphorus.

Indian Chicken and Rice

ONION KNOCKWURSTS

The quick-to-make tomato-onion relish makes these knockwursts special—

- 2 cups frozen chopped onion
- 1¼ cups water
- 1 6-ounce can tomato paste
- 1 teaspoon dried oregano, crushed
- ½ teaspoon pepper
- 8 fully cooked knockwursts *or* bratwursts
- 1 small green pepper, cut into strips
- 8 slices American cheese
- 8 hoagie buns *or* frankfurter buns, split
- Mustard (optional)

In a 10-inch skillet combine onion, water, tomato paste, oregano, and pepper. Bring to boiling, then reduce heat. Cover and simmer about 5 minutes or till onion is thawed.

Slash one side of knockwursts or bratwursts ¼ inch deep at ¾-inch intervals (if extra large, also slash lengthwise). Place in skillet, spooning onion mixture over. Cover and simmer for 5 minutes. Add green pepper. Cover and simmer 5 minutes more or till sausages are hot and green pepper is tender.

Place 1 cheese slice inside each bun. Add a sausage, then top with some onion mixture. If desired, pass mustard. Makes 8 servings.

Nutrition information per sandwich: 511 cal., 23 g pro., 31 g carbo., 33 g fat, 79 mg chol., 1,229 mg sodium, 3 g dietary fiber. U.S. RDA: 18% vit. A, 29% vit. C, 44% thiamine, 23% riboflavin, 24% niacin, 26% calcium, 19% iron, 39% phosphorus.

Onion Knockwursts

PLUM DELICIOUS CHICKEN

If you start with boneless chicken breasts, you'll have this fruity stir-fry on the table in less than 20 minutes—

- 2 whole large chicken breasts (about 1½ pounds total), skinned, boned, and halved lengthwise
- 2 tablespoons sugar
- 1 tablespoon rice wine vinegar *or* white wine vinegar
- 1 tablespoon soy sauce
- 2 teaspoons cornstarch
- 2 tablespoons cooking oil
- 1 small onion, thinly sliced and separated into rings
- 1 6-ounce package frozen pea pods
- 6 plums, pitted and quartered
- Chow mein noodles (optional)

Rinse chicken; pat dry. Cut into thin bite-size strips. For sauce, in a small bowl stir together sugar, vinegar, soy sauce, and cornstarch. Set aside.

Preheat a wok or 12-inch skillet over high heat; add oil. Stir-fry onion in hot oil for 1 minute. Add chicken; stir-fry for 2 minutes or till chicken and onion are tender. Push mixture from the center of the wok. Stir sauce; add to the center of the wok. Cook and stir till thickened and bubbly. Add pea pods; stir to coat. Cook and stir for 2 minutes more or till heated. Stir in plums. If desired, serve with noodles. Serves 4.

Nutrition information per serving: 303 cal., 29 g pro., 25 g carbo., 10 g fat, 71 mg chol., 321 mg sodium, 3 g dietary fiber. U.S. RDA: 9% vit. A, 40% vit. C, 11% thiamine, 14% riboflavin, 63% niacin, 4% calcium, 9% iron, 24% phosphorus.

SPINACH AND POTATO PIE

Keep your kitchen cool by "baking" this quichelike pie on top of the range—

- 4 beaten eggs
- 1 tablespoon milk
- ½ teaspoon garlic salt
- ⅛ teaspoon pepper
- 1½ cups frozen hash brown potatoes with onion and peppers
- 1 10-ounce package frozen chopped spinach, thawed and well drained
- ½ cup shredded Swiss cheese (2 ounces)

Grease an 8-inch skillet. In a medium mixing bowl combine eggs, milk, garlic salt, and pepper. Stir in potatoes, spinach, and cheese. Pour egg mixture into the greased skillet.

Cook, covered, over medium heat for 10 to 12 minutes or till center is soft-set and bottom is golden. Remove from heat. Let stand, covered, for 5 minutes. Cut into wedges to serve. Serves 3.

Nutrition information per serving: 354 cal., 23 g pro., 24 g carbo., 19 g fat, 401 mg chol., 576 mg sodium, 3 g dietary fiber. U.S. RDA: 134% vit. A, 18% vit. C, 15% thiamine, 31% riboflavin, 11% niacin, 52% calcium, 28% iron, 44% phosphorus.

Spinach and Potato Pie

ITALIAN ARTICHOKES AND CHICKEN

Elegance and fast cooking do go together. Here's the proof—

- 3 whole medium chicken breasts (about 2¼ pounds total), skinned, boned, and halved lengthwise
- 1 clove garlic, minced *or* ½ teaspoon bottled minced garlic
- 2 tablespoons margarine *or* butter
- 1 10¾-ounce can condensed cream of chicken soup
- 1 8-ounce carton dairy sour cream
- ½ cup shredded mozzarella cheese (2 ounces)
- ¼ cup dry white wine
- 2 tablespoons grated Parmesan cheese
- 1 6-ounce jar marinated artichoke hearts, drained and halved
- Hot cooked corkscrew macaroni *or* noodles (optional)
- 2 tablespoons snipped parsley

Rinse chicken; pat dry. In a 12-inch skillet cook garlic in hot margarine or butter for 15 seconds. Add chicken. Cook for 5 minutes or till light brown, turning once.

Meanwhile, in a medium mixing bowl stir together condensed soup, sour cream, mozzarella cheese, wine, and Parmesan cheese. Add to skillet. Cover and cook for 5 to 7 minutes more or till chicken is tender. Transfer chicken to a serving platter or dinner plates. Cover to keep chicken warm.

Stir sauce mixture in skillet. Add artichokes. Cover and cook for 1 to 2 minutes more or till heated through. If desired, serve with hot cooked macaroni or noodles. Sprinkle with snipped parsley. Makes 6 servings.

Nutrition information per serving: 353 cal., 33 g pro., 8 g carbo., 20 g fat, 100 mg chol., 627 mg sodium, 0 g dietary fiber. U.S. RDA: 17% vit. A, 5% vit. C, 6% thiamine, 15% riboflavin, 61% niacin, 17% calcium, 7% iron, 31% phosphorus.

PEPPER HAM

A colorful veggie topping you also can use to jazz up boneless chicken breasts, burgers, or pork chops—

- 8 ounces fresh mushrooms, halved (about 3 cups)
- 2 yellow *or* green sweet peppers, cut into bite-size strips
- 1 medium onion, sliced
- 2 tablespoons margarine *or* butter
- 1 1-pound fully cooked boneless ham slice, cut about ¾ inch thick
- ½ cup water
- 1 tablespoon brown sugar
- 2 teaspoons cornstarch
- 1 tablespoon dry sherry

In a medium skillet cook mushrooms, peppers, and onion in hot margarine or butter about 5 minutes or till pepper is crisp-tender. Remove vegetables from skillet, then cover to keep warm.

Place ham in skillet. Cook ham over medium heat for 10 to 14 minutes or till heated through, turning once. Transfer ham to platter. Return vegetables to skillet.

In a small mixing bowl combine water, brown sugar, and cornstarch. Add to skillet. Cook and stir till thickened and bubbly. Cook and stir for 2 minutes more. Stir in sherry. Serve over ham. Makes 4 servings.

Nutrition information per serving: 274 cal., 26 g pro., 14 g carbo., 13 g fat, 60 mg chol., 1,436 mg sodium, and 2 g dietary fiber. U.S. RDA: 11% vit. A, 12% vit. C, 65% thiamine, 30% riboflavin, 36% niacin, 3% calcium, 18% iron, 30% phosphorus.

Pepper Ham

FRESH FRUIT DESSERTS

THE YUMMIEST IDEAS YET!

By Joy Taylor

SWEET CHERRY-NUT TART
What a scrumptious concoction!

● Tender pastry . . . toasted pecans . . . sweet cherries: an enticing trio. One forkful and you'll promise yourself to bake a tart every cherry season.

FRESH-FRUIT ALEXANDERS
Peach, strawberry, or mango? You choose!

● You may get a creamy mustache while sipping this dessert. But, who cares when you're in dessert heaven? A second glassful is tempting, but the brandy may surprise you!

PEACH-ALMOND KUCHEN
Serve warm, and watch it go fast—

● Twice is always nice. That's why we put both fresh peaches and peach yogurt in this homestyle dish. The toughest part of the recipe is waiting for it to come out of the oven.

FOR FRESH-FRUIT RECIPES SEE PAGE 99.

MELON CREAM WITH BERRIES
Chill overnight then dress up with fruit—

●How can so few ingredients create such a sensation? To start, pick a ripe, juicy melon for the fluffy cream. Then, choose your prettiest dessert cups to showcase this summer sparkler.

SUMMER SAMPLER WITH CUSTARD
It's no flap to fix or serve!

●Here's a pass-around-the-table dessert that will bring smiles. Pile a platter with poached plums, raspberries, figs, and orange sections, then serve chilled custard alongside.

▲ Seal fruits in freezer bags by pressing out air and closing with a twist tie.

▲ Treat cherries, peaches, and plums with ascorbic acid color keeper.

▲ Pack fruit (but don't crush) into rigid containers, leaving a ½-inch headspace.

USING FROZEN FRUITS

● Thaw fruit in sealed container in a bowl of cool water. Or, thaw fruit in an uncovered microwave-safe bowl in the microwave oven on 30% power for 7 to 9 minutes (30 minutes for fruits in water).

● For cooking, fruits need to be thawed only enough to separate. Serve uncooked fruits when there are a few ice crystals still remaining.

FRESH FRUIT
FREEZE NOW— ENJOY LATER!
■ SUGAR FREE! ■

● **Berries, plums, peaches—all the fruits of summer are naturally wonderful. That's why you shouldn't add a bit of sugar to freeze any of them. Come winter, enjoy low-calorie, juicy fruits.**

GATHER EQUIPMENT

The most important item for freezing is the container or wrapping. You'll want a tightly sealed product so the food won't develop off-flavors, or lose color, moisture, or nutritive value. The best containers for freezing unsweetened fruits are rigid plastic containers or freezer bags. If packed properly and stored at zero degrees or below, frozen fruits maintain quality for eight to 12 months.

BERRIES

Choose berries that are plump, firm, and brightly colored.

Allow 1½ to 3 pounds *blackberries, blueberries, boysenberries, gooseberries, loganberries, raspberries,* or *strawberries* for each quart. Rinse berries; remove stems and leaves. Drain.

Slice berries, if desired. Pack into moisture- and vaporproof freezer containers or bags, leaving a ½-inch headspace. Lightly shake to pack berries closely. Seal, label, and freeze.

CHERRIES

Choose tart red or dark sweet cherries that are firm and bright.

Allow 2 to 2½ pounds unpitted *dark sweet* or *tart red cherries* for each quart. Rinse cherries; remove stems and leaves. Pit the cherries, if desired. Drain.

Dip cherries into *water* containing *ascorbic acid color keeper* (follow package directions for proportions of color keeper to water). Drain. Pack cherries into moisture- and vaporproof freezer containers or bags, leaving a ½-inch headspace. Lightly shake containers or bags to pack cherries closely. Seal, label, and freeze.

MELONS

Choose firm-fleshed, well-colored ripe melons.

Allow about 4 pounds *cantaloupe, Crenshaw melon, watermelon, Persian melon,* or *honeydew melon* for each quart. Cut melons in half. Remove seeds and rind. Cut melons into slices, cubes, or balls.

Pack melon pieces tightly into moisture- and vaporproof freezer containers or freezer bags, leaving a ½-inch headspace. Seal, label, and freeze.

PEACHES/NECTARINES

Choose plump fruits with a soft, creamy-to-yellow color.

Allow 2 to 3 pounds fruit for each quart. Rinse peaches or nectarines in cold water. To peel, immerse in *boiling water* for 20 to 30 seconds. Plunge into *cold water*. Carefully remove skins. Halve fruit; pit.

Prevent darkening during preparation by dipping fruit into *water* containing *ascorbic acid color keeper*. Drain fruit well.

Slice fruit, if desired. Stir 1 teaspoon *ascorbic acid color keeper* into each 4 cups *cold water;* allow 1 to 1½ cups of the water for each quart. Pack fruit tightly into moisture- and vaporproof freezer containers; leave headspace. Add the water to cover the fruit; leave a ½-inch headspace. Seal, label, and freeze.

PLUMS

Choose meaty varieties, which are usually larger. Plums should be fairly firm.

Allow 1¼ to 2½ pounds of *plums* for each quart. Thoroughly rinse plums in cold water and remove stems. Drain well. Halve and pit plums.

Dip halved plums into *water* containing *ascorbic acid color keeper*. Drain well. Pack plums tightly into moisture- and vaporproof freezer containers or bags, leaving a ½-inch headspace. Seal, label, and freeze.

FRESH-FRUIT ALEXANDERS

A popular bar drink, creamy Alexanders always have a splash of brandy—

  2 **ripe peaches** *or* **nectarines, peeled, pitted, and chopped;** *or* **2 cups halved strawberries;** *or* **1 large mango, peeled, pitted, and chopped (2 cups)**
  ¼ **cup brandy**
  2 **tablespoons orange schnapps**
  1 **cup vanilla ice cream**
  6 **to 10 ice cubes**

In a blender container combine desired fruit, brandy, and schnapps. Cover and blend till fruit is pureed.

Add ice cream to the fruit mixture in the blender container. Cover and blend till smooth.

With blender running, add the ice cubes through the opening in the lid, blending till drink is smooth and of desired consistency.

To serve, pour the drink mixture into tall wineglasses. Serve immediately. If desired, garnish each serving with whole strawberries, peach slices, or citrus slices. Makes 4 servings.

Nutrition information per drink: 146 cal., 2 g pro., 19 g carbo., 4 g fat, 15 mg chol., 29 mg sodium, 1 g dietary fiber. U.S. RDA: 7% vit. A, 5% vit. C, 1% thiamine, 6% riboflavin, 2% niacin, 5% calcium, 4% phosphorus.

MELON CREAM WITH BERRIES

Has blueberry season come and gone? Serve the melon cream with sugar cookies, peach slices, or orange sections—

  1 **medium cantaloupe** *or* **honeydew melon**
  ⅓ **cup sugar***
  1 **envelope unflavored gelatin**
  ½ **cup milk**
  1 **3-ounce package cream cheese**
  ¼ **cup whipping cream**
  2 **to 3 cups fresh blueberries**

Halve cantaloupe or melon, then remove seeds. Chill *half* of the melon till serving time. Peel and chop remaining melon (you should have about 2 cups).

In a small saucepan combine the sugar and the gelatin. Add the milk. Heat and stir mixture over low heat till gelatin is dissolved.

In a blender container combine chopped melon, gelatin mixture, and cream cheese. Cover and blend till smooth. Transfer to a medium mixing bowl. Cover and chill for 30 to 45 minutes or till the mixture mounds.

In a mixer bowl beat whipping cream till soft peaks form. Fold whipped cream into gelatin mixture.

Place about ¼ cup blueberries in *each* dessert dish. Top *each* dish of blueberries with ½ *cup* of the melon-cream mixture. Cover and chill about 4 hours or till set.

To serve, cut remaining melon into long thin slices. Top each serving with more blueberries and melon slices. Makes 6 servings.

**Note:* If using honeydew melon, increase the sugar to ½ *cup.*

Nutrition information per serving: 198 cal., 4 g pro., 27 g carbo., 9 g fat, 31 mg chol., 68 mg sodium, and 4 g dietary fiber. U.S. RDA: 66% vit. A, 73% vit. C, 4% thiamine, 7% riboflavin, 6% calcium, 3% iron, 6% phosphorus.

PEACH-ALMOND KUCHEN

Kuchen is German for cake. In America, it describes coffee-cakelike desserts—

  ½ **cup all-purpose flour**
  3 **tablespoons brown sugar**
  ½ **teaspoon ground cinnamon**
  3 **tablespoons margarine** *or* **butter**
  ¼ **cup sliced almonds, toasted**
  1¼ **pounds medium peaches, peeled, pitted, and sliced (4 cups)**
  1 **8-ounce carton peach yogurt**
  1 **3-ounce package cream cheese, softened**
  2 **eggs**
  ¼ **cup sugar**
  ¼ **cup all-purpose flour**

For crumb topping, in a small mixing bowl stir together the ½ cup flour, brown sugar, and cinnamon. Cut in margarine or butter till mixture resembles fine crumbs. Stir in almonds. Set crumb topping aside.

Spoon peaches into an ungreased 10x6x2-inch baking dish. In a medium mixer bowl use an electric mixer or rotary beater to beat together yogurt and cream cheese. Add eggs, sugar, and ¼ cup flour, beating till smooth. Pour mixture over fruit in dish. Sprinkle crumb topping around edge of dish.

Bake in a 375° oven for 30 minutes or till filling is set. Serve warm, cut into squares. Makes 6 to 8 servings.

Nutrition information per serving: 353 cal., 8 g pro., 48 g carbo., 15 g fat, 109 mg chol., 157 mg sodium, 2 g dietary fiber. U.S. RDA: 23% vit. A, 9% vit. C, 10% thiamine, 17% riboflavin, 11% niacin, 11% calcium, 10% iron, and 14% phosphorus.

SWEET CHERRY-NUT TART

During July and August look for Rainier cherries to prepare this luscious tart. These golden cherries with a pink blush are the pride of cherry growers in the Northwest. They're sweeter tasting and extra large—

- ¼ **cup dairy sour cream**
- 1 **egg yolk**
- 1 **package active dry yeast**
- 2 **tablespoons sugar**
- ¼ **teaspoon salt**
- ¼ **teaspoon vanilla**
- ⅓ **cup margarine *or* butter**
- 1¼ **cups all-purpose flour**
- 1 **cup chopped pecans, toasted**
- ¼ **cup sugar**
- 1 **tablespoon milk**
- ½ **teaspoon vanilla**
- 1½ **pounds dark *or* light sweet cherries (about 5 cups)**
- ¼ **cup sugar**
- 4 **teaspoons cornstarch**

Powdered sugar

For crust, in a small mixing bowl stir together sour cream, egg yolk, yeast, 2 tablespoons sugar, salt, and ¼ teaspoon vanilla. Let mixture stand about 10 minutes to soften yeast.

In a medium mixing bowl use a pastry blender to cut margarine or butter into flour till pieces are the size of small peas. Make a well in the center of the flour mixture. Add yeast mixture, then stir till combined. Wrap dough in plastic wrap. Chill at least 2 hours.

Press dough evenly over the bottom and 1½ inches up the sides of a 9-inch springform pan. Bake in a 350° oven for 15 minutes.

Meanwhile, for nut filling, combine pecans, ¼ cup sugar, milk, and ½ teaspoon vanilla. Spoon the nut filling evenly over partially baked crust. Bake for 15 to 20 minutes more or till the crust is golden.

For fruit filling, stem and pit cherries. As you work, dip pitted cherries in water containing ascorbic acid color keeper (follow the package directions for the proportions of color keeper to water). Drain the cherries well.

In a large saucepan combine cherries and ¼ cup sugar. Let stand 10 to 15 minutes to draw out juices. Stir in cornstarch. Cook and stir till thickened and bubbly. Cook and stir 2 minutes more.

Spoon cherry mixture over nut filling. Cool on wire rack. Remove sides of pan. Just before serving, sift powdered sugar over tart. Makes 8 servings.

Nutrition information per serving: 404 cal., 5 g pro., 52 g carbo., 21 g fat, 38 mg chol., 164 mg sodium, 2 g dietary fiber. U.S. RDA: 13% vit. A, 12% vit. C, 22% thiamine, 13% riboflavin, 9% niacin, 4% calcium, 10% iron, and 11% phosphorus.

ORANGE CUSTARD SAUCE

- 2 **tablespoons sugar**
- 2 **teaspoons cornstarch**
- ½ **teaspoon finely shredded orange peel**
- ⅛ **teaspoon salt**
- 1½ **cups milk**
- 1 **beaten egg yolk**
- 1 **to 2 tablespoons orange liqueur**
- 1 **teaspoon vanilla**

In a 2-quart saucepan stir together sugar, cornstarch, orange peel, and salt. Stir in milk. Cook and stir till thickened and bubbly. Cook and stir for 2 minutes more.

Gradually stir about *half* of the hot mixture into the egg yolk. Return the egg yolk mixture to the remaining mixture in the saucepan. Cook and stir till bubbly. Cook and stir for 2 minutes more. Remove from heat.

Stir in orange liqueur and vanilla. Cover the surface of the sauce with clear plastic wrap. Cool without stirring. Place sauce in the refrigerator to chill thoroughly before serving. Makes 1⅓ cups sauce.

SUMMER SAMPLER WITH CUSTARD

Pick up different plum varieties when you shop—the juiciness and color of the flesh differs in each variety, ranging from creamy yellow to light pink. Your summer sampler will be all the more enticing—

- 6 **ripe plums**
- ½ **cup water**
- ½ **cup orange juice**
- ¼ **cup sugar**
- 2 **oranges**
- 1 **cup fresh raspberries, chilled**
- 4 **fresh figs, quartered**
- 1 **recipe Orange Custard Sauce (see recipe, *below left*)**

Halve, pit, and peel plums. Cut any large plums into quarters.

In a 10-inch skillet combine water, orange juice, and sugar. Bring to boiling. Carefully add plum pieces. Reduce heat. Simmer, uncovered, for 5 to 8 minutes or till plums can be easily pierced with a fork, turning plums over halfway through the cooking time. Using a slotted spoon, transfer plums to a bowl. Cover and chill.

To serve, peel and section oranges. On a large platter arrange the plums, orange sections, raspberries, and figs. Serve fruits with the Orange Custard Sauce. Makes 4 servings.

Nutrition information per serving: 301 cal., 6 g pro., 64 g carbo., 4 g fat, 75 mg chol., 116 mg sodium, 4 g dietary fiber. U.S. RDA: 17% vit. A, 110% vit. C, 13% thiamine, 20% riboflavin, 6% niacin, 18% calcium, 5% iron, 14% phosphorus.

AUGUST

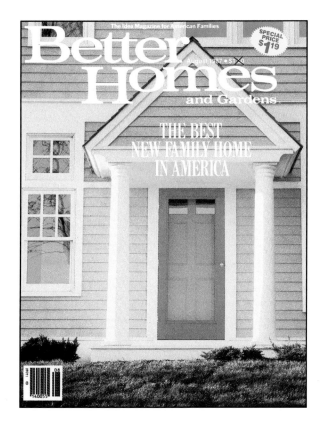

STUFFED FLOUNDER FLORENTINE

TIP: To defrost frozen fish, put fillets in the dish. Micro-cook, covered, on 30% power (medium-low) 6 to 8 minutes or till pliable, but still icy. Turn fish over after 3 minutes cooking. Let stand 10 minutes.

MICROWAVE
ONE-DISH MEALS
OUT OF THE OVEN IN 15 MINUTES OR LESS!

By Barbara Greenwood

STUFFED FLOUNDER FLORENTINE

- **4** fresh *or* individually frozen sole *or* flounder fillets
- **1** 10-ounce package frozen chopped spinach, thawed and well drained
- **1½** cups garlic croutons, coarsely crushed
- **1** 7-ounce can whole kernel corn with sweet peppers, well drained
- **1** beaten egg
- **⅓** cup chicken broth
- **1** large tomato, cut into thin wedges
- **½** of a 12-ounce jar (⅔ cup) chicken gravy
- **1** tablespoon lemon juice

Thaw fillets, if frozen (see tip, opposite). For stuffing, combine spinach, croutons, and corn. Add egg and broth; toss to mix well.

Lay the fillets in a single layer in a 12x7½x2-inch microwave-safe baking dish. (They may hang over edge.) Season with *pepper*. Spoon *one-fourth* of the stuffing over *half* of *each* fillet. Fold remaining fillet half over stuffing. Cover with vented microwave-safe plastic wrap. Micro-cook on 100% power (high) 4 minutes. Place tomato at ends of dish; cook, covered, on high 1 to 2 minutes or till fish flakes easily with fork. Cover; let stand while preparing sauce.

In a 2-cup glass measure combine gravy and juice. Micro-cook, uncovered, on high 2 to 3 minutes or till heated through; stir once. Spoon over fish. Makes 4 servings.

Nutrition information per serving: 214 cal., 26 g pro., 15 g carbo., 6 g fat, 118 mg chol., 601 mg sodium, 4 g dietary fiber. U.S. RDA: 107% vit. A, 18% vit. C, 17% riboflavin, 16% niacin, 12% calcium, 18% iron, 29% phosphorus.

PHOTOGRAPHS: JIM HEDRICH. FOOD STYLIST: PAT GODSTED

CORDON BLEU CASSEROLE
TIP: Make-ahead convenience! Layer and chill this dish one night; cook it the next.

- **1** 10-ounce package frozen cut broccoli
- **4** slices rye *or* whole wheat bread
- **1** 2½-ounce package thinly sliced smoked chicken
- **1** 6-ounce package sliced fully cooked ham
- **¼** teaspoon onion powder
- **1** 10¾-ounce can ready-to-eat chunky creamy mushroom soup
- **½** of a 6-ounce package shredded Swiss cheese

Rinse broccoli under water to thaw and separate; pat dry. Line bottom of 8x8x2-inch microwave-safe baking dish with bread. Top with chicken, ham, and broccoli.

Stir onion powder into soup; pour over all. Sprinkle with cheese. Cover; chill overnight, if desired.

To cook, cover dish with vented microwave-safe plastic wrap. Micro-cook on 50% power (medium) 13 to 15 minutes for unchilled casserole (18 to 20 minutes for chilled casserole) or till heated through, giving dish a half-turn once. Makes 4 servings.

Nutrition information per serving: 277 cal., 24 g pro., 21 g carbo., 12 g fat, 48 mg chol., 1,229 mg sodium, 4 g dietary fiber. U.S. RDA: 27% vit. A, 40% vit. C, 30% thiamine, 18% riboflavin, 22% niacin, 27% calcium, 11% iron, 35% phosphorus.

SUMMER FOODS
TO GO!

- **EASY TO MAKE**
- **EASY TO TAKE**
- **EASY TO ENJOY**

By Lynn Hoppe

POTLUCK FAVORITES

TAKE-ALONG SIDE DISHES FOR A FAMILY REUNION OR BLOCK PARTY

KEEP POTLUCK FOODS IN TIP-TOP SHAPE

● Wrap a hot casserole in foil or a heavy towel and stow it in a plastic-foam container to keep it hot up to 3 hours. Or, inexpensive square or round foam containers often are sized just right for a 1- or 2-quart casserole.

The casserole in its insulated container can go straight to the table for serving.

● Of course, pack cold food in an ice-filled cooler, and plan on eating it within 4 to 6 hours.

SPINACH-PASTA SALAD
▲ *Light and fresh—every potlucker will dig into this side salad. The simple chutney dressing adds the oomph!*

RAINBOW FRUIT BOWL
▼ *Like bees to honey, picnickers will swarm to this fresh-fruit bowl topped with a spicy peach sauce.*

HAWAIIAN BAKED BEANS
▲ *Dump, stir, and bake! Canned three-bean salad and pineapple provide the ultraeasy, ultragood, sweet-sour flavor.*

PARMESAN POTATO SALAD
▲ *Show up with this show-off potato salad with Parmesan, hazelnuts, artichokes, and green beans.*

PEPPER CHEESE VEGETABLES
▼ *Brace yourself. The four-ingredient, easy-to-make cheese sauce is a real tongue-tingler.*

CARROT-COCONUT CAKE
▼ *Spruce up a cake-mix cake with this smear-resistant frosting—it stays on the cake, not on the lid!*

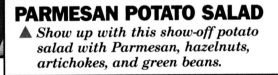

CASUAL PICNIC

A KID-PLEASIN' FEAST FOR A FAMILY OUTING

●OUTSIDE-IN BURGERS
The condiments are tucked inside the patties.

●WONTON CHIPS
These spicy chips quick-bake in 10 minutes.

●LEMON-FRESH WALDORF SALAD
A salad that's fun, good, and nutritious, too!

●CHERRY-CHOCOLATE SMILES
A gooey filling between wedges of piecrust.

●FRUIT JUICE
Pack plenty of your favorite thirst quencher.

PREPARE FOR AN AWAY-FROM-HOME GRILL-OUT

● The night before the picnic, shape and freeze burgers. The frozen burgers help keep the rest of the food chilled in the cooler.

● Cooler packing strategy: Pack a frozen ice pack first, then your salad. The frozen burgers go on top.

● Don't forget the grilling accessories: Grill, long-handled spatula, hot pad, charcoal, lighter fluid, matches.

- **SESAME CHICKEN AND RICE SALAD**
  A make-ahead main dish with oriental flair.

- **MELON-PROSCIUTTO KABOBS**
  Tailored for packing, serving, and eating.

- **HARD ROLL**
  Your bakery's contribution to the meal.

- **RASPBERRY-GLAZED POUND CAKE**
  Drench the cake with a luscious liqueur glaze.

- **CHENIN BLANC WINE**
  Chilled, of course.

PACK A PICNIC WITH FIRST-CLASS AMBIENCE

● Make your picnic special with sturdy, yet fancy dinnerware. Cushion it in your picnic basket with layers of paper towels between each plate. Acrylic stemware is a care-free addition. And because the foods are easy to eat, just pack forks.

● Here's how to easily transport the cake: Remove the cake from the loaf pan; line the pan with foil. Slice cake and return to pan.

107

ROADSIDE PICNIC

LIGHT FARE TO BREAK ON-THE-ROAD TEDIUM

- **TUNA-CUCUMBER SPREAD**
  Deli vegetable salad adds punch to tuna.

- **FRESH VEGGIES, FRUIT, CRACKERS**
  Pack up what's left for in-the-car munching.

- **SLICED FRENCH BREAD**
  Spread the tuna-cucumber topper on thick.

- **CARAMEL-BANANA CUPS**
  A chilled filling caps a cookie crust.

- **MINERAL WATER**
  A no-stain whistle-wetter that travels well.

CHOOSE FINGER FOODS FOR A HELP-YOURSELF MENU

- Tender, baby vegetables are great for munching. No need to cut them up; they're already nibble size.

- The hot sun does a number on food. When packing perishable foods such as the spread and pie cups, take just enough for one meal—no leftovers.

- Be prepared for cleanup. Take a large plastic bag for disposables.

SPINACH PASTA SALAD

Tortellini are rings of stuffed pasta—

- 1 7-ounce package frozen *or* refrigerated cheese-filled egg tortellini *or* 1 cup dried tortellini
- 6 cups torn fresh spinach
- 1 cup shredded red cabbage
- 6 slices bacon, crisp-cooked, drained, and crumbled
- 4 green onions, sliced
- ¼ cup chutney
- ⅓ cup red wine vinegar and oil salad dressing

Cook pasta according to package directions. Drain; rinse with cold water. Drain again. In a large salad bowl toss together pasta, spinach, cabbage, bacon, and onions. Cover and chill.

For dressing, cut up large pieces of chutney. In a screw-top jar combine chutney and salad dressing. Cover and chill. To serve, shake dressing well. Toss with salad. Makes 12 servings.

Nutrition information per serving: 85 cal., 5 g pro., 10 g carbo., 3 g fat, 23 mg chol., 155 mg sodium. U.S. RDA: 38% vit. A, 21% vit. C.

HAWAIIAN BAKED BEANS

- 2 16-ounce cans pork and beans with tomato sauce
- 2 15-ounce cans three-bean salad, drained
- 2 8-ounce cans crushed pineapple (juice pack)
- ⅔ cup bottled barbecue sauce
- 2 tablespoons Worcestershire sauce
Bacon curls
Fresh herbs

In a 3-quart casserole combine first 5 ingredients. Bake, uncovered, in a 350° oven about 1 hour or till hot. Stir; top with bacon curls and herbs. Serves 12.

Microwave directions: In a 3-quart microwave-safe casserole combine ingredients as above. Micro-cook, covered, on 100% power (high) for 18 to 20 minutes or till heated through; stir 3 times. Serve as above.

Nutrition information per serving: 177 cal., 6 g pro., 33 g carbo., 2 g fat, 3 mg chol., 817 mg sodium, 11 g dietary fiber. U.S. RDA: 14% vit. C, 21% iron, 10% phosphorus.

RAINBOW FRUIT BOWL

- 6 medium peaches *or* nectarines, peeled, pitted, and sliced
- 3 tablespoons lemon juice
- 3 tablespoons sugar
- 1 tablespoon cornstarch
Dash ground cinnamon
Dash ground cloves
- 1 banana, sliced
- 1 pound plums, pitted and quartered
- 1 cup seedless green grapes, halved
- ½ cup sliced strawberries
- 1½ cups blueberries

In a large mixing bowl toss *half* of the peaches or nectarines with *1 tablespoon* of the lemon juice. Set aside.

In a medium saucepan combine remaining peaches, ½ cup *water,* and *1 tablespoon* of the lemon juice. Bring to boiling; reduce heat. Cover; simmer about 5 minutes or till very tender. *Do not drain.* In a blender container or food processor bowl process peaches and liquid till smooth. Return to pan.

Combine sugar, cornstarch, cinnamon, and cloves. Add to saucepan. Cook and stir till thickened and bubbly; cook and stir 2 minutes more. Cool. Toss banana with remaining lemon juice.

Layer fruits in a 2-quart straight-side glass bowl, using *half* of the remaining peaches or nectarines, all of the plums, and all of the grapes. Alternate bananas and strawberries around outside of bowl with cut side toward glass. Add remaining peaches and all of the blueberries. Spoon peach sauce atop. Cover; chill. Serves 8.

Microwave directions: For sauce, in a 2-quart microwave-safe casserole combine remaining half of the peaches, water, and *1 tablespoon* lemon juice. Micro-cook, covered, on 100% power (high) for 3 to 5 minutes or till tender, stirring twice. *Do not drain.* Blend or process peach mixture as directed. Return to casserole. Combine sugar, cornstarch, cinnamon, and cloves. Add to casserole. Cook, uncovered, on high for 2 to 3 minutes or till thickened and bubbly, stirring after every minute till slightly thickened, then after every 30 seconds. Cook, uncovered, on high for 1 minute more.

Nutrition information per serving: 121 cal., 1 g pro., 31 g carbo., 1 g fat, 0 mg chol., 2 mg sodium, 4 g dietary fiber. U.S. RDA: 12% vit. A, 29% vit. C.

PARMESAN POTATO SALAD

After cooking, chill the potatoes for 1 hour. That way, they'll slice easier—

- 6 medium potatoes (2 pounds) *or* three 16-ounce cans sliced potatoes
- 1 9-ounce package frozen French-style green beans
- 2 tablespoons chopped hazelnuts (filberts)
- 1 cup creamy cucumber salad dressing
- ⅓ cup snipped parsley
- ¼ cup grated Parmesan cheese
- 1 13¾-ounce jar marinated artichoke hearts, drained and quartered

Cook fresh potatoes, uncovered, in boiling salted water for 25 to 30 minutes or till tender; drain well. Let cool; slice. (Or, drain canned potatoes.) Cook beans according to package directions. Drain.

In a blender container place hazelnuts. Cover and blend till ground. In a bowl combine hazelnuts, salad dressing, parsley, and Parmesan cheese.

In a large salad bowl combine potatoes, green beans, and artichokes. Toss gently with dressing mixture. Cover and chill at least 1 hour. Transport in an insulated cooler with an ice pack. Makes 6 to 8 servings.

Microwave directions: Cut fresh potatoes in half crosswise. In a 3-quart microwave-safe casserole cook potatoes and 1 cup *water,* covered, on 100% power (high) for 8 minutes. Add green beans. Cook, covered, for 8 to 10 minutes more or till vegetables are tender. Drain. Continue as directed above.

Nutrition information per serving: 336 cal., 8 g pro., 38 g carbo., 19 g fat, 6 mg chol., 450 mg sodium. U.S. RDA: 10% vit. A, 50% vit. C, 15% thiamine, 13% riboflavin, 15% niacin, 11% calcium, 11% iron, 14% phosphorus.

PEPPER CHEESE VEGETABLES

No jicama available? Try sliced water chestnuts— ·

- 1 10-ounce package frozen cut broccoli
- 1 10-ounce package frozen peas and carrots
- 1 cup milk
- 1 1¾-ounce envelope white sauce mix
- 1 1¼-ounce envelope cheese sauce mix
- 8 ounces jicama, cut into thin strips (1½ cups)
- ½ cup shredded Monterey Jack cheese with jalapeño peppers (2 ounces)

In a medium saucepan cook frozen vegetables, covered, in ½ cup *boiling water* about 5 minutes or till crisp-tender. *Do not drain.* Stir in milk and sauce mixes. Bring to boiling. Remove from heat. Stir in jicama and cheese. Turn into a 10x6x2-inch baking dish. Bake, uncovered, in a 350° oven for 30 minutes or till heated through. Makes 10 servings.

Microwave directions: In a 2-quart microwave-safe casserole combine frozen vegetables and ¼ cup *water.* Cover with clear plastic wrap; vent by leaving a small area unsealed at the edge of the dish. Micro-cook on 100% power (high) about 8 minutes or till crisp-tender, rearranging dish once. *Do not drain.* Stir in milk and sauce mixes. Cook on high for 1 to 2 minutes or till boiling. Cook for 2 minutes more. Stir in jicama and cheese. Cook for 1 to 2 minutes or till heated through.

Nutrition information per serving: 104 cal., 6 g pro., 12 g carbo., 5 g fat, 9 mg chol., 386 mg sodium, 3 g dietary fiber. U.S. RDA: 65% vit. A, 21% vit. C, 16% calcium, 12% phosphorus.

CARROT-COCONUT CAKE

- 3 medium carrots, sliced
- 1 1-inch-square orange peel
- 1 cup orange juice
- ¼ cup cooking oil
- 1 package 2-layer-size yellow cake mix
- 3 eggs
- 1⅓ cups coconut
- ¾ cup packed brown sugar
- ¾ cup chopped pecans
- ⅓ cup milk
- ¼ cup margarine *or* butter, melted
- 1 teaspoon vanilla

Combine carrots, orange peel, juice, and oil in a blender container or food processor bowl. Cover and blend or process till carrots are finely chopped.

In a large mixer bowl combine carrot mixture, cake mix, and eggs. Beat just till blended. Beat on medium speed for 2 minutes, scraping sides occasionally. Turn batter into a greased and floured 13x9x2-inch baking pan. Bake in a 350° oven for 35 to 40 minutes or till a wooden toothpick inserted in the center comes out clean. Remove from oven. Turn oven to broil.

Mix coconut, brown sugar, and pecans. Stir in milk, margarine, and vanilla. Using the back of a spoon or a small spatula, quickly spread coconut topping over hot cake in pan. Broil cake 4 to 5 inches from heat for 2 to 3 minutes or till coconut topping is golden brown. Serve warm or cool. Serves 12.

Nutrition information per serving: 438 cal., 5 g pro., 57 g carbo., 22 g fat, 69 mg chol., 375 mg sodium, and 3 g dietary fiber. U.S. RDA: 107% vit. A, 11% vit. C, 15% thiamine, 10% iron, and 19% phosphorus.

OUTSIDE-IN BURGERS

- 2 pounds lean ground beef
- 1 cup shredded Swiss cheese (4 ounces)
- 3 tablespoons catsup-style hamburger relish, mustard-style hot dog relish, *or* horseradish mustard
- 8 kaiser rolls *or* hamburger buns, split
- Lettuce leaves
- Tomato slices

Shape beef into sixteen ¼-inch-thick patties. For filling, in a medium bowl combine cheese and relish or mustard. Place about *2 tablespoons* filling on *each* of 8 patties. Spread to within ½ inch of edges. Top with remaining patties. Press beef around edges to seal well. Wrap patties individually in foil. Chill at least 3 hours or freeze up to 6 months. Transport in an insulated cooler with an ice pack.

Grill chilled patties, on an uncovered grill, directly over *medium-hot* coals for 13 to 14 minutes or till done, turning once. (Or, grill frozen patties for 18 to 20 minutes or till done, turning once.) Serve burgers on buns with lettuce and tomato slices. Serves 8.

Nutrition information per serving: 369 cal., 31 g pro., 24 g carbo., 16 g fat, 95 mg chol., 338 mg sodium. U.S. RDA: 16% thiamine, 21% riboflavin, 33% niacin, 18% calcium, 24% iron, 32% phosphorus.

WONTON CHIPS

Pack chips in a self-sealing clear plastic bag, leaving some air in the bag—

- ¼ cup margarine *or* butter, melted
- ¾ teaspoon dry mustard
- ¾ teaspoon onion powder
- ¾ teaspoon garlic salt
- ⅛ teaspoon ground red pepper
- ½ of a 16-ounce package wonton skins
- Nonstick spray coating
- Salsa, mustard sauce, avocado dip, *or* sour cream dip (optional)

Combine margarine, mustard, onion powder, garlic salt, and red pepper. Separate wonton skins. Fold skins to form interesting shapes. Place in a single layer on 2 baking sheets sprayed with nonstick spray coating. Brush with margarine mixture.

Bake wonton skins in a 350° oven for 8 to 10 minutes or till crisp and golden brown. Repeat till all wontons are baked. Cool on a wire rack. Store in a tightly closed container up to 2 weeks. Serve with salsa, mustard sauce, or dips, if desired. Makes about 32.

Nutrition information per chip: 32 cal., 1 g pro., 4 g carbo., 2 g fat, 0 mg chol., 46 mg sodium.

LEMON-FRESH WALDORF SALAD

    1 cup wagon wheel *or*
      bow tie macaroni
    ¾ cup chopped celery
    ¼ cup raisins
    3 small apples, cored and chopped
    ½ cup mayonnaise *or* salad
      dressing
    ½ cup lemon yogurt
    2 tablespoons sunflower nuts

Cook the wagon wheels or bow ties according to package directions. Drain macaroni. Rinse with cold water. Drain the macaroni again. Cover and chill.

In a large plastic container with a sealable lid toss together the cooked pasta, chopped celery, and raisins.

For dressing, stir together the chopped apples, mayonnaise or salad dressing, and yogurt. Spread the mayonnaise mixture over the pasta mixture. Sprinkle with the sunflower nuts. Cover and chill at least 4 hours.

Transport the salad in an insulated cooler with an ice pack. To serve, fold the dressing into the pasta mixture. Makes 8 to 10 servings.

Nutrition information per serving: 221 cal., 3 g pro., 26 g carbo., 12 g fat, 9 mg chol., 98 mg sodium, 2 g dietary fiber. U.S. RDA: 13% thiamine.

MELON-PROSCIUTTO KABOBS

    4 cups honeydew melon *or*
      cantaloupe balls
    8 ounces sliced prosciutto, cut into
      thin strips (about 1½ cups)
   12 6-inch wooden skewers

Arrange melon balls and thread prosciutto accordion-style on wooden skewers. Store in an airtight container. Chill at least 2 hours. Transport in insulated cooler with ice pack. Serves 6.

Nutrition information per serving: 101 cal., 9 g pro., 13 g carbo., 2 g fat, 20 mg chol., 468 mg sodium, 2 g dietary fiber. U.S. RDA: 68% vit. C, 26% thiamine, 12% niacin.

CHERRY-CHOCOLATE SMILES

Next time, try strawberry or raspberry preserves instead of cherry—

    1 15-ounce package folded
      refrigerated unbaked piecrusts
      (2 crusts)
    ½ cup cherry preserves
    ¼ cup milk chocolate pieces
    ¼ cup chopped pecans
    ¼ teaspoon ground cinnamon
    1 beaten egg white
    1 tablespoon water

Let piecrusts stand at room temperature for 20 minutes.

Meanwhile, for cherry filling, in a small mixing bowl combine cherry preserves, milk chocolate pieces, chopped pecans, and cinnamon.

Unfold piecrusts; cut *each* piecrust into 8 wedges. Place about *1 tablespoon* of filling on *8* of the piecrust wedges, leaving ½ inch around edges. Make cutouts in remaining wedges or prick with a fork. Moisten the edges of each wedge with filling. Place the remaining wedges atop filling, then use a fork to seal edges well.

In a small mixing bowl use a fork to beat together the egg white and water. Brush egg white mixture on *each* filled wedge. Place filled wedges in a lightly greased shallow baking pan.

Bake filled wedges in a 375° oven about 20 minutes or till golden brown. Cool on wire rack. Place the wedges in an airtight container for transporting. Makes 8 servings.

Nutrition information per serving: 340 cal., 2 g pro., 39 g carbo., 20 g fat, 1 mg chol., 339 mg sodium.

SESAME CHICKEN AND RICE SALAD

    ¾ cup wild rice
   1½ cups water
    2 cups fresh pea pods *or* one
      6-ounce package frozen pea
      pods
    2 cups diced cooked chicken
    1 11-ounce can mandarin orange
      sections, drained
    ½ cup sliced water chestnuts,
      halved
    ¼ cup rice wine vinegar *or* vinegar
    1 tablespoon sesame oil
    1 tablespoon salad oil
    ¼ teaspoon salt
    ¼ teaspoon ground red pepper
    ⅛ teaspoon garlic powder

Run cold water over rice in a strainer about 1 minute, lifting rice to rinse well. In a medium saucepan bring rice and water to boiling; reduce heat. Cover and simmer for 40 to 50 minutes or till done. Drain. Rinse with cold water. Drain again.

In a bowl toss together rice, pea pods, chicken, mandarin orange sections, and water chestnuts. Cover; chill rice mixture for 6 hours or overnight.

In a screw-top jar combine vinegar, sesame oil, salad oil, salt, red pepper, and garlic powder. Cover and chill at least 6 hours or overnight.

Transport the vinegar and oil mixture and rice mixture separately in an insulated cooler with an ice pack. At the picnic, shake vinegar and oil mixture well. Pour over rice mixture; toss well. Makes 6 main-dish servings.

Nutrition information per serving: 234 cal., 18 g pro., 24 g carbo., 8 g fat, 42 mg chol., 136 mg sodium, 3 g dietary fiber. U.S. RDA: 25% vit. C, 13% thiamine, 14% riboflavin, 30% niacin, 11% iron, 18% phosphorus.

RASPBERRY-GLAZED POUND CAKE

1	16-ounce package pound cake mix
½	teaspoon finely shredded orange peel
⅔	cup orange juice
1½	cups fresh raspberries, blueberries, *or* boysenberries
¼	cup sugar
¼	cup orange juice *or* triple sec
⅛	teaspoon ground ginger

Lemon curd *or* frozen whipped dessert topping, thawed (optional)
Fresh raspberries, blueberries, *or* boysenberries (optional)

Prepare and bake pound cake according to package directions *except* add orange peel and substitute the ⅔ cup orange juice for the water.

While cake is still warm, prick cake several times with fork. *Do not remove cake from pan.*

For glaze, in a medium saucepan combine the 1½ cups raspberries, blueberries, or boysenberries; sugar; the ¼ cup orange juice or triple sec; and ginger. Cook and stir till thickened and bubbly. Cook and stir 2 minutes more. Strain warm berry mixture through a sieve to remove seeds and skin. Spoon over pound cake. Cool.

To serve, spoon lemon curd or thawed whipped dessert topping and additional raspberries, blueberries, or boysenberries over sliced pound cake, if desired. Makes 12 servings.

Nutrition information per serving:
225 cal., 3 g pro., 42 g carbo., 5 g fat, 46 mg chol., 197 mg sodium, 2 g dietary fiber. U.S. RDA: 17% vit. C.

TUNA-CUCUMBER SPREAD

For a decorative touch, reserve ¼ cup of the chopped vegetables from the salad and arrange them on the bottom of the lined mold before spooning in the tuna-gelatin mixture—

1	teaspoon unflavored gelatin
1	cup deli marinated cucumber *or* mixed vegetable salad
½	of an 8-ounce package cream cheese, softened
2	tablespoons mayonnaise *or* salad dressing
1	tablespoon snipped fresh dill or ½ teaspoon dried dillweed
1	3½-ounce can tuna (water pack), drained and flaked

Sliced French bread, Melba toast, *or* desired crackers

In a small saucepan combine unflavored gelatin and 2 tablespoons *cold water*. Let stand 5 minutes. Cook and stir over low heat till gelatin is dissolved. Set aside.

Drain the marinated cucumber or mixed vegetable salad, reserving *1 tablespoon* of the marinade. Finely chop the vegetables.

In small mixer bowl beat reserved marinade, softened cream cheese, mayonnaise or salad dressing, and dill with an electric mixer on medium speed till combined. Stir in the dissolved gelatin, chopped vegetables, and tuna.

Line a 2-cup mold or airtight container with clear plastic wrap. Transfer the tuna-gelatin mixture to prepared mold. Chill salad at least 6 hours or overnight till set. Transport spread in an insulated cooler with an ice pack.

To serve, invert spread. Remove mold and carefully peel off the plastic wrap. Serve spread with French bread Melba toast, or crackers. Serves 6.

Nutrition information per serving:
174 cal., 7 g pro., 2 g carbo., 15 g fat, 34 mg chol., 170 mg sodium. U.S. RDA: 12% niacin.

CARAMEL-BANANA CUPS

Don't like banana pudding? How about using vanilla, butterscotch, or chocolate pudding instead?—

2	5-ounce containers banana pudding
⅓	cup dairy sour cream
¼	teaspoon rum flavoring

Dash salt

6	foil bake cups
6	vanilla wafers *or* gingersnaps
¼	cup chopped pecans*
¼	cup caramel ice cream topping

In a small mixing bowl combine banana pudding, sour cream, rum flavoring, and salt; set mixture aside.

Line a muffin tin with foil bake cups. Place one vanilla wafer or gingersnap on bottom of each bake cup. Spoon about *2 tablespoons* of the pudding mixture atop each cookie.

In a small mixing bowl combine pecans and caramel topping. Spoon *half* of the caramel mixture atop pudding. Repeat pudding and caramel layers once more. Cover; freeze overnight.

Transport the frozen cups in an insulated container with an ice pack. Makes 6 servings.

**Note:* For even more pecan flavor, toast the nuts before you chop them. Place the pecans in a single layer in a shallow baking pan. Bake in a 350° oven for 6 to 7 minutes or till nuts are light brown. *(Or,* to toast pecans in the microwave oven, micro-cook ½ cup nuts in a 2-cup glass measure, uncovered, on 100% power (high) for 2 to 3 minutes till toasted; stir every minute.)

Nutrition information per serving:
191 cal., 2 g pro., 24 g carbo., 9 g fat, 7 mg chol., 67 mg sodium.

SEPTEMBER

The Idea Magazine for American Families

Better Homes and Gardens

September 1987
$1.50

TELL US ABOUT YOUR FAMILY'S RELATIONSHIP WITH GOD
Page 19

MAKE-AHEAD GIFTS!

25 COUNTRY CRAFTS

DECORATING WITH SHEETS!

AFFORDABLE LANDSCAPING
▼ ▼ ▼
50 PRIZEWINNING RECIPES
▲ ▲ ▲

PRIZE TESTED RECIPES®
50 WINNERS FROM 50 YEARS

By Terri Pauser Wolf

Join our celebration! The Prize Tested Recipes contest, a monthly reader recipe exchange devoted to home cooking, turns 50 this month. We chose 50 of the very best winning recipes since 1937 to honor this Better Homes and Gardens® tradition. The recipes are oldies but goodies whether brownies, breads, or pot roast. Enjoy them all!

- Appetizers
- Main Dishes
- Side Dishes
- Desserts
- Breads

APPETIZERS

CLARET PUNCH
November 1975
Mrs. John Langlois, Miami, Fla.
The holiday beverage category showcased this wine-spiked punch 12 years ago. It's equally suitable for a formal cocktail party or a casual picnic in the park.

SPARKLING PEACHES AND CREAM
December 1981
Clara Beth Negoro, Hawthorne, Calif.
Whip up an off-the-shelf milk shake. Canned peach slices provide the flavor and carbonated water adds unexpected effervescence.

ICED ALMONDS
December 1961
Mrs. C. Mason Mize, Lakeland, Fla.
This recipe is so popular that you have to be careful—the sugar-glazed nuts are irresistible. Serve a small bowlful before or after a meal.

ARTICHOKE-CHILI DIP
July 1981
Mary Bergeron, Seattle, Wash.
The call went out for easy snack recipes, and the winning result was a last-minute dip with only four ingredients.

RECIPES BEGIN ON PAGE 123.

CHEESE AND SPINACH PUFFS

November 1982
Elaine W. Sanders, Blackstone, Va.
Make-ahead appetizers are the ticket to hassle-free hosting. Bake and freeze these one-bite puffs for last-minute oven reheating.

FRENCH MUSTARD SLICES

April 1967
Mrs. Robert R. Harwick,
Vienna, Va.
Mustard lovers, here's a recipe for you. Buttery, mustard-covered bread slices are baked till golden brown. What a way to start a meal!

CHICKEN HAM PINWHEELS

December 1969
Lucille Howell, Washington, D.C.
A party planner's favorite—an elaborate appetizer that is sinfully easy to make. And, it has a minimum of ingredients (chicken, ham, and a few seasonings).

MEET A WINNER

WM. HOPKINS

"A neighbor shared this recipe with me 35 years ago, and I've been making it ever since."

MARY MARGARET BARROW

Lanett, Ala.
Bursting with nutrition and taste-appeal, this fruit spread is a good partner with crackers, celery, carrots, or toasted bread. Or, do as Mary does: give it as a holiday gift.

NUT AND RAISIN SPREAD,   SEPTEMBER 1984

PRIZEWINNING RECIPES
MAIN DISHES

A dozen answers to the "What's for dinner?" question from *BH&G* families just like yours!

CHICKEN À LA MARIA
November 1981
Mrs. John Coder, Timonium, Md.
Praises go to this entrée because it's as elegant as stuffed chicken breasts, but minus the work.

ORANGE 'N' SPICE POT ROAST
October 1979
Mrs. Ghita Carter, Houston, Tex.
Sunday afternoons and pot roast—for years, they've gone hand in hand. A main dish from '79, it perks up a plain roast with a delicious citrus sauce.

LASAGNA IN A BUN
September 1983
Agnes B. Kleinhenz,
Willoughby Hills, Ohio
Americans' love affair with Italian food is as strong as ever. This meal in a bun captures the flavors of one favorite food—no wonder it came out on top!

TURKEY WITH CURRY SAUCE, NOVEMBER 1983

MEET A WINNER

WM. HOPKINS

"The BH&G recipe contest gives me the inspiration to enter contests and create new recipes."

ROXANNE E. CHAN
Albany, Calif.
An avid gardener and cook, Roxanne enjoys devising quick recipes with an ethnic twist. A surplus of leftover turkey spurred her to invent this extraordinary entrée.

ORIENTAL-STYLE PORK STEAKS

January 1981
Mary E. Druce, Lubbock, Tex.
In 45 minutes or less you can turn pork, vegetables, and pineapple into a colorful skillet supper.

RECIPES BEGIN ON PAGE 124.

PEPPER STEAK SALAD

July 1976
Mickey Strang, China Lake, Calif.
Health-conscious diners in the 1950s turned to salads for a main meal. Exciting recipes like this tangy whole-meal salad have been coming to our office ever since!

RED SNAPPER VERACRUZ

January 1976
Jan Toole, Vail, Colo.
As more and more readers add microwave ovens to their homes, we publish more microwave recipes for you to try. This one is ideal for today's busy family; it cooks in 12 minutes.

LEMON SHRIMP ORIENTAL

May 1975
Helen M. McPhail,
Lake Oswego, Oreg.
A presidential trip to China in the early '70s popularized oriental cooking, especially stir-frying, in the States.

BARBECUED PORK RIBS

July 1942
Mrs. T. R. Harrington,
Des Moines, Iowa
Outdoor cooking in the early '40s kindled the grilling craze of the '80s. Fire up the coals and try these saucy ribs.

CAMEMBERT SOUFFLÉ

August 1979
Marlene McCall,
Overland Park, Kans.
Here's a champion that continues to receive kudos. A tower of fresh eggs and creamy camembert cheese, the soufflé literally melts in your mouth.

POTATO-SHELL TACO PIE

July 1977
Betty S. Judy, Rockville, Md.
This kid-pleasing pie couldn't be easier. The crust features instant potatoes; the filling is refried beans and ground beef spiced up with seasonings.

SAVORY SAUSAGE STEW

November 1967
Mrs. Bruce Prevatt,
Saint Simons Island, Ga.
Combine this hearty one-dish meal with crisp crackers or warm bread for a festive fall meal.

PRIZEWINNING RECIPES
SIDE DISHES

From casseroles to soups to salads, side dishes always add a special touch to any meal, any time of the day.

HONEY SAUTERNE JELLY
August 1974
Mrs. Allen C. Davis, Sr.,
Smyrna, Ga.
Our editors rated this jelly superb and noted that it would make a great gift.

FIVE-FRUIT SALAD WITH PEANUT BUTTER DRESSING
April 1981
Jolie Steckart, De Pere, Wis.
"Eat your fruits and vegetables." It's not a hard rule to live by when you can add a favorite, peanut butter, to the dressing and serve it over a fruit salad.

MARINATED MUSHROOMS AND VEGETABLES
June 1981
Mrs. Doris Knoke, Chester, Ill.
Zesty marinated salads fill the deli case, but here's one that you can toss together at home.

TOMATO AND BROCCOLI BAKE, JULY 1984

MEET A WINNER

WM. HOPKINS

"A winning recipe in our house is one that is easy to prepare, versatile, and liked by the entire family."

TERRY MITCHUM
Overland Park, Kans.
For this dish, Terry changed an existing recipe by adding ingredients and seasonings her family likes. She serves this vegetable casserole with baked chicken, a salad, and Italian bread.

RECIPES BEGIN ON PAGE 128.

SARAH'S SALAD
July 1962
Mrs. David Thompson,
La Crosse, Wis.
This novel layered salad was a winner 25 years ago, but its popularity continues today.

CREAMY CELERY-ZUCCHINI SOUP
August 1978
Floy Schrage, Webster Groves, Mo.
In 1973 the food processor revolutionized food preparation. By using the handy appliance, you can have a garden-fresh soup in 30 minutes.

BAKED POTATOES WITH CHEF'S CHEESE SAUCE
November 1961
Mrs. T. A. Milner, Hopkins, Minn.
In our Test Kitchen, this cheese-capped spud received the distinction of being rated outstanding—the best in its class. It's so delectable you'll want to make it ahead so it's always on hand.

SPAGHETTI RING FLORENTINE
September 1974
Lynn Steuer, Hawley, Pa.
Imaginative recipes win at *BH&G*. Lynn turned the ingredients from a common recipe for spaghetti into something spectacular.

CURRY SLICES
August 1965
Mrs. Frank Wilkuski,
East Tawas, Mich.
In 1965, few of us had the chance to sample Indian food, but in 1987 it's a stylish cuisine. Using curry as a seasoning in the '60s put this zesty pickle ahead of its time.

BROCCOLI AND WILD RICE BAKE
July 1975
Mrs. Glenn Hunter, St. Louis, Mo.
Today's cooks will applaud this recipe for its convenience. Rice mix, soup mix, and sour cream mix give it an off-the-shelf head start.

MARSHMALLOW-PECAN SQUASH
January 1979
Mrs. F. Luana Rockwell,
Seattle, Wash.
Even kids will eat squash when the nutty filling is crowned with tiny marshmallows.

COLESLAW SOUFFLÉ SALAD
June 1956
Mrs. Betty Smith, Kalamazoo, Mich.
In the '50s, this recipe was the rage. Stirring mayonnaise into gelatin creates a creamy soufflélike salad.

PRIZEWINNING RECIPES
DESSERTS

Dessert will never go out of style. Neither will any of these irresistible sweet temptations.

LEMON-NUT ICE CREAM
June 1938
Mrs. R. H. Shinew, Cleveland, Ohio
Always watching food trends, *BH&G* searched for innovative frozen desserts like this one, when electric refrigerators with freezers became common appliances in the late '30s.

MARBLE CHEESECAKE
April 1974
Mrs. Peter Porcaro, Hawthorne, N.J.
One of the creamiest cheesecakes you'll ever sink your teeth into. The swirled chocolate layer creates a different design each time you make it.

STRAWBERRY PIE DELUXE
May 1937
Thomas F. Goss, Los Angeles, Calif.
In the '30s, we challenged the "pants in the family" to give cooking a try. This striking pie captured top honors in our first recipe contest.

WM. HOPKINS

MEET A WINNER

"I'm always inventing recipes in my mind. I like to do the unexpected with foods."

JACQUELINE McCOMAS
Frazer, Pa.
A food enthusiast, Jacqueline brings her creations to the office for her co-workers to sample. The two-tone tarts won rave reviews, so she entered the recipe and received the same praise from *BH&G* taste panelists.

CHOCOLATE AND VANILLA TARTS, SEPTEMBER 1982

PUMPKIN CAKE ROLL
November 1974
Lucy Feldkamp, Ann Arbor, Mich.
The lightly spiced, tender cake with a cream cheese filling is a snap to make, but it looks as if you worked for hours.

RECIPES BEGIN ON PAGE 131.

BANANA SPLIT CAKE
February 1975
Mrs. Milton Brooks, Chelsea, Okla.
A favorite ice-cream concoction turns into an ingenious, moist cake. How could anyone resist this blue-ribbon dessert?

BURNT-SUGAR CHIFFON CAKE
April 1951
Mrs. William J. Young, Evansville, Ind.
The first new cake in 100 years hit the scene in the '40s—a chiffon cake. This mile-high version is a grand example of these featherweight cakes.

SWISS NUT TORTE
December 1980
Mrs. Jeanne Howard, Monterey Park, Calif.
Impressive—the best way to describe this European-style torte with a liqueur-laced nut filling. It adds elegance to any meal or occasion.

CHOCOLATE-COVERED CHERRY COOKIES
December 1981
Mary Pickard, Tampa, Fla.
A fun, sophisticated cookie that you can take to a kid's party or serve at a holiday open house. Chocolate fanatics love the rich cookie base and frosting that holds a surprise center.

CARAMEL PECAN BROWNIES
September 1966
Mary B. Lundegard, Sunnyvale, Calif.
We were deluged with brownie recipes in 1966. This delightful winner emerged with its slightly chewy, caramel texture.

FROSTY STRAWBERRY SQUARES
June 1964
Mrs. Rodney Everson, Austin, Minn.
Marion Viall, *BH&G* recipe editor for 27 years, picks this as a favorite. Why? You can make it ahead and it's a snap to fix.

RAISIN PUFFS WITH ORANGE SAUCE
January 1946
Mrs. J. W. Hunter, Tavares, Fla.
The feathery muffinlike puffs with their bright orange sauce won praise in the '40s and continue to do so in the '80s.

RECIPES BEGIN ON PAGE 135.

PRIZEWINNING RECIPES
BREADS

Who can resist fresh baked breads? Sample these classics and they're sure to become most-requested recipes—just try to keep them around the house.

WHOLE WHEAT AND COTTAGE CHEESE ROLLS
March 1973
Mrs. Charlie Lovelace, Danville, Va.
Eating right has always been a concern for Americans and the editors of *BH&G.* This wholesome recipe is an example of our commitment to healthful eating.

CORN-RYE BISCUITS
April 1978
Susan E. Cornwall, Crofton, Md.
Biscuits have been around forever, but there's always room for improvement. Serve this hearty version tonight with soup or stew.

APPLE-CINNAMON SWIRL LOAF
March 1975
Mrs. Conrad R. Appledorn, Artesia, N.Mex.
Why measure every ingredient when you can personalize a mix and still produce a tastes-like-scratch bread? This bread starts with a white cake mix.

MOLASSES CORN BREAD
March 1965
Mrs. Howard J. Garman, Wilmington, Ohio
Sweet, buttery goodness. A great breakfast bread or main-dish addition, this gingerbreadlike recipe is slightly sweet from the molasses and nutty from the cornmeal.

RASPBERRY CREAM-CHEESE COFFEE CAKE
October 1970
Carol Jensen, East Hazelcrest, Ill.
This cake may look complicated but the recipe is really meant for the on-the-go cook. You can assemble it in minutes.

RASPBERRY BRAN MUFFINS
July 1938
Mrs. Lester G. Engelson, Shafter, Calif.
Muffins may be the rage today, but they've been popular for a long time. We published this winning muffin recipe almost 50 years ago!

Appetizers

CLARET PUNCH

- 1 750-ml bottle claret *or* dry red wine, chilled
- 1 cup cold water
- 1 6-ounce can frozen red fruit punch concentrate
- ½ cup orange liqueur
- 1 32-ounce bottle lemon-lime carbonated beverage *or* carbonated water, chilled

In a punch bowl mix wine, water, punch concentrate, and orange liqueur.

Slowly pour carbonated beverage or water down the side of bowl. Stir gently with an up-and-down motion to mix. Serve immediately. Makes 18 (4-ounce) servings.

Nutrition information per each 4-ounce serving of punch: 84 cal., 0 g pro., 14 g carbo., 0 g fat, 0 mg chol., and 4 mg sodium. U.S. RDA: 2% iron, 1% phosphorus.

SPARKLING PEACHES AND CREAM

- 1 16-ounce can peach slices, chilled
- ½ cup unsweetened pineapple juice, chilled
- 1 egg
- 4 ice cubes (½ cup)
- 1 tablespoon sugar
- 1 tablespoon lemon juice
- 1 teaspoon vanilla
- ⅓ cup light cream *or* milk
- 1 10-ounce bottle sparkling mineral water *or* carbonated water, chilled (1¼ cups)

In a blender container combine *undrained* peaches, pineapple juice, egg, ice cubes, sugar, lemon juice, and vanilla. Cover and blend till smooth.

Stir in light cream or milk. Slowly pour mineral water down the side of the blender. Stir gently with an up-and-down motion to mix. Pour into chilled punch cups. Makes 5 (6-ounce) servings.

Nutrition information per serving: 112 cal., 2 g pro., 17 g carbo., 4 g fat, 66 mg chol., 24 mg sodium, and 2 g dietary fiber. U.S. RDA: 10% vit. A, 12% vit. C, 2% thiamine, 4% riboflavin, 3% niacin, 3% calcium, 3% iron, and 5% phosphorus.

ICED ALMONDS

- 1½ cups blanched whole almonds, pecan halves, walnut halves, *or* cashews
- ½ cup sugar
- 2 tablespoons margarine *or* butter
- ½ teaspoon vanilla

Line a baking sheet with foil. Butter the foil, then set the baking sheet aside.

In a heavy 8-inch skillet combine nuts, sugar, and margarine. Cook over medium heat, stirring constantly, for 9 minutes or till sugar melts and turns a rich brown color. (Mixture may splatter.) Remove from heat.

Immediately stir in the vanilla. Spread mixture onto the prepared baking sheet. Cool completely. Break into small clusters. Store tightly covered. Makes about 10 ounces (2¾ cups).

Nutrition information per ounce: 198 cal., 5 g pro., 15 g carbo., 15 g fat, 0 mg chol., 29 mg sodium. U.S. RDA: 2% vit. A, 3% thiamine, 11% riboflavin, 4% niacin, 6% calcium, 5% iron, 12% phosphorus.

ARTICHOKE-CHILI DIP

- 1 14-ounce can artichoke hearts, drained and chopped
- 1 cup grated Parmesan cheese
- 1 cup mayonnaise *or* salad dressing
- 1 4-ounce can green chili peppers, rinsed, seeded, and chopped
- Dippers such as toasted pita wedges *or* tortilla chips

In a mixing bowl combine artichokes, cheese, mayonnaise or salad dressing, and chili peppers.

Transfer the mixture to an 8-inch round baking dish. Bake, uncovered, in a 350° oven about 20 minutes or till heated through. Serve warm with pita wedges or chips. Makes about 2⅔ cups.

Microwave directions: Prepare dip as directed above, *except* transfer mixture to an 8-inch microwave-safe baking dish. Micro-cook, uncovered, on 70% power (medium-high) for 4 to 6 minutes or till heated through, stirring after 2 minutes. Stir before serving.

Nutrition information per tablespoon dip: 51 cal., 1 g pro., 1 g carbo., 5 g fat, 5 mg chol., and 78 mg sodium.

CHEESE AND SPINACH PUFFS

- 1 10-ounce package frozen chopped spinach
- ½ cup chopped onion
- 2 slightly beaten eggs
- ½ cup grated Parmesan cheese
- ½ cup shredded cheddar cheese
- ⅓ cup blue cheese salad dressing
- 2 tablespoons margarine *or* butter, melted
- ⅛ teaspoon garlic powder
- 1 8½-ounce package corn muffin mix
- Dijon-style *or* coarse-grain mustard

Cook spinach according to package directions, *except* add onion. Drain well, pressing out excess liquid. In a bowl combine eggs, cheeses, salad dressing, margarine, and garlic. Stir in spinach mixture and muffin mix. Cover; chill about 1 hour or till easy to handle.

Shape into 1-inch balls. Arrange balls on a baking sheet. Cover and chill till serving time. (Or, place in a freezer container; seal, label, and freeze.)

To serve, place on a baking sheet. Bake in a 350° oven for 10 to 12 minutes for chilled balls (12 to 15 minutes for frozen balls) or till light brown. Serve warm with mustard. Makes 50.

Nutrition information per puff: 47 cal., 2 g pro., 4 g carbo., 3 g fat, 17 mg chol., and 111 mg sodium.

FRENCH MUSTARD SLICES

- ½ cup margarine *or* butter, softened
- ¼ cup snipped parsley
- 2 tablespoons sliced green onion
- 2 tablespoons prepared mustard
- 1 tablespoon toasted sesame seed
- 1 teaspoon lemon juice
- 2 9-inch loaves French bread, sliced

In a bowl stir together all ingredients *except* bread. Spread the mixture on both sides of bread slices. Arrange bread on a baking sheet. Bake in a 350° oven 20 minutes or till golden brown and toasted. (Or, reassemble prepared slices into a loaf; wrap loosely in foil. Bake in a 375° oven 10 to 15 minutes or till heated.) Makes about 36 slices.

Nutrition information per slice: 76 cal., 2 g pro., 10 g carbo., 3 g fat, 1 mg chol., and 142 mg sodium.

CHICKEN HAM PINWHEELS

2 **whole large chicken breasts, skinned and boned**
⅛ **teaspoon dried basil, crushed**
Dash garlic salt
4 **thin slices fully cooked ham (about 3 ounces)**
2 **teaspoons lemon juice**
Paprika
Sliced party bread
Assorted crackers

Rinse chicken, then pat dry. Place 1 whole chicken breast, boned side up, between 2 pieces of clear plastic wrap. Working from the center to the edges, pound lightly with the flat side of a meat mallet to ¼-inch thickness. Repeat with remaining chicken breast.

In a custard cup combine basil, garlic salt, *⅛ teaspoon salt,* and *dash pepper.* Sprinkle on chicken. Place 2 slices of ham on each chicken breast. Roll up, jelly-roll style, starting from a long side. Place rolls, seam side down, in a 10x6x2-inch baking dish.

Drizzle with the lemon juice, then sprinkle with paprika. Bake in a 350° oven about 30 minutes or till tender and no longer pink. Cover and chill.

To serve, cut into ½-inch-thick slices. Serve with party bread slices and crackers. Makes about 24 slices.

Nutrition information per slice: 36 cal., 7 g pro., 0 g carbo., 1 g fat, 18 mg chol., and 73 mg sodium. U.S. RDA: 2% vit. C, 3% thiamine, 2% riboflavin, 14% niacin, 1% iron, 5% phosphorus.

NUT AND RAISIN SPREAD

1 **medium orange**
1 **cup broken pecans**
2½ **cups light raisins**
¾ **cup mayonnaise *or* salad dressing**
Orange slices, celery sticks, *or* assorted crackers

Do not peel orange. Quarter and seed orange. In a food processor bowl place orange and nuts. Cover and process till finely chopped. Add *half* of the raisins and all of the mayonnaise or salad dressing. Cover and process till raisins are chopped. Add remaining raisins. Cover and process till finely chopped.

Transfer to a covered container; chill. (Or, place mixture in a moisture- and vaporproof freezer container; seal, label, and freeze up to 3 months. Thaw in refrigerator for several hours.)

To serve, spread on orange slices, celery, or crackers. Makes 3½ cups.

Food grinder directions: Run the quartered and seeded orange, pecans, and raisins through fine blade of food grinder. Stir in mayonnaise or salad dressing. Store as directed above.

Nutrition information per tablespoon spread: 56 cal., 0 g pro., 6 g carbo., 4 g fat, 2 mg chol., and 18 mg sodium. U.S. RDA: 3% vit. C, 1% thiamine, 1% riboflavin, 1% niacin, 1% calcium, 1% iron, 1% phosphorus.

Main Dishes

CHICKEN À LA MARIA

¾ **cup fine dry Italian-seasoned bread crumbs**
2 **tablespoons grated Parmesan cheese**
6 **whole large chicken breasts (about 6 pounds total), skinned, boned, and halved lengthwise**
½ **cup sliced green onion**
2 **tablespoons margarine *or* butter**
2 **tablespoons all-purpose flour**
1 **cup milk**
1 **10-ounce package frozen chopped spinach, thawed and well drained**
¾ **cup diced fully cooked ham**

In shallow dish mix crumbs and cheese. Set half of the crumb mixture aside. Rinse chicken; pat dry. Roll chicken in crumb mixture to coat lightly. Place chicken in a 13x9x2-inch baking dish.

In a small saucepan cook green onion in margarine till tender. Stir in flour till blended. Add milk. Cook and stir over medium heat till thickened and bubbly. Stir in spinach and ham.

Spoon spinach mixture over chicken. Sprinkle with the reserved crumb mixture. Bake, uncovered, in a 350° oven for 40 to 45 minutes or till chicken is tender and no longer pink. Serves 12.

Nutrition information per serving: 271 cal., 39 g pro., 7 g carbo., 8 g fat, 103 mg chol., and 339 mg sodium. U.S. RDA: 33% vit. A, 12% thiamine, 14% riboflavin, 80% niacin, 11% iron, and 32% phosphorus.

ORANGE 'N' SPICE POT ROAST

1 **3½- to 4-pound beef chuck pot roast**
2 **tablespoons lemon juice**
1 **teaspoon salt**
3 **slices bacon**
1 **8-ounce can stewed tomatoes**
1 **cup orange juice**
⅔ **cup chopped onion**
¼ **cup snipped fresh parsley *or* 1 tablespoon dried parsley flakes**
1 **teaspoon sugar**
½ **teaspoon ground cinnamon**
1 **clove garlic, minced**
4 **whole cloves**
1 **small bay leaf**
2 **tablespoons all-purpose flour**
¼ **cup cold water**

Sprinkle roast with lemon juice and salt. In a 12-inch ovenproof skillet cook bacon till crisp. Remove bacon from pan; crumble bacon, then set it aside. Brown roast in bacon drippings in skillet. Drain off fat.

In a medium bowl combine bacon, *undrained* tomatoes, orange juice, onion, parsley, sugar, cinnamon, garlic, cloves, and bay leaf. Pour over roast.

Bake, covered, in a 325° oven for 2 to 2½ hours or till roast is tender. Transfer roast to serving platter. Cover roast with foil to keep warm.

For gravy, remove cloves and bay leaf from pan juices. Then skim off fat. Stir flour into water, then stir flour mixture into pan juices. Cook and stir till thickened and bubbly. Cook and stir for 1 minute more. Pass gravy with meat. Makes 6 to 8 servings.

Nutrition information per serving: 360 cal., 43 g pro., 12 g carbo., 15 g fat, 125 mg chol., and 584 mg sodium. U.S. RDA: 34% vit. C, 12% thiamine, 21% riboflavin, 35% niacin, 33% iron, and 25% phosphorus.

LASAGNA IN A BUN

- 8 hoagie buns
- ¾ pound ground beef
- 1 8-ounce can tomato sauce
- ½ of a 1⅓-ounce envelope dry onion soup mix (¼ cup)
- ¼ teaspoon dried oregano, crushed
- ¼ teaspoon dried basil, crushed
- 1 beaten egg
- ¾ cup ricotta *or* cream-style cottage cheese, drained
- 1 cup shredded mozzarella cheese (4 ounces)

Cut thin slice off tops of buns. Hollow out centers, leaving ½-inch-thick shells; set aside. Reserve bread crumbs for another use.

In a skillet cook beef till brown; drain off fat. Add tomato sauce, soup mix, and herbs. Cook, covered, over low heat for 5 minutes. Uncover; cook 5 minutes more or till of desired consistency, stirring frequently.

Meanwhile, in a bowl combine egg, ricotta or cottage cheese, and ½ *cup* of the mozzarella cheese. Spoon *half* of the meat mixture into bottom of rolls. Top with cheese mixture, then remaining meat mixture. Top with remaining mozzarella cheese. Replace bun tops. Wrap sandwiches individually in foil. Bake in a 400° oven for 20 to 25 minutes or till hot. Makes 8 servings.

Nutrition information per sandwich: 257 cal., 18 g pro., 19 g carbo., 12 g fat, 79 mg chol., 659 mg sodium. U.S. RDA: 10% vit. A, 11% thiamine, 16% riboflavin, 15% niacin, 19% calcium, 12% iron, 23% phosphorus.

TURKEY WITH CURRY SAUCE

- 1 pound fresh turkey breast tenderloin slices, cut ½ inch thick
- 2 tablespoons margarine *or* butter
- 2 tablespoons all-purpose flour
- ½ teaspoon curry powder
- 1 cup chicken broth
- ¼ cup milk
- ½ of a small banana, diced (½ cup)
- ¼ cup chopped pitted dates *or* raisins
- ¼ cup chopped cashews
- ½ teaspoon finely shredded lemon peel
- 3 cups hot cooked rice *or* bulgur

Wrap turkey slices in foil; place in a shallow baking pan. Cook in a 350° oven for 25 minutes or till turkey is no longer pink.

Meanwhile, for sauce, in a small saucepan melt margarine or butter. Stir in flour and curry powder till blended. Add broth and milk. Cook and stir over medium heat till thickened and bubbly. Cook and stir for 1 minute more. Stir in banana, dates or raisins, cashews, and lemon peel.

Arrange turkey over rice or bulgur. Pour sauce over turkey. Serves 6.

Nutrition information per serving: 316 cal., 23 g pro., 38 g carbo., 8 g fat, 48 mg chol., 214 mg sodium, 2 g dietary fiber. U.S. RDA: 12% thiamine, 10% riboflavin, 34% niacin, 14% iron, 24% phosphorus.

ORIENTAL-STYLE PORK STEAKS

- 4 pork shoulder steaks, cut ½ inch thick (about 1½ pounds)
- 1 tablespoon cooking oil
- 1 8-ounce can crushed pineapple (juice pack)
- 2 tablespoons vinegar
- 2 tablespoons soy sauce
- 1 teaspoon sugar
- ½ teaspoon ground ginger
- 2 medium carrots, bias-sliced ¼ inch thick (1 cup)
- ½ of a small onion, cut into wedges
- 1 small green pepper, cut into bite-size strips
- 1½ teaspoons cornstarch
- Warm chow mein noodles

In a 10-inch skillet brown pork on both sides in hot oil. Remove from skillet; set aside. Drain off fat.

Drain pineapple, reserving juice. Add *water* to juice to make ½ *cup*. Add vinegar, soy sauce, sugar, and ginger. Add to skillet. Add carrots and onion. Return pork to skillet; cover and simmer for 20 to 25 minutes or till pork and carrots are tender. Stir green pepper into sauce. Cover and simmer for 3 minutes. Remove pork from skillet.

Combine pineapple and cornstarch; add to mixture in skillet. Cook and stir till thickened and bubbly. Cook and stir for 2 minutes more. Serve pork and sauce over noodles. Serves 4.

Nutrition information per serving: 360 cal., 24 g pro., 18 g carbo., 21 g fat, 81 mg chol., 590 mg sodium, 2 g dietary fiber. U.S. RDA: 174% vit. A, 57% vit. C, 42% thiamine, 21% riboflavin, 26% niacin, 12% iron, 23% phosphorus.

PEPPER STEAK SALAD

- 1 pound rare-cooked roast beef, cut into thin strips (3 cups)
- 2 small tomatoes, cut into wedges
- 1 large green pepper, cut into strips
- 1 cup sliced celery
- ⅓ cup green onion sliced into 1-inch pieces
- ⅓ cup sliced fresh mushrooms
- ½ cup teriyaki sauce
- ⅓ cup dry sherry
- ⅓ cup salad oil *or* olive oil
- 3 tablespoons white *or* rice vinegar
- ½ teaspoon ground ginger
- 1 cup fresh bean sprouts *or* canned bean sprouts, drained and rinsed
- 4 cups shredded Chinese cabbage

In a plastic bag combine beef, tomatoes, green pepper, celery, green onion, and mushrooms; place in a shallow dish.

In a screw-top jar combine teriyaki sauce, sherry, oil, vinegar, and ginger; cover and shake well. Pour over beef mixture. Seal bag. Turn bag to coat well. Marinate for 2 to 3 hours in the refrigerator, turning the bag occasionally. Drain and reserve marinade. Add bean sprouts to mixture in bag.

In a large salad bowl arrange Chinese cabbage; top with meat and vegetables. Toss to combine. Pass reserved marinade for dressing. Serves 6.

Nutrition information per serving:
330 cal., 25 g pro., 11 g carbo., 20 g fat, 69 mg chol., 862 mg sodium, 2 g dietary fiber. U.S. RDA: 27% vit. A, 62% vit. C, 16% riboflavin, 25% niacin, 24% iron, 26% phosphorus.

LEMON SHRIMP ORIENTAL

- 1¼ pounds fresh *or* frozen shrimp in shells
- 1 cup water
- 2 tablespoons cornstarch
- 2 tablespoons soy sauce
- 1 teaspoon sugar
- 1 teaspoon instant chicken bouillon granules
- ½ teaspoon finely shredded lemon peel
- 3 to 4 tablespoons lemon juice
- ⅛ teaspoon pepper
- 2 tablespoons cooking oil
- 2 cups sliced fresh mushrooms (5 ounces)
- 3 stalks celery, bias-sliced
- 1 medium pepper cut into strips
- ¼ cup sliced green onion
- 1 6-ounce package frozen pea pods, thawed

Hot cooked rice

Thaw shrimp, if frozen, and drain well. Peel and devein shrimp. For sauce, stir together water, cornstarch, soy sauce, sugar, bouillon granules, lemon peel, lemon juice, and pepper. Set aside.

Preheat a wok or large skillet over high heat. Add *1 tablespoon* of the oil. Add mushrooms, celery, and green pepper; stir-fry for 3 minutes. Add green onion and stir-fry for 1 minute more. Remove vegetables from wok.

Add remaining oil to wok. Add *half* of the shrimp. Stir-fry for 2 to 3 minutes or till shrimp turn pink. Remove shrimp. Stir-fry the remaining shrimp. Return all shrimp to wok. Push from center of wok.

Stir sauce; add to center of the wok. Cook and stir till thickened and bubbly. Add vegetables and pea pods to wok. Stir to coat mixture with sauce. Cook and stir for 1 minute. Serve over hot cooked rice. Makes 6 servings.

Nutrition information per serving with ½ cup rice: 244 cal., 14 g pro., 35 g carbo., 5 g fat, 59 mg chol., 495 mg sodium, 3 g dietary fiber. U.S. RDA: 55% vit. C, 15% thiamine, 21% niacin, 16% iron, 19% phosphorus.

RED SNAPPER VERACRUZ

- 1½ pounds skinless fresh *or* frozen red snapper *or* cod fillets
- 1 small tomato, peeled, seeded, and chopped
- ½ cup chopped onion
- ½ cup chopped green pepper
- 1 4-ounce can sliced mushrooms, drained
- 3 tablespoons chili sauce
- 2 tablespoons margarine *or* butter
- 2 tablespoons lemon juice
- 1 tablespoon snipped parsley
- 1 tablespoon capers, drained
- 1 clove garlic, minced
- ½ teaspoon dried thyme, crushed
- ¼ teaspoon salt

Several dashes bottled hot pepper sauce
- 1 4½-ounce can shrimp, drained
- ¼ cup dry white wine

Thaw fish, if frozen. In a 12x7½x2-inch glass baking dish combine tomato, onion, green pepper, mushrooms, chili sauce, margarine or butter, lemon juice, parsley, capers, garlic, thyme, salt, and hot pepper sauce.

Micro-cook, covered with waxed paper, on 100% power (high) for 5 to 6 minutes or till vegetables are tender, stirring twice. Stir in shrimp and wine. Place fish fillets atop mixture, folding thin edges under; spoon some of the vegetable mixture over fillets. Cook, covered, on high for 5 to 7 more or till fish flakes easily with a fork. Transfer to dinner plates, using a slotted spoon. Makes 6 servings.

Nutrition information per serving:
234 cal., 29 g pro., 6 g carbo., 9 g fat, 77 mg chol., and 469 mg sodium. U.S. RDA: 12% vit. A, 28% vit. C, 12% thiamine, 15% niacin, 11% iron, and 24% phosphorus.

BARBECUED PORK RIBS

- 1 cup catsup
- 1 cup water
- 2 to 3 tablespoons Worcestershire sauce
- 1 teaspoon chili powder
- 1 teaspoon celery seed
- ¼ teaspoon salt
- ¼ teaspoon bottled hot pepper sauce
- 3 to 4 pounds meaty spareribs, cut into serving-size pieces

For sauce, in a small saucepan combine catsup, water, Worcestershire sauce, chili powder, celery seed, salt, and hot pepper sauce. Bring to boiling; reduce heat. Simmer, uncovered, for 5 minutes. Remove from heat.

In a covered grill, arrange preheated coals around a drip pan; test for *medium* heat* above the pan. Place spareribs on grill rack over drip pan but not over coals. Lower grill hood. Grill for 25 minutes. Turn and grill, covered, for 20 minutes more.

Brush sauce onto both sides of the spareribs. Continue grilling the spareribs, on an *uncovered* grill, about 15 minutes more or till no pink remains, brushing occasionally with the sauce. Makes 4 servings.

Note: To test for medium heat, hold your hand, palm side down, above the pan. Start counting seconds: "one thousand one, one thousand two." If you need to withdraw your hand after four seconds, the coals are medium.

Nutrition information per serving:
288 cal., 36 g pro., 5 g carbo., 13 g fat, 110 mg chol., 296 mg sodium. U.S. RDA: 16% riboflavin, 29% niacin, 27% iron, 19% phosphorus.

CAMEMBERT SOUFFLÉ

- ¼ cup chopped celery
- 2 tablespoons thinly sliced green onion
- 1 clove garlic, minced
- 3 tablespoons margarine *or* butter
- 3 tablespoons all-purpose flour
- 1 teaspoon dry mustard
- ¼ teaspoon salt
- Dash pepper
- 1 cup milk
- 4½ ounces Camembert cheese, rind removed and cheese cubed (½ cup)
- ½ cup grated Parmesan *or* Romano cheese (2 ounces)
- 5 egg yolks
- 7 egg whites

In a medium saucepan cook celery, green onion, and garlic in margarine or butter till tender. Stir in flour, mustard, salt, and pepper. Add milk. Cook and stir till thickened and bubbly. Stir in cheeses till just melted. Remove from heat.

Beat egg yolks slightly with a fork. Gradually stir in cheese mixture.

In a large mixer bowl beat egg whites with an electric mixer on high speed till stiff peaks form (tips stand straight). Fold in yolk mixture.

Transfer mixture to a 2- or 2½-quart ungreased soufflé dish. For a "top hat" that puffs in the oven, use a spatula to trace a 1-inch-deep circle through the mixture about 1 inch from the edge of the soufflé dish. Bake in a 350° oven for 35 to 40 minutes or till a knife inserted near the center comes out clean. Serve immediately. Makes 6 servings.

Nutrition information per serving:
268 cal., 16 g pro., 7 g carbo., 19 g fat, 250 mg chol., 604 mg sodium. U.S. RDA: 17% vit. A, 23% riboflavin, 30% calcium, and 28% phosphorus.

POTATO-SHELL TACO PIE

- ¼ cup margarine *or* butter
- ⅔ cup milk
- 1 1¼-ounce package taco seasoning mix
- 2½ cups packaged instant mashed potato flakes
- 1 pound ground beef
- ½ cup chopped onion
- 1 16-ounce can refried beans
- ½ cup bottled barbecue sauce
- 1 cup shredded lettuce
- 1 medium tomato, chopped
- 1 cup shredded cheddar cheese (4 ounces)
- Dairy sour cream (optional)

In a medium saucepan melt margarine or butter. Add milk and *2 tablespoons* of the taco seasoning mix. Remove saucepan from heat; stir in potato flakes. Press potato mixture over the bottom and up the sides of an ungreased 10-inch quiche dish or pie plate.

In a 10-inch skillet cook beef and onion till beef is brown and onion is tender. Drain off fat. Stir in remaining taco mix, beans, and barbecue sauce. Cook and stir till bubbly. Turn into prepared crust. Bake, uncovered, in a 350° oven for 30 to 35 minutes. Let stand for 5 minutes. Top with lettuce, tomato, and cheese. Cut into wedges. Serve with sour cream. Makes 6 servings.

Nutrition information per serving:
556 cal., 27 g pro., 32 g carbo., 36 g fat, 73 mg chol., 760 mg sodium, 9 g dietary fiber. U.S. RDA: 21% vit. A, 25% vit. C, 17% thiamine, 18% riboflavin, 24% niacin, 22% calcium, 21% iron, 37% phosphorus.

SAVORY SAUSAGE STEW

- 1 12-ounce package fully cooked smoked sausage links *or* 1 pound skinless pork sausage links
- 1 14½-ounce can tomatoes, cut up
- 1 10½-ounce can condensed French onion soup
- 2 medium potatoes, peeled and cubed
- ½ teaspoon Worcestershire sauce
- 1 10-ounce package frozen peas and carrots, *or* one 10-ounce package frozen peas with pearl onions
- 3 tablespoons all-purpose flour
- ½ cup water

Cut each sausage link into 4 or 5 pieces. In a large saucepan brown sausage; drain off fat. Add *undrained* tomatoes, condensed soup, potatoes, and Worcestershire sauce. Bring to boiling; reduce heat. Cover and simmer for 10 minutes.

Stir in the frozen vegetables. Cook about 10 minutes more or till potatoes are tender. Stir flour into water; stir into stew. Cook and stir till thickened and bubbly. Cook and stir for 1 minute more. Makes 6 servings.

Nutrition information per serving: 226 cal., 14 g pro., 24 g carbo., 9 g fat, 39 mg chol., 1,025 mg sodium, and 4 g dietary fiber. U.S. RDA: 97% vit. A, 43% vit. C, 16% thiamine, 13% riboflavin, 23% niacin, 14% iron, and 15% phosphorus.

Side Dishes

HONEY SAUTERNE JELLY

- 1½ cups sauterne *or* other sweet white wine
- ½ of a 1¾-ounce package (2 tablespoons) powdered fruit pectin
- 2 tablespoons lemon juice
- 2 teaspoons finely shredded orange peel
- ½ cup orange juice
- 3 cups honey

In an 8-quart kettle combine sauterne, pectin, lemon juice, orange peel, and orange juice. Bring to a full rolling boil. Stir in honey; return to boiling. Boil for 5 minutes, stirring constantly. Remove from heat.

Skim off foam with a metal spoon. Pour into clean, hot jars; seal at once. Serve with ham, poultry, lamb, bread, or rolls. Makes 4 half-pints.

Note: Do not double recipe. If desired, make a second batch.

Nutrition information per tablespoon: 50 cal., 0 g pro., 14 g carbo., 0 g fat, 0 mg chol., 1 mg sodium.

MARINATED MUSHROOMS AND VEGETABLES

- ⅔ cup vinegar
- ½ cup olive oil *or* salad oil
- ¼ cup chopped onion
- 2 cloves garlic, minced
- 1 teaspoon sugar
- 1 teaspoon dried basil, crushed
- 1 teaspoon dried oregano, crushed
- ½ teaspoon salt
- ¼ teaspoon pepper
- 1 16-ounce can whole small carrots, drained, *or* one 10-ounce package frozen tiny whole carrots, cooked and drained
- 1 14-ounce can artichoke hearts, drained and quartered
- 8 ounces fresh mushrooms, halved
- 1 cup sliced celery
- 1 cup pitted ripe olives, halved
- 1 2-ounce jar sliced pimiento, drained and chopped (¼ cup)

Lettuce leaves (optional)

For marinade, combine vinegar, oil, onion, garlic, sugar, basil, oregano, salt, and pepper. Set aside.

Halve large carrots. Combine carrots, artichoke hearts, mushrooms, celery, olives, and pimiento. Pour the marinade over the vegetables; stir. Cover; chill for 6 hours or overnight, stirring occasionally. Drain the vegetables. Serve on lettuce-lined plates, if desired. Makes 10 to 12 servings.

Nutrition information per serving: 70 cal., 2 g pro., 7 g carbo., 5 g fat, 0 mg chol., 179 mg sodium, 3 g dietary fiber. U.S. RDA: 124% vit. A, 15% vit. C, and 10% riboflavin.

FIVE-FRUIT SALAD WITH PEANUT BUTTER DRESSING

- ½ of a 6-ounce can (⅓ cup) frozen pineapple juice concentrate, thawed
- 2 tablespoons creamy peanut butter
- ⅓ cup salad oil
- 1 cup fresh *or* canned pineapple chunks, drained
- 1 cup frozen unsweetened peach slices, thawed, *or* one 8-ounce can peach slices (juice pack), drained
- ¼ of a medium cantaloupe, peeled and cut into wedges
- ½ cup seedless green grapes, halved
- ½ cup strawberries, halved

For dressing, in a blender container combine pineapple juice and peanut butter. Cover; blend till smooth. With blender running on high, gradually add oil through opening in lid or with lid ajar. Blend well. Transfer to a covered container. Store in refrigerator.

To serve, arrange fruit on individual salad plates. Stir dressing; serve over fruit. Makes 8 servings.

Nutrition information per serving: 159 cal., 2 g pro., 14 g carbo., 11 g fat, 2 mg chol., 21 mg sodium, 2 g dietary fiber. U.S. RDA: 14% vit. A, 42% vit. C.

BAKED POTATOES WITH CHEF'S CHEESE SAUCE

```
    5 or 6 large baking potatoes
Shortening (optional)
    1 cup shredded sharp American
      cheese (4 ounces)
    ½ cup dairy sour cream
    ¼ cup margarine or butter,
      softened
    2 tablespoons sliced green onion
```

Scrub potatoes with a brush. For soft skins, rub potatoes with shortening. Prick potatoes with a fork. Bake in a 425° oven for 40 to 60 minutes or till tender. (Or, prepare potatoes as directed, omitting shortening. Micro-cook, uncovered, on 100% power (high) for 17 to 20 minutes or till tender, rearranging potatoes once.)

Using a pot holder, gently roll potatoes to lightly mash inside. Immediately cut a crisscross in the top of each; press ends, pushing up to fluff.

For sauce, in a mixing bowl combine cheese, sour cream, margarine or butter, and green onion. Dollop on warm potatoes. Makes 5 or 6 servings.

Nutrition information per serving with ¼ cup sauce: 423 cal., 12 g pro., 47 g carbo., 22 g fat, 34 mg chol., 276 mg sodium, 5 g dietary fiber. U.S. RDA: 16% vit. A, 57% vit. C, 16% thiamine, 12% riboflavin, 19% niacin, 21% calcium, 12% iron, 26% phosphorus.

SARAH'S SALAD

```
    2 cups torn lettuce
    2 cups torn curly endive
    2 cups torn romaine
    4 ounces Swiss cheese, cut into
      thin strips
    1½ cups cooked peas
    6 slices bacon, crisp-cooked,
      drained, and crumbled
    1 medium red onion, thinly sliced
    ⅓ cup mayonnaise or salad
      dressing
    1 teaspoon sugar
Dash salt
```

In a large glass bowl with straight sides toss together lettuce, endive, and romaine. Top with cheese, peas, *half* of the bacon, and all of the onion.

In a small bowl stir together mayonnaise or salad dressing, sugar, and salt. Spoon dressing over onion. *Do not* toss. Cover; chill at least 2 hours or up to 24 hours. Just before serving, sprinkle with remaining bacon and toss. Makes 6 to 8 servings.

Nutrition information per serving: 250 cal., 11 g pro., 10 g carbo., 19 g fat, 31 mg chol., 303 mg sodium, 3 g dietary fiber. U.S. RDA: 30% vit. A, 25% vit. C, 15% thiamine, 10% riboflavin, 22% calcium, 20% phosphorus.

TOMATO AND BROCCOLI BAKE

```
    4 ounces cavatelli or elbow
      macaroni (1½ cups)
    1 medium onion, thinly sliced
    1 clove garlic, minced
    2 tablespoons margarine or butter
    5 medium tomatoes, peeled,
      seeded, and chopped
    2 cups fresh chopped broccoli
    1 cup snipped parsley
    1 teaspoon instant chicken
      bouillon granules
    ¼ teaspoon dried oregano,
      crushed
    ¼ teaspoon dried basil, crushed
    1 cup shredded cheddar cheese
      (4 ounces)
```

In a large kettle or Dutch oven cook pasta, uncovered, in boiling salted water for 8 to 10 minutes or till tender; drain. Set aside.

In a 3-quart saucepan cook onion and garlic in hot margarine or butter. Add tomatoes, broccoli, parsley, bouillon granules, oregano, basil, and ¼ teaspoon *salt*. Bring to boiling; reduce heat. Cover; simmer 3 minutes. Stir in pasta and ½ *cup* of the cheese. Transfer to an 8x8x2-inch baking dish.

Bake, covered, in a 375° oven for 15 minutes. Sprinkle with the remaining cheese. Bake, uncovered, for 5 minutes more. Makes 6 to 8 servings.

Nutrition information per serving: 216 cal., 9 g pro., 21 g carbo., 11 g fat, 38 mg chol., 332 mg sodium, 3 g dietary fiber. U.S. RDA: 44% vit. A, 58% vit. C, 16% thiamine, 13% riboflavin, 18% calcium, 11% iron, 18% phosphorus.

CREAMY CELERY-ZUCCHINI SOUP

```
    3 stalks celery
    3 green onions, cut into 1-inch
      pieces
    2 tablespoons margarine or butter
    2 medium zucchini, halved
      lengthwise
    1 cup water
    1 tablespoon instant chicken
      bouillon granules
    1½ cups milk
    1 tablespoon cornstarch
    3 slices bacon, crisp-cooked,
      drained, and crumbled (optional)
```

In a food processor bowl slice celery with slicing blade; remove. In processor bowl finely chop green onions with chopping blade. In a 3-quart saucepan cook celery and green onion, covered, in hot margarine or butter over medium-low heat for 5 to 10 minutes or till the vegetables are tender but not brown, stirring occasionally.

Meanwhile, slice zucchini in food processor. Add zucchini, water, and chicken bouillon granules to saucepan. Bring to boiling; reduce heat. Cover; simmer for 10 minutes.

Combine milk and cornstarch; add to saucepan. Cook and stir till thickened and bubbly. Cook and stir for 2 minutes more. Season to taste with salt and pepper. Sprinkle each serving with bacon, if desired. Makes 6 servings.

Nutrition information per serving: 84 cal., 3 g pro., 7 g carbo., 5 g fat, 5 mg chol., and 289 mg sodium. U.S. RDA: 10% calcium.

SPAGHETTI RING FLORENTINE

- 8 ounces spaghetti
- 2 10-ounce packages frozen chopped spinach
- ½ cup chopped onion
- 2 slightly beaten eggs
- ½ cup grated Parmesan cheese (2 ounces)
- 6 tablespoons margarine *or* butter, softened
- 1 4-ounce jar pimiento, chopped
- 2 cups sliced fresh mushrooms (5 ounces)
- 1 15½-ounce jar meatless spaghetti sauce

Line a 6½-cup ring mold with foil. Grease with *margarine;* set aside.

Cook spaghetti according to package directions; drain. Cook spinach according to package directions, adding onion. Drain, pressing out liquid with the back of a spoon.

In a mixing bowl stir together the eggs, cooked spaghetti, spinach mixture, cheese, *4 tablespoons* of the margarine or butter, and pimiento. Press mixture into the prepared mold. Cover and bake in a 375° oven for 25 minutes. Let stand for 5 minutes; unmold.

For sauce, in a saucepan cook mushrooms in remaining margarine or butter till tender. Add spaghetti sauce; heat through. To serve, cut the ring into wedges. Spoon some sauce over each serving. Makes 8 servings.

Nutrition information per serving: 304 cal., 12 g pro., 33 g carbo., 14 g fat, 74 mg chol., 666 mg sodium, and 3 g dietary fiber. U.S. RDA: 103% vit. A, 17% vit. C, 23% thiamine, 23% riboflavin, 14% niacin, 22% calcium, 22% iron, 18% phosphorus.

CURRY SLICES

- 2½ pounds pickling cucumbers, thinly sliced (8 cups)
- 1 medium onion, thinly sliced
- 1 tablespoon salt
- 1 green pepper, cut into thin strips
- 2 cups vinegar
- 1⅓ cups sugar
- 1 tablespoon curry powder
- 2 teaspoons pickling spice
- 1 teaspoon celery seed
- 1 teaspoon mustard seed
- ½ teaspoon pepper

In a large mixing bowl combine the cucumbers and onion. Sprinkle with salt; cover with ice water and let stand for 3 hours. Drain well. Rinse and drain cucumber mixture again.

In a 4½-quart Dutch oven or kettle combine green pepper, vinegar, sugar, curry powder, pickling spice, celery seed, mustard seed, and pepper; add drained cucumber and onion. Heat just to boiling. Fill hot, clean pint jars; leave ½-inch headspace. Wipe the rims; adjust the lids.

Process in a boiling water bath for 10 minutes (start timing when the water boils). Makes 4 pints.

Nutrition information per ¼ cup: 42 cal., 0 g pro., 11 g carbo., 0 g fat, 0 mg chol., and 201 mg sodium. U.S. RDA: 14% vit. C.

BROCCOLI AND WILD RICE BAKE

- 1 to 1¼ pounds broccoli, cut into 1-inch pieces
- 1 6¾-ounce package quick-cooking long grain and wild rice mix
- 1 1-ounce envelope sour cream sauce mix
- 1 single-serving envelope *instant* cream of chicken soup mix
- 2 cups milk
- ¾ cup soft bread crumbs (1 slice)
- 1 tablespoon margarine *or* butter, melted
- ¼ teaspoon paprika

Cook broccoli stems in enough boiling salted water to cover for 5 minutes. Add flowerets; cook for 4 to 5 minutes or till tender. Drain. Prepare rice mix according to package directions. Combine sauce and soup mixes. Stir in milk.

In a 2-quart casserole combine rice and milk mixture; fold in broccoli. Combine bread crumbs, margarine or butter, and paprika; sprinkle over top. Bake, uncovered, in a 350° oven for 35 to 40 minutes or till heated through. Makes 8 servings.

Nutrition information per serving: 134 cal., 6 g pro., 17 g carbo., 4 g fat, 5 mg chol., 402 mg sodium, 2 g dietary fiber. U.S. RDA: 24% vit. A, 63% vit. C.

MARSHMALLOW-PECAN SQUASH

- 2 medium acorn squash (2 pounds)
- ⅓ cup saltine cracker crumbs
- ¼ cup chopped pecans
- 3 tablespoons margarine *or* butter, melted
- 1 tablespoon brown sugar
- ⅛ teaspoon ground nutmeg
- 1 cup tiny marshmallows

Halve squash; remove and discard the seeds and fibers. Place squash, cut side up, in a 12x7½x2-inch baking dish.

Combine cracker crumbs, pecans, *2 tablespoons* of the margarine or butter, brown sugar, and nutmeg. Brush the squash halves with remaining margarine or butter. Spoon *one-fourth* of the pecan mixture into *each* squash half. Bake, covered, in a 400° oven for 50 to 55 minutes.

Uncover the baking dish; top *each* squash half with ¼ cup of the marshmallows. Bake 4 to 5 minutes more or till marshmallows are golden. Serves 4.

Nutrition information per serving: 274 cal., 3 g pro., 37 g carbo., 15 g fat, 0 mg chol., 188 mg sodium, 5 g dietary fiber. U.S. RDA: 19% vit. A, 31% vit. C, 22% thiamine, 11% iron.

COLESLAW SOUFFLÉ SALAD

- 1 3-ounce package lemon-flavored gelatin
- 1 cup boiling water
- ½ cup mayonnaise *or* salad dressing
- 2 tablespoons vinegar
- ½ cup cold water
- ¼ teaspoon salt
- 1½ cups finely shredded green cabbage
- ½ cup diced celery
- 2 to 4 tablespoons diced red *or* green sweet pepper
- 1 tablespoon diced onion
- Shredded red and green cabbage (optional)

In a large mixer bowl dissolve gelatin in boiling water. Stir in mayonnaise, vinegar, cold water, and salt. Chill till partially set (consistency of unbeaten egg whites).

Beat with an electric mixer on medium speed till fluffy. Fold in cabbage, celery, red or green pepper, and onion. Pour into a 1-quart mold; chill at least 6 hours or till set.

Unmold salad onto a cabbage-lined platter, if desired. Serves 6 to 8.
Nutrition information per serving: 192 cal., 2 g pro., 15 g carbo., 15 g fat, 11 mg chol., 251 mg sodium.

Desserts

LEMON-NUT ICE CREAM

- 2 eggs
- ½ cup sugar
- 2 cups light cream
- ½ cup light corn syrup
- 2 teaspoons finely shredded lemon peel
- ¼ cup lemon juice
- ½ cup chopped walnuts

In a small mixer bowl beat eggs with an electric mixer on high speed till thick and lemon-colored, about 5 minutes. Gradually add sugar, beating till thick. Add cream, corn syrup, lemon peel, and lemon juice; mix well. Pour mixture into a 9x9x2-inch pan. Cover; freeze till partially frozen, about 2 hours.

Break frozen mixture into chunks. Place in a chilled large mixer bowl. Beat with an electric mixer on medium speed for 1 to 2 minutes or till smooth. Stir in walnuts.

Return mixture to cold pan. Freeze about 3 hours or till firm. (Or, pour unfrozen mixture and nuts into a 2- to 4-quart ice-cream freezer container and freeze according to manufacturer's directions). Makes 8 servings.
Nutrition information per serving: 296 cal., 4 g pro., 32 g carbo., 18 g fat, 109 mg chol., 56 mg sodium.

STRAWBERRY PIE DELUXE

- 1 quart fresh strawberries *or* one 16-ounce package frozen unsweetened whole strawberries
- ½ cup sugar
- 1 envelope unflavored gelatin
- 1 tablespoon lemon juice
- 1 baked 9-inch pastry shell
- 1 large banana

Thaw frozen strawberries, reserving juices. Using a potato masher, crush *3 cups* of the strawberries. Halve or slice remaining berries; set aside.

Strain crushed strawberries; add water to juice to equal *1 cup* liquid. Reserve crushed strawberries.

In a medium saucepan stir together sugar and gelatin. Add the 1 cup liquid. Cook and stir over medium heat till gelatin and sugar are dissolved. Stir in reserved crushed strawberries and lemon juice. Transfer mixture to a mixing bowl. Chill till partially set (the consistency of unbeaten egg whites).

Pour *half* of the mixture into the cooled pastry shell. Thinly slice banana; arrange in a single layer over berry mixture. Top with remaining berry mixture. Arrange the reserved strawberry halves or slices on top. Chill several hours or till firm. Serves 6 to 8.
Nutrition information per serving: 283 cal., 3 g pro., 45 g carbo., 11 g fat, 0 mg chol., 221 mg sodium, 3 g dietary fiber. U.S. RDA: 100% vit. C.

MARBLE CHEESECAKE

You may be tempted to pour the melted chocolate into the reserved cheesecake batter (rather than vice versa), but the result will be an unattractive speckled chocolate mixture. Be sure to follow the recipe directions exactly as given for the best-looking marble effect—

- 1½ cups graham cracker crumbs
- 1½ cups sugar
- 6 tablespoons margarine *or* butter, melted
- 3 8-ounce packages cream cheese, softened
- 1½ teaspoons vanilla
- 4 eggs
- 1 cup light cream
- 2 squares (2 ounces) unsweetened chocolate, melted and cooled

Combine cracker crumbs, *¼ cup* sugar, and margarine or butter. Press in bottom and 1¾ inches up the sides of a 9-inch springform pan; set aside.

In a large mixer bowl beat the remaining sugar, cream cheese, and vanilla with an electric mixer on medium speed till fluffy. Add eggs; beat on low speed just till blended. Add cream; beat on low speed till blended.

Using *1½ cups* of the batter, stir a small amount at a time into the melted chocolate, stirring briskly after each addition till smooth.

Pour *half* of the plain mixture into crust; gradually pour in half of the chocolate mixture, using a zigzag motion. Repeat layers. Draw a knife or narrow metal spatula through the batter to marble the layers.

Bake in a 325° oven for 60 to 70 minutes or till the center appears nearly set when shaken. Cool in the pan on a wire rack for 15 minutes; loosen sides of pan. Cool for 30 minutes more on rack, then remove sides of pan. Chill cake. Makes 16 servings.
Note: Typically, the top of this cheesecake cracks during cooling.
Nutrition information per serving: 357 cal., 6 g pro., 27 g carbo., 26 g fat, 126 mg chol., and 254 mg sodium. U.S. RDA: 19% vit. A, 12% riboflavin, and 11% phosphorus.

CHOCOLATE AND VANILLA TARTS

1½ cups all-purpose flour
3 tablespoons granulated sugar
3 tablespoons unsweetened cocoa powder
½ cup margarine *or* butter
2 tablespoons shortening
3 to 4 tablespoons cold water
2 3-ounce packages cream cheese
¼ cup sifted powdered sugar
1 8-ounce carton vanilla yogurt
1 teaspoon vanilla
½ of a 4-ounce container frozen whipped dessert topping, thawed
Sliced kiwi fruit *or* assorted fresh fruit, sliced
Colored mint wafers (optional)

In a mixing bowl combine flour, granulated sugar, and cocoa. Cut in margarine or butter and shortening till the mixture resembles coarse crumbs. Sprinkle water over flour mixture, *1 tablespoon* at a time, tossing with a fork till moistened. Form into a ball.

On a floured surface roll dough ⅛ inch thick. Cut into *twelve* 4½-inch circles. Fit pastry circles into muffin cups; flute edges. Prick bottom and sides of *each* with a fork. Bake in a 400° oven for 12 minutes. Remove from pans; cool on wire racks.

In a small mixer bowl beat cream cheese and powdered sugar with an electric mixer on medium speed till well blended. Stir in yogurt and vanilla. Fold in dessert topping; spoon into pastry shells. Chill. Top with fruit just before serving. If desired, make candy curls by drawing a vegetable peeler across bottom of a mint wafer, forming a curl. Makes 12 servings.

Nutrition information per serving: 273 cal., 4 g pro., 26 g carbo., 17 g fat, 17 mg chol., 159 mg sodium. U.S. RDA: 12% vit. A, 24% vit. C.

BANANA SPLIT CAKE

3 cups all-purpose flour
2 teaspoons baking powder
¼ teaspoon baking soda
¼ teaspoon salt
1 cup margarine *or* butter
1½ cups granulated sugar
4 eggs
1 large banana
½ cup dairy sour cream
½ cup milk
1 teaspoon vanilla
½ cup strawberry preserves
Few drops red food coloring (optional)
½ cup presweetened cocoa powder *or* instant cocoa mix
Powdered sugar (optional)

Grease and lightly flour a 10-inch fluted tube pan; set aside. In a medium mixing bowl stir together flour, baking powder, baking soda, and salt; set aside.

In a large mixer bowl beat margarine or butter with an electric mixer on medium speed for 30 seconds. Add granulated sugar and beat till fluffy. Add eggs, one at a time, beating well on medium speed after each addition.

In a medium mixing bowl mash banana (you should have about ½ cup). Add sour cream, milk, and vanilla; stir till combined.

Add dry ingredients and banana mixture alternately to beaten mixture, beating on low speed after each addition till well blended.

Reserve *2 cups* of the batter. Stir strawberry preserves and food coloring into *1 cup* of this reserved batter. Stir cocoa powder or instant cocoa mix into *1 cup* of this reserved batter.

Spoon *half* of the remaining plain batter into the prepared pan. Top with strawberry batter. Top with the remaining plain batter. Spoon cocoa batter over all.

Bake in a 350° oven for 60 to 65 minutes or till cake tests done. Cool for 10 minutes on a wire rack. Remove from pan; cool thoroughly. Sift powdered sugar over cooled cake, if desired. Makes 16 servings.

Nutrition information per serving: 343 cal., 5 g pro., 49 g carbo., 15 g fat, 73 mg chol., and 256 mg sodium. U.S. RDA: 12% vit. A, 11% thiamine, and 10% riboflavin.

PUMPKIN CAKE ROLL

3 eggs
1 cup granulated sugar
⅔ cup canned pumpkin
1 teaspoon lemon juice
¾ cup all-purpose flour
2 teaspoons ground cinnamon
1 teaspoon baking powder
1 teaspoon ground ginger
½ teaspoon salt
½ teaspoon ground nutmeg
1 cup finely chopped walnuts
Sifted powdered sugar
1 cup sifted powdered sugar
2 3-ounce packages cream cheese
¼ cup margarine *or* butter
½ teaspoon vanilla

In a large mixer bowl beat eggs with an electric mixer on high speed for 5 minutes; gradually beat in granulated sugar. Stir in pumpkin and lemon juice.

In a small bowl stir together flour, cinnamon, baking powder, ginger, salt, and nutmeg. Fold into the pumpkin mixture. Spread the batter in a greased and floured 15x10x1-inch jelly-roll pan. Sprinkle with walnuts.

Bake in a 375° oven for 15 minutes. Immediately invert cake onto a towel sprinkled with powdered sugar. Roll up cake and towel, jelly-roll style, starting from a short side. Cool completely.

For filling, in a small mixer bowl combine the 1 cup powdered sugar, cream cheese, margarine or butter, and vanilla; beat with an electric mixer on medium speed till smooth. Unroll the cooled cake. Spread filling over cake; reroll cake. Cover and chill.

To serve, cut cake crosswise into 1-inch slices. Makes 10 to 12 servings.

Nutrition information per serving: 325 cal., 6 g pro., 33 g carbo., 20 g fat, 101 mg chol., 264 mg sodium. U.S. RDA: 82% vit. A, 10% phosphorus.

BURNT-SUGAR CHIFFON CAKE

¾ cup sugar
¾ cup hot water
2¼ cups sifted cake flour *or* 2 cups all-purpose flour
1¼ cups sugar
1 tablespoon baking powder
⅛ teaspoon salt
5 egg yolks
½ cup cooking oil
⅓ cup water
1 teaspoon vanilla
8 egg whites
½ teaspoon cream of tartar
1 recipe Burnt-Sugar Frosting (see recipe, below)
Toasted coconut (optional)

In a heavy skillet melt the ¾ cup sugar over medium-low heat without stirring till it just begins to melt. Heat and stir for 6 to 8 minutes or till clear and a deep golden color. Remove from heat; carefully stir in ¾ cup hot water. Return to heat; cook and stir over low heat till lumps dissolve and mixture is reduced to ⅔ cup. Remove from heat.

In a large mixer bowl sift together flour, 1¼ cups sugar, baking powder, and salt; make a well in the center. Add ½ *cup* of the burnt-sugar syrup (reserve remaining for frosting), egg yolks, oil, ⅓ cup water, and vanilla. Beat with an electric mixer on low speed just till combined, then on high speed about 5 minutes or till satin smooth.

Transfer batter to a another bowl. Thoroughly wash mixer bowl and beaters. In the same mixer bowl beat egg whites and cream of tartar with electric mixer on high speed till stiff peaks form (tips stand straight). Pour batter in a thin stream over entire surface of egg whites, folding in gently by hand. Pour into ungreased 10-inch tube pan.

Bake on the bottom rack in a 325° oven for 55 to 60 minutes or till cake springs back when lightly touched with fingers. Invert cake in pan; cool completely. Loosen cake; remove from pan.

Drizzle with Burnt-Sugar Frosting. Sprinkle with toasted coconut, if desired. Makes 16 servings.

Burnt-Sugar Frosting: In a medium saucepan melt 2 tablespoons *margarine* or *butter;* remove from heat. Blend in 4 teaspoons *all-purpose flour* and ⅛ teaspoon *salt.* Stir in remaining *burnt-sugar syrup.* Heat to boiling, stirring constantly. Cook and stir 1 minute

more. Remove the saucepan from heat. Beat 1½ cups sifted *powdered sugar* and 2 tablespoons *milk* alternately into syrup mixture. Beat in 3 tablespoons *margarine* or *butter.* Add ½ teaspoon *vanilla.* Beat mixture till of drizzling consistency. If necessary, stir in 1 to 2 teaspoons *milk.*

Nutrition information per serving: 312 cal., 4 g pro., 47 g carbo., 12 g fat, 85 mg chol., 161 mg sodium.

CHOCOLATE-COVERED CHERRY COOKIES

1½ cups all-purpose flour
½ cup unsweetened cocoa powder
¼ teaspoon baking powder
¼ teaspoon baking soda
¼ teaspoon salt
½ cup margarine *or* butter, softened
1 cup sugar
1 egg
1½ teaspoons vanilla
2 10-ounce jars *small* maraschino cherries (about 48)
1 6-ounce package (1 cup) semisweet chocolate pieces (*not* imitation)
½ cup *sweetened condensed* milk

Stir together flour, cocoa powder, baking powder, soda, and salt; set aside.

In a mixer bowl beat margarine with electric mixer on medium speed for 30 seconds. Add sugar and beat on low speed till fluffy. Add egg and vanilla; beat well on medium speed. Gradually add the flour mixture, beating on low speed till blended.

Shape into 1-inch balls; place 2 inches apart on ungreased cookie sheet. Press down center of each with thumb.

Drain maraschino cherries, reserving the juice. Press a cherry into the center of each ball of cookie dough.

For frosting, in small heavy saucepan melt chocolate and sweetened condensed milk over low heat, stirring often. Stir in *4 teaspoons* of the reserved juice. Spoon *1 teaspoon* frosting over each cherry, spreading to cover cherry. If necessary, add additional juice, 1 teaspoon at a time, to thin frosting.

Bake in a 350° oven for 10 minutes or till done. Transfer to wire rack; cool. Makes 48 cookies.

Nutrition information per cookie: 83 cal., 1 g pro., 12 g carbo., 4 g fat, 7 mg chol., 53 mg sodium.

SWISS NUT TORTE

2⅔ cups all-purpose flour
1½ cups sugar
Dash salt
⅔ cup margarine *or* butter
1 beaten egg
2 tablespoons rum *or* water
1 teaspoon finely shredded lemon peel
1 cup whipping cream, at room temperature
3 tablespoons honey
1 to 2 tablespoons kirsch
2¾ cups coarsely chopped walnuts
1 slightly beaten egg yolk
1 tablespoon milk

Stir together flour, ½ *cup* of the sugar, and salt; set aside.

In a large mixer bowl beat margarine with an electric mixer on medium speed till fluffy. Add flour mixture; beat till crumbly. Combine whole egg, rum, and lemon peel. Stir into flour mixture till moistened.

Divide dough into thirds. Pat *one-third* onto bottom of a 10-inch springform pan. Pat another *third* of dough 1 inch up the sides of pan. On waxed paper roll remaining dough into a 10x4-inch rectangle about ¼ inch thick; cover. Chill dough for 30 minutes.

In a heavy large skillet heat the remaining sugar over medium-low heat without stirring till it just begins to melt. Heat and stir 6 to 8 minutes more or till golden, stirring constantly. Remove from heat; slowly stir in cream. Heat and stir 5 minutes or till sugar dissolves. Add honey and kirsch. Stir in nuts. Remove from heat; cool 5 minutes. Spread nut mixture over crust.

Using a fluted pastry wheel or a knife, cut the rectangle of dough into seven ½-inch-wide strips. Halve one strip; place a half strip at one edge of torte. Place the remaining half strip on the opposite edge. Crisscross remaining strips on top of torte. Combine egg yolk and milk; brush over crust. Bake in a 350° oven about 40 minutes or till crust is golden. Cool for 1 hour. Serve warm or chilled. Makes 16 servings.

Nutrition information per serving: 427 cal., 6 g pro., 42 g carbo., 27 g fat, 55 mg chol., and 102 mg sodium. U.S. RDA: 12% vit. A, 15% thiamine, and 11% phosphorus.

CARAMEL PECAN BROWNIES

⅔ cup vanilla caramels
  (12 caramels)
⅓ cup margarine *or* butter
2 tablespoons milk
¾ cup sugar
2 eggs
½ teaspoon vanilla
¾ cup all-purpose flour
½ teaspoon baking powder
¼ teaspoon salt
½ cup chopped pecans

In a 2-quart saucepan combine the caramels, margarine or butter, and milk. Heat and stir over low heat just till caramels are melted. Remove the saucepan from the heat. Stir in the sugar. Add the eggs and vanilla; stir till well blended. Set aside.

In a mixing bowl combine flour, baking powder, and salt. Add to saucepan mixture, stirring till blended. Stir in pecans. Turn into a greased 9x9x2-inch baking pan.

Bake in a 350° oven for 20 to 25 minutes or till a wooden toothpick inserted in the center comes out clean. Cool in pan on a wire rack; cut into bars. Makes about 20 bars.

Nutrition information per bar: 124 cal., 2 g pro., 16 g carbo., 6 g fat, 28 mg chol., 93 mg sodium.

RAISIN PUFFS WITH ORANGE SAUCE

1½ cups all-purpose flour
2 teaspoons baking powder
⅓ cup shortening
⅓ cup sugar
1 beaten egg
1 teaspoon vanilla
¾ cup milk
1 cup raisins
1 recipe Orange Sauce

In a small bowl stir together flour and baking powder; set aside. In a small mixer bowl beat shortening with an electric mixer on medium speed for 30 seconds. Add sugar and beat till fluffy. Add egg and vanilla, beating well on medium speed. Add flour mixture and milk alternately to beaten mixture, beating on low speed after each addition just till combined. Fold in raisins.

Grease six 6-ounce custard cups; arrange cups in a shallow baking pan. Fill custard cups ⅔ full.

Bake in a 350° oven for 25 to 30 minutes or till puffs test done. Cool for 10 minutes in cups. Remove from cups. Serve warm with Orange Sauce. Makes 6 servings.

Orange Sauce: In a small saucepan stir together ⅓ cup *sugar*, 2 tablespoons *cornstarch*, and ⅛ teaspoon *salt*. Add ⅓ cup *light corn syrup*, 1 to 2 teaspoons finely shredded *orange peel*, and 1 cup *orange juice*. Cook and stir till thickened and bubbly. Cook and stir 2 minutes more. Stir in 2 tablespoons *margarine* or *butter* till melted. Serve warm. Makes about 1⅔ cups sauce.

Nutrition information per serving: 515 cal., 6 g pro., 87 g carbo., 17 g fat, 48 mg chol., 232 mg sodium, 3 g dietary fiber. U.S. RDA: 21% vit. C, 19% thiamine, 13% riboflavin, 10% niacin, 14% calcium, 16% iron, 12% phosphorus.

FROSTY STRAWBERRY SQUARES

1 cup all-purpose flour
¼ cup packed brown sugar
½ cup chopped walnuts
½ cup margarine *or* butter, melted
2 egg whites
2 cups sliced fresh strawberries *or* one 10-ounce package frozen sliced strawberries, partially thawed
1 cup granulated sugar*
2 tablespoons lemon juice
1 cup whipping cream

For crumb mixture, in a small bowl combine flour, brown sugar, walnuts, and margarine or butter. Spread the crumb mixture evenly in a shallow baking pan. Bake in a 350° oven for 20 minutes, stirring occasionally. Sprinkle *two-thirds* of the crumbs in a 13x9x2-inch baking pan; set the pan aside.

In a large mixer bowl combine egg whites, strawberries, granulated sugar, and lemon juice. Beat with an electric mixer on high speed about 10 minutes or till stiff peaks form (the tips stand straight).

In a small mixer bowl beat whipping cream till soft peaks form. Fold whipped cream into strawberry mixture. Spoon mixture over crumbs in the baking pan; sprinkle remaining crumbs on top. Freeze for 6 hours or overnight. Let stand a few minutes before serving. Cut into squares to serve. Makes 10 to 12 servings.

Note: If you use frozen strawberries, decrease the sugar to just ⅔ cup.

Nutrition information per serving: 365 cal., 4 g pro., 41 g carbo., 22 g fat, 33 mg chol., 129 mg sodium, 2 g dietary fiber. U.S. RDA: 15% vit. A, 51% vit. C.

Breads

WHOLE WHEAT AND COTTAGE CHEESE ROLLS

- 3¾ to 4 cups whole wheat flour
- 2 packages active dry yeast
- 1½ cups cream-style cottage cheese
- ½ cup water
- ¼ cup packed brown sugar
- 2 tablespoons margarine *or* butter
- 1 teaspoon salt
- 2 eggs

In a small mixer bowl stir together *1½ cups* of the flour and yeast. In a small saucepan heat cottage cheese, water, brown sugar, margarine or butter, and salt just till warm (120° to 130°), stirring constantly to melt the margarine or butter. Add to the flour mixture; add eggs. Beat with an electric mixer on low speed for 30 seconds, scraping sides of bowl constantly. Beat on high speed for 3 minutes more. Using a spoon, stir in as much of remaining flour as you can.

Turn dough out onto a lightly floured surface. Knead in enough of the remaining flour to make a stiff dough that is smooth and elastic (8 to 10 minutes total). Shape into a ball. Place in a lightly greased bowl; turn to grease the surface. Cover and let rise in a warm place till double (30 to 45 minutes).

Punch dough down. Divide in half. Cover and let rest for 10 minutes. Shape dough as desired (see directions, below). Let rise till nearly double, about 20 minutes.

Bake in a 375° oven for 12 to 15 minutes. Makes 24 rolls.

Shortcut Cloverleafs: Lightly grease 24 muffin cups. Divide each dough-half into 12 pieces. Shape *each* piece into a ball, pulling the edges under to make a smooth top. Place one ball in each muffin cup, smooth side up. Using scissors dipped in flour, snip top of each roll in half, then snip across the first cut, making 4 points.

Butterhorns: Lightly grease baking sheets. On a lightly floured surface roll each dough-half into a 12-inch circle. Brush with melted *butter.* Cut each circle into 12 wedges. To shape, begin at wide end of wedge and roll toward point. Place, point-side down, 2 to 3 inches apart on baking sheets.

Rosettes: Lightly grease 2 baking sheets. Divide each dough-half into 12 pieces. On a lightly floured surface roll each piece of dough into a 12-inch rope. Tie in a loose knot, leaving two long ends. Tuck top end of dough under roll. Bring bottom end up; tuck into center of roll. Place rolls 2 to 3 inches apart on baking sheets.

Nutrition information per roll: 100 cal., 5 g pro., 16 g carbo., 2 g fat, 24 mg chol., 165 mg sodium, 2 g dietary fiber. U.S. RDA: 11% phosphorus.

CORN-RYE BISCUITS

- 1 cup all-purpose flour
- ⅓ cup rye flour
- ¼ cup yellow cornmeal
- 1 tablespoon baking powder
- ½ teaspoon salt
- ½ teaspoon sugar
- ½ teaspoon caraway seed
- ¼ cup shortening
- ⅔ cup milk
- Yellow cornmeal

In a large mixing bowl stir together all-purpose flour, rye flour, the ¼ cup cornmeal, baking powder, salt, sugar, and caraway seed. Cut in shortening till the mixture resembles coarse crumbs. Make a well in the center; add milk all at once. Stir just till the dough clings together.

Turn dough onto a lightly floured surface. (The dough should be soft.) Knead dough gently, 10 to 12 strokes. Roll or pat dough to a ½-inch thickness. Cut dough with a floured 2½-inch biscuit cutter. Dip tops and bottoms of biscuits in cornmeal. Transfer to an ungreased baking sheet. Bake in a 450° oven for 10 to 12 minutes or till golden. Serve warm. Makes 8 biscuits.

Nutrition information per biscuit: 153 cal., 3 g pro., 20 g carbo., 7 g fat, 2 mg chol., and 256 mg sodium. U.S. RDA: 10% calcium.

APPLE-CINNAMON SWIRL LOAF

- 3¾ to 4¼ cups all-purpose flour
- 1 package 1-layer-size white cake mix
- 1 package active dry yeast
- 1¼ cups warm water (120° to 130°)
- ½ teaspoon salt
- 1 egg
- 2½ cups finely chopped and peeled apple
- ⅓ cup sugar
- ⅓ cup finely chopped pecans
- 2 teaspoons ground cinnamon
- 3 tablespoons margarine *or* butter, melted

In large mixer bowl stir together *1½ cups* of the flour, cake mix, and yeast. Combine warm water and salt; add to flour mixture. Add egg. Beat with an electric mixer on low speed for 30 seconds. Beat at high speed for 3 minutes. Using a spoon, stir in as much of the remaining flour as you can.

Turn dough out onto a lightly floured surface. Knead in enough of the remaining flour to make a moderately stiff dough that is smooth and elastic (6 to 8 minutes total). Shape dough into a ball. Place in a lightly greased bowl; turn once to grease surface. Cover and let rise in a warm place till double (about 1¼ hours).

Punch dough down; divide in half. Cover and let rest for 10 minutes. Meanwhile, in a medium mixing bowl stir together chopped apple, sugar, pecans, and cinnamon. Roll *half* of the dough into a 12x8-inch rectangle. Brush surface with *some* of the margarine or butter. Sprinkle with *half* of the apple mixture.

Roll up jelly-roll style, beginning with one of the narrow ends; seal edge and ends. Place in a greased 8x4x2-inch loaf pan. Repeat with the remaining dough, filling, and margarine to make a second loaf. Brush top of loaves with remaining margarine.

Cover; let rise in warm place till nearly double (about 1 hour).

Bake in a 375° oven about 35 minutes or till top is golden. Remove from pans immediately; cool on a wire rack. Makes 2 loaves (36 slices).

Nutrition information per slice: 139 cal., 2 g pro., 25 g carbo., 4 g fat, 8 mg chol., 137 mg sodium.

MOLASSES CORN BREAD

1½ cups whole bran cereal
1 cup all-purpose flour
½ cup yellow cornmeal
1 tablespoon baking powder
¼ teaspoon salt
⅓ cup shortening
½ cup sugar
2 eggs
1 cup milk
⅓ cup molasses

In a small mixing bowl stir together bran cereal, flour, cornmeal, baking powder, and salt; set aside.

In small mixer bowl beat shortening with an electric mixer on medium speed for 30 seconds. Add the sugar and beat till fluffy. Add the eggs, one at a time, beating well on medium speed after each addition. Stir in milk and molasses. Add flour mixture to beaten mixture, stirring just till combined.

Turn batter into a greased 9x9x2-inch baking pan. Bake in a 375° oven about 30 minutes or till the top is golden. Cut into squares to serve. Serve warm. Makes 8 servings.

Nutrition information per serving:
302 cal., 6 g pro., 48 g carbo., 11 g fat, 71 mg chol., 337 mg sodium. U.S. RDA: 13% vit. A, 19% thiamine, 19% riboflavin, 15% niacin, 17% calcium, 20% iron, 21% phosphorus.

RASPBERRY CREAM-CHEESE COFFEE CAKE

1 3-ounce package cream cheese
¼ cup margarine *or* butter
2 cups packaged biscuit mix
¼ cup milk
½ cup raspberry preserves
1 cup sifted powdered sugar
1 to 2 tablespoons milk
½ teaspoon vanilla

In a medium mixing bowl cut the cream cheese and the margarine or butter into the biscuit mix till the mixture is crumbly. Stir in the ¼ cup milk. Turn dough onto a lightly floured surface; knead 8 to 10 strokes.

On waxed paper, roll the dough to a 12x8-inch rectangle. Invert onto a greased baking sheet; remove waxed paper. Spread raspberry preserves down center of dough. Make 2½-inch-long cuts at 1-inch intervals on long sides. Fold strips over the filling.

Bake, uncovered, in a 375° oven about 20 minutes or till golden brown. Let the coffee cake cool for 5 minutes before frosting.

For frosting, in a small mixing bowl stir together sugar, the 1 to 2 tablespoons milk, and vanilla; drizzle over slightly cooled coffee cake. Serve warm. Makes 8 to 10 servings.

Nutrition information per serving:
317 cal., 4 g pro., 47 g carbo., 13 g fat, 12 mg chol., 486 mg sodium. U.S. RDA: 10% thiamine, 10% phosphorus.

RASPBERRY BRAN MUFFINS

1 cup fresh *or* frozen raspberries
1 cup all-purpose flour
1 cup unprocessed wheat bran
¼ cup sugar
3 teaspoons baking powder
¼ teaspoon salt
1 beaten egg
1 cup milk
¼ cup cooking oil

Partially thaw frozen raspberries. *Do not* completely thaw. In a medium mixing bowl stir together flour, bran, sugar, baking powder, and salt. Make a well in the center.

In a small mixing bowl combine egg, milk, and oil; add all at once to flour mixture. Stir just till moistened. Fold in raspberries. Grease *bottoms* of muffin cups or line with paper bake cups. Fill ⅔ full.

Bake in a 400° oven about 20 minutes or till done. Remove from pan. Cool slightly on wire racks. Makes 12.

Nutrition information per muffin:
128 cal., 3 g pro., 18 g carbo., 6 g fat, 24 mg chol., 136 mg sodium, 2 g dietary fiber. U.S. RDA: 11% phosphorus.

THE MAGAZINE FOR AMERICAN FAMILIES

OCTOBER 1987
$1.50

Better Homes and Gardens.

PIZZA!

HOMEMADE AND SCRUMPTIOUS

By Terri Pauser Wolf

PIZZA TURNOVERS

Pizza can be a nutritious coup. These pockets rely on lean meat and a low-fat cheese to keep calories and fat in hand—

- 1 **tablespoon cornmeal**
- 1 **10-ounce package refrigerated pizza crust dough**
- 1½ **cups shredded mozzarella cheese (6 ounces)**
- ½ **cup pizza sauce**
- 1 **4-ounce package sliced Canadian-style bacon, halved**
- 1 **medium carrot, coarsely shredded (½ cup)**
- 2 **tablespoons grated Parmesan cheese**

●**Lightly grease a baking sheet;** sprinkle with cornmeal. Unroll dough onto baking sheet. Pat or press dough into a 12-inch square; cut into quarters.

●**Sprinkle one-fourth of the cheese** on a diagonal half of each piece of dough. Top each with the pizza sauce, bacon, and carrot.

●**Fold each dough portion in half** to form a triangle and press edges firmly to seal. Cut slits in top of dough to allow steam to escape. Sprinkle Parmesan cheese over triangles. Bake in a 350° oven for 25 to 30 minutes or till golden. Makes 4 main-dish servings.

Nutrition information per turnover: 389 cal., 26 g pro., 40 g carbo., 13 g fat, 40 mg chol., 1,206 mg sodium. U.S. RDA: 111% vit. A, 18% vit. C, 34% thiamine, 25% riboflavin, 24% niacin, 38% calcium, 37% phosphorus, and 16% iron.

Photograph: Ron Crofoot
Food stylist: Janet Pittman

MAKE IN 10 MINUTES BAKE FOR 25

READY IN 33 MINUTES

CHEESE AND VEGETABLE PIZZA

This pizza has about half the calories of conventional pizza—

- 1 6½-ounce package pizza crust mix
- 1 10-ounce package frozen cut broccoli
- 1 5-ounce jar sharp American cheese spread
- 1 teaspoon Italian seasoning, crushed
- ¼ cup sliced pitted ripe olives
- 1 small red *or* green sweet pepper, cut into thin rings
- 4 ounces sliced provolone *or* mozzarella cheese, cut into triangles

●**Prepare pizza crust mix** according to package directions; press into a greased 12-inch pizza pan. Bake in a 425° oven for 15 minutes or till light brown.

●**Meanwhile, cook broccoli** according to package directions; drain.

●**Dollop cheese spread** by teaspoonfuls evenly over crust. Sprinkle with broccoli, seasoning, and olives. Arrange pepper rings in a circle. Place cheese triangles around edge of pizza.

●**Bake in a 425° oven** for 5 to 8 minutes or till heated through and cheese just melts. Cut into wedges to serve. Makes 4 to 6 servings.

Nutrition information per serving: 405 cal., 20 g pro., 44 g carbo., 17 g fat, 39 mg chol., 1,134 mg sodium, 4 g dietary fiber. U.S. RDA: 69% vit. A, 102% vit. C, 24% thiamine, 32% riboflavin, 16% niacin, 48% calcium, 16% iron, and 48% phosphorus.

3 BREADS & 3 SOUPS IN 3 HOURS

By Barbara Greenwood

Stock up for busy days ahead with these hearty soups and breads. Our timetable weaves the way to fix them all in a three-hour cooking spree. The trick? Make a master stock and a yeast dough, then split each three ways. Your payoff: a freezerful of meals ready to heat on autumn days.

CRUSTY OAT BREAD
Moist and scrumptious loaf that's healthful, too—

HOCK 'N' BEAN SOUP
A mingling of black beans and pork hocks that makes taste buds dance—

TIMETABLE

9:00 READ RECIPES AND TIMETABLE

9:05 GATHER UTENSILS

UTENSILS

- 3 large bowls
- 1½-, 2-, and 3-quart saucepans with lids
- 4½-quart Dutch oven
- colander
- 2 baking sheets
- 12 muffin cups
- wire rack
- cutting board
- paring and chef's knives
- rolling pin
- wooden spoon and rubber spatula
- fork
- custard cup
- pastry brush
- pin or wooden toothpick
- dry and liquid measuring cups; measuring spoons
- electric mixer
- can opener
- blender or food processor
- string and cheesecloth
- two 2-quart and one 1½-quart freezer containers
- scissors
- thermometer
- plastic wrap; freezer wrap; waxed paper; freezer tape; marking pen

BROWN 'N' SERVE CLOVERLEAVES

*Flavor these rolls with
your favorite herbs and seeds—*

CHEESE TWIST

*Buttery bread wrapped around
tunnels of cheddar cheese—*

SEAFOOD GUMBO

*Hot and spicy tasting—
just the way gumbo should be!*

CHICKEN SPAETZLE CHOWDER

*A comforting blend of tender pasta
and vegetables in a rich broth—*

Timetable continued

TIMETABLE *continued*

9:15 GATHER INGREDIENTS

■ INGREDIENTS ■

Meat and Seafood
- 2 smoked pork hocks
- 1½ cups chopped cooked chicken *or* turkey
- 1 8-ounce package frozen, peeled, and deveined shrimp*
- 1 8-ounce package frozen salad-style crab-flavored fish*

Dairy Products
- 1½ cups buttermilk
- ¾ cup margarine *or* butter
- 5 eggs
- ½ cup shredded cheddar cheese
- Dairy sour cream*

Fresh Produce
- 1 onion
- 1 carrot
- 1 green pepper
- Leaves from 1 celery stalk
- 2 sprigs parsley
- Green onions*

Packaged and Canned Goods
- 2 packages quick-rising active dry yeast
- 1 49½-ounce can chicken broth
- 1 14½-ounce can chicken broth
- 1 14½-ounce can stewed tomatoes
- 1 10-ounce package frozen cut okra
- 1 5½-ounce can tomato juice
- ½ pound dry black beans
- ½ of a 16-ounce package loose-pack frozen mixed vegetables
- 1 12-ounce can evaporated milk
- ¾ cup packaged spaetzle

Staples
- All-purpose and whole wheat flours
- Bay leaf and dried dillweed
- Bottled hot pepper sauce
- Bottled minced garlic
- Cooking oil and shortening
- Ground red pepper
- Poppy seed, sesame seed, and fines herbes
- Quick-cooking tapioca
- Rice*
- Rolled oats
- Sugar and salt
- Whole black peppercorns and cloves
- Worcestershire sauce

*You'll need these ingredients when you serve the soups.

9:25 START COOKING
OK, time to start on Hock 'n' Bean Soup. In the colander, rinse beans. In a 3-quart saucepan bring beans and water to boiling.

As beans come to boiling, make bouquet garni (see photo A) for Basic Soup Stock (see recipe, *page 144*).

A. For bouquet garni, tie the seasonings in cheesecloth.

When beans boil, reduce heat and simmer 2 minutes. Remove from heat. Cover and let stand for 1 hour.

In a 4½-quart Dutch oven combine all ingredients for Basic Soup Stock; bring to boiling. Cover and simmer for 30 minutes.

9:35 MIX YEAST DOUGH
With the stock and a soup underway, move right on to the breads. In a large mixer bowl mix up Basic Yeast Dough (see recipe, *page 144*). Turn on your oven; raise bread dough as recipe directs (see photo B).

B. To speed-raise dough, place in a briefly preheated oven 20 minutes.

9:50 GET SET FOR GUMBO
Back to soups; start another! In 2-quart saucepan cook flour-oil mixture for Seafood Gumbo (see photo C). Stir in tomatoes, tomato juice, okra, and red pepper. Set aside.

C. For Seafood Gumbo, cook flour-oil mixture till golden brown.

10:05 SHAPE 2 BREADS
Stir down Basic Yeast Dough; divide into thirds and chill one portion. Shape the Crusty Oat Bread (see photo D). Cover and chill. Shape Brown 'n' Serve Cloverleaves; let rolls rise 10 to 15 minutes while you preheat your oven to 325°.

D. For Crusty Oat Bread, shape a 6-inch dough circle; slash top.

10:25 STRAIN STOCK; COOL
You're half done! Remove the pork hocks from Basic Soup Stock; cool. Remove bouquet garni and discard. Strain Basic Soup Stock over a large container, reserving vegetables. Go ahead, sample the tasty broth you've made!

10:35 FINISH GUMBO

Add *one-third* of the Basic Soup Stock to Seafood Gumbo in pan. Bring to boiling; reduce heat. Cover; simmer 15 minutes. Remove from heat; cool. One soup down!

Meanwhile, bake Brown 'n' Serve Cloverleaves; cool on a wire rack. One bread down!

During simmering and baking, fill Cheese Twist (see photo E). Shape, cover, and let rise 20 to 25 minutes.

E. For Cheese Twist, sprinkle cheese down center of the two 14x5-inch dough rectangles.

The black beans for Hock 'n' Bean Soup should have finished soaking for 60 minutes by now. Drain them into the colander.

10:50 SIMMER BEAN SOUP

Remove and cut up meat from smoked pork hocks (see photo F). Discard bones.

F. Remove as much meat as you can from pork hock bones. Use meat in Hock 'n' Bean Soup.

In the 3-quart saucepan combine ingredients for Hock 'n' Bean Soup. Bring to boiling; reduce heat. Cover and simmer 1 hour. Cool. You're coming around to the home stretch!

11:00 CHOWDER TIME

In a blender grind tapioca for Chicken Spaetzle Chowder (see photo G). Remove and set aside.

G. Blend tapioca, covered, till finely ground. This will thicken Chicken Spaetzle Chowder.

In same blender container puree vegetables from Basic Soup Stock (see photo H). In a 2-quart freezer container combine all ingredients for Chicken Spaetzle Chowder. Seal, label, and freeze. Two soups down!

H. Puree vegetables from Basic Soup Stock in blender.

11:10 BAKE MORE BREAD

Bake Cheese Twist; cool. Meanwhile, tidy up your kitchen. When Cheese Twist has 10 minutes of

baking left, remove Crusty Oat Bread from refrigerator; let stand at room temperature on counter.

11:30 FREEZE YOUR WORK

Place Seafood Gumbo in 2-quart freezer container. Seal; label. Freeze. Puncture air bubbles in Crusty Oat Bread; bake bread. Cool. When breads cool, wrap in freezer wrap (see photo I). Seal; label. Freeze.

I. Fold edges of wrap in a series of locked folds. Crease ends; seal.

When Hock 'n' Bean Soup cools, place in 1½-quart freezer container. Seal, label, and freeze (see photo J).

J. Apply lid to container, pressing out air. Date and label contents.

12:00 YOU'RE DONE!

Congratulations! You're ready for hectic days.

BASIC SOUP STOCK

Use this simple, flavorful stock to make the three soups on the following pages: Hock 'n' Bean Soup, Seafood Gumbo, and Chicken Spaetzle Chowder—

Leaves from 1 celery stalk *or* ½ teaspoon celery seed
2 sprigs parsley
4 whole cloves
4 whole black peppercorns
1 bay leaf
1 49½-ounce can chicken broth
1 14½-ounce can chicken broth
2 smoked pork hocks *or* one meaty ham bone (about 1 to 1¼ pounds total)
1 medium onion, quartered
1 medium carrot, cut up
1½ teaspoons bottled minced garlic

For bouquet garni, place the celery leaves or celery seed, parsley sprigs, cloves, black peppercorns, and bay leaf in the center of an 8-inch square of several layers of cheesecloth. Bring edges together; tie with string (see photo A, page 142).

In a 4½-quart Dutch oven combine bouquet garni, all of the chicken broth, smoked pork hocks or meaty ham bone, onion, carrot, and garlic. Bring to boiling; reduce heat. Cover and simmer about 30 minutes or till meat is tender. Remove the smoked pork hocks or meaty ham bone and cool.

When cool enough to handle, remove meat from bones. Chop meat and discard bones (see photo F, page 143). Reserve meat for Hock 'n' Bean Soup. Remove bouquet garni and discard. Drain stock in a colander, reserving vegetables. Place vegetables in a blender container or food processor bowl (see photo H, page 143). Cover and blend or process till pureed. Reserve pureed vegetables for Chicken Spaetzle Chowder. Makes about 7 cups stock.

BASIC YEAST DOUGH

Use this fast-rising bread dough to make the following three breads: Crusty Oat Bread, Brown 'n' Serve Cloverleaves, and Cheese Twist—

3¼ cups all-purpose flour
2 packages quick-rising active dry yeast
1½ cups buttermilk
¾ cup margarine *or* butter
½ cup sugar
½ teaspoon salt
5 eggs
3½ cups whole wheat flour

In a large mixer bowl stir together the all-purpose flour and yeast. In 1½-quart saucepan heat the buttermilk, margarine or butter, sugar, and salt just till warm (120° to 130°) and the margarine or butter is almost melted, stirring constantly. Add to the flour mixture along with *4* of the eggs and 1 *egg yolk* (reserve the remaining egg white for use later).

Beat with an electric mixer on low speed for ½ minute. Beat on high speed for 3 minutes. Stir in whole wheat flour to make a soft dough.

Place the dough in a greased oven-proof bowl; grease the top of the dough lightly. Cover the dough with waxed paper. Turn the oven to 200° for *1 minute* for an electric oven, *2 minutes* for a gas oven. Turn the oven off. *Quickly* place the covered bowl of dough in the oven; close the door (see photo B, page 142). Let rise till dough is nearly double (20 to 25 minutes).

Stir dough down (it will be sticky). Divide the dough into thirds (about 1¼ pounds each). Return *one* portion to the bowl for Cheese Twist; cover and chill while shaping Crusty Oat Bread and Brown 'n' Serve Cloverleaves.

Microwave directions: To test your microwave oven for raising yeast bread dough, place 2 tablespoons cold *stick margarine* in a microwave-safe custard cup in the center of the microwave oven cavity. Micro-cook, uncovered, on 10% power (low) for 4 minutes. If the margarine is *not* completely melted, you can use your microwave oven to raise yeast bread dough.

In a large mixer bowl combine all-purpose flour and yeast. Cut margarine into chunks. In a 4-cup glass measure combine margarine, buttermilk, sugar, and salt. Micro-cook, uncovered, on

100% power (high) for 2 to 2¼ minutes or till margarine is almost melted, stirring once. Add to flour mixture along with *four* of the eggs and 1 *egg yolk* (reserve the remaining egg white for use later). Beat with an electric mixer on low speed for ½ minute. Beat on high speed for 3 minutes. Stir in whole wheat flour to make a soft dough.

In a 4-cup glass measure micro-cook 3 cups *water*, uncovered, on high for 6 to 8 minutes or till boiling. Set water to the side in the oven. Place dough in a greased microwave-safe mixing bowl; cover loosely with waxed paper. Cook on 10% power (low) to 7 minutes or till double. Stir down (dough will be sticky). Divide as directed.

Tips for Freezing Soups and Breads

For successful freezing, keep these hints in mind.

● Maintain your freezer temperature at 0°F or lower. (Use a freezer thermometer to check it.) These low temperatures help maintain the best color, flavor, and texture in your food.

● Label each package you place in the freezer with the date and contents so you'll know what's in it months later.

● When you add food to the freezer, keep the packages separate until they're frozen solid. This allows cold air to circulate around the packages.

Soups

● It's best to undercook the vegetables slightly before freezing. They'll become tender as you reheat the soup.

● Some seasonings and vegetables, such as green pepper and garlic, become more intense with freezing. You may want to cut down on the amount of these that you normally add to a soup or simply add them after freezing.

● Cool soups before placing in a freezer container. Placing a pan of hot soup in an ice-water bath can cool it to room temperature quickly.

● Freeze soups up to six months.

Breads

● Bake breads as usual, then cool completely before wrapping for freezing. If you wrap your bread warm, it may become soggy.

● Wait to frost sweet breads after freezing and thawing.

● Thaw yeast breads, loosely covered, at room temperature. A loose covering lets some moisture from freezing escape without the bread drying out.

● Freeze breads four to eight months.

HOCK 'N' BEAN SOUP

- **½ pound dry black beans (1¼ cups)**
- **3 cups water**
- **⅓ recipe (about 2⅓ cups) Basic Soup Stock (see recipe, page 144)**
- **2 cups hot water**
- **Meat from Basic Soup Stock's smoked pork hocks (1 cup)**
- **1 tablespoon Worcestershire sauce**
- **¼ to ½ teaspoon bottled hot pepper sauce**
- **Dairy sour cream**
- **Sliced green onion**

In a colander rinse beans. In a 3-quart saucepan combine beans and 3 cups water. Bring to boiling; reduce heat. Simmer for 2 minutes. Remove from heat. Cover; let stand for 1 hour.

Drain beans. In the same saucepan combine beans, Basic Soup Stock, 2 cups hot water, smoked pork hock meat, Worcestershire sauce, and hot pepper sauce. Bring to boiling; reduce heat. Cover and simmer for 1 hour or till beans are tender.

Cool. Transfer to a 1½-quart freezer container. Seal, label, and freeze up to 6 months (see photo J, page 143).

Stove-top reheating: Transfer frozen mixture to a 3-quart saucepan. Cover and cook over medium heat for 15 to 20 minutes or till thawed, stirring occasionally to break up frozen chunks. Cook over high heat about 10 minutes or till bubbly, stirring occasionally. Mash beans slightly. Top each serving with sour cream and green onion. Makes 4 servings.

Microwave reheating: Transfer frozen mixture to a 2-quart microwave-safe casserole. Micro-cook, covered, on 70% power (medium-high) for 15 to 17 minutes or till thawed, stirring twice to break up frozen chunks. Cook, covered, on 100% power (high) for 10 to 12 minutes more or till heated through. Mash beans slightly. Serve as directed.

Nutrition information per serving: 276 cal., 23 g pro., 38 g carbo., 3 g fat, 19 mg chol., 949 mg sodium, 7 g fiber. U.S. RDA: 49% thiamine, 13% riboflavin, 24% niacin, 25% iron, and 37% phosphorus.

SEAFOOD GUMBO

For those with brave taste buds, pass the bottled hot pepper sauce—

- **1 medium green pepper, chopped**
- **2 tablespoons cooking oil**
- **2 tablespoons all-purpose flour**
- **⅓ recipe (about 2⅓ cups) Basic Soup Stock (see recipe, page 144)**
- **1 14½-ounce can stewed tomatoes**
- **1 10-ounce package frozen cut okra**
- **1 5½-ounce can tomato juice**
- **¼ to ½ teaspoon ground red pepper**
- **1 8-ounce package frozen peeled and deveined shrimp**
- **1 8-ounce package frozen salad-style crab-flavored fish**
- **2 cups hot cooked rice**

In a 2-quart saucepan cook green pepper in hot oil about 3 minutes or till tender. Stir in flour. Cook, stirring constantly, over medium heat about 3 minutes or till mixture is golden brown (see photo C, page 142).

Stir in Basic Soup Stock, *undrained* tomatoes, okra, tomato juice, and red pepper. Bring to boiling; reduce heat. Cover and simmer for 15 minutes. Remove from heat. Cool.

Spoon the soup into a 2-quart freezer container. Seal, label, and freeze for up to 6 months.

Stove-top reheating: Transfer frozen mixture to a 3-quart saucepan. Cover and cook over medium-low heat about 30 minutes or till thawed, stirring occasionally and breaking up frozen chunks. Add shrimp and crab-flavored fish. Cook, covered, over high heat till boiling; reduce heat. Simmer, covered, for 3 to 5 minutes more or till shrimp turn pink, stirring occasionally. Serve over rice.

Microwave reheating: Transfer frozen mixture to a 3-quart microwave-safe casserole. Micro-cook, covered, on 70% power (medium-high) for 13 to 15 minutes or till thawed, stirring twice to break up frozen chunks. Add shrimp and crab-flavored fish. Cook, covered, on 100% power (high) for 15 to 20 minutes more or till the shrimp turn pink and mixture is heated through, stirring after 10 minutes. Serve the gumbo over hot cooked rice.

To serve immediately: Prepare and simmer the soup for 15 minutes as directed. Add shrimp and crab-flavored fish; return to boiling. Simmer, covered, for 3 to 5 minutes or till the shrimp turn pink. Serve over rice. Makes 4 servings.

Nutrition information per serving: 399 cal., 31 g pro., 44 g carbo., 11 g fat, 136 mg chol., 1,059 mg sodium, 4 g dietary fiber. U.S. RDA: 40% vit. A, 80% vit. C, 24% thiamine, 15% riboflavin, 42% niacin, 17% calcium, 26% iron, 36% phosphorus.

CRUSTY OAT BREAD

So quick and easy! Take 2 to 3 minutes to shape the round, then stash it in the refrigerator to rise unattended—

- **⅓ recipe Basic Yeast Dough (see recipe, page 144)**
- **1 egg white (reserved from Basic Yeast Dough)**
- **1 tablespoon water**
- **Rolled oats**

On a greased baking sheet shape Basic Yeast Dough into a 6-inch round loaf. With a sharp knife, gently cut a large shallow cross in the top of the loaf (see photo D, page 142).

Stir together egg white and water; lightly brush over loaf. (Reserve remaining egg white mixture for Brown 'n' Serve Cloverleaves and Cheese Twist.) Sprinkle round loaf with oats. Cover loosely with clear plastic wrap. Chill dough in the refrigerator for 1 to 2 hours or till double.

To bake, let loaf stand at room temperature for 10 minutes. Carefully puncture any air bubbles on surface with a pin or wooden toothpick. Bake in a 325° oven for 25 to 30 minutes or till loaf sounds hollow when tapped. Cool on a wire rack. Wrap in moisture- and vaporproof wrap. Seal, label, and freeze for up to 8 months.

To serve: Partially uncover frozen loaf and let stand at room temperature several hours or till thawed. (Or, wrap frozen loaf in foil. Place in a 300° oven for 30 to 40 minutes or till warm.) Makes 1 loaf, 16 servings.

Nutrition information per serving: 108 cal., 3 g pro., 16 g carbo., 4 g fat, 29 mg chol., 71 mg sodium, and 1 g dietary fiber.

CHICKEN SPAETZLE CHOWDER

The tapioca, which looks like translucent beads after cooking, helps thicken and stabilize the chowder during freezing. If you don't have tapioca, see the note below on how to thicken the chowder with cornstarch after thawing—

- ½ of a 16-ounce package (2½ cups) loose-pack frozen mixed vegetables
- ⅓ recipe (about 2⅓ cups) Basic Soup Stock (see recipe, page 144)
- 1 12-ounce can (1½ cups) evaporated milk
- 1½ cups chopped cooked chicken *or* turkey
- ¾ cup packaged spaetzle *or* tiny shell macaroni
   Pureed vegetables from Basic Soup Stock
- 2 tablespoons quick-cooking tapioca, finely ground (see photo G, page 143)
- 1 teaspoon dried dillweed
- 1 cup water

In a 2-quart freezer container combine frozen mixed vegetables, Basic Soup Stock, evaporated milk, chicken or turkey, spaetzle or macaroni, pureed vegetables from Basic Soup Stock, tapioca, and dillweed. Seal, label, and freeze up to 6 months.

Stove-top reheating: Transfer frozen mixture to a 3-quart saucepan. Add water. Cover and cook over medium heat for 25 minutes, stirring occasionally to break up frozen chunks. Increase heat to medium-high; cook about 5 minutes more or till mixture is heated through and spaetzle is tender.

Microwave reheating: Transfer the frozen mixture to a 3-quart microwave-safe casserole. Cover and micro-cook on 70% power (medium-high) for 35 to 40 minutes or till thawed, stirring every 10 minutes to break up frozen chunks. Add water. Cook, covered, on 100% power (high) for 5 to 7 minutes more or till heated through and spaetzle is tender, stirring once.

To serve immediately: In a 3-quart saucepan combine the mixed vegetables, Basic Soup Stock, evaporated milk, chicken or turkey, pureed vegetables, tapioca, dillweed, and water. Bring to boiling, stirring occasionally.

Add spaetzle. Reduce heat. Simmer, covered, for 12 to 15 minutes or till spaetzle is tender, stirring occasionally. Makes 4 servings.

Note: If desired, omit the tapioca and thicken with cornstarch when you thaw and heat the frozen mixture. (If you would freeze cornstarch in the mixture, it would break down and lose its ability to thicken.) Here's how: In a 2-quart freezer container combine all ingredients *except* tapioca and water. Seal, label, and freeze up to 6 months.

To serve, add water and heat through on stove top as directed. Stir together ¼ cup *water* and 2 tablespoons *cornstarch;* stir into heated chowder. Cook and stir till thickened and bubbly. Cook and stir for 2 minutes more. (Or, thaw chowder in the microwave as directed. Stir 2 tablespoons *cornstarch* into the 1 cup water; stir into thawed chowder. Micro-cook on 100% power (high) for 10 to 12 minutes or till thickened and bubbly, stirring every 2 minutes. Cook on high for 1 minute more.)

Nutrition information per serving: 397 cal., 30 g pro., 40 g carbo., 13 g fat, 75 mg chol., 656 mg sodium, 3 g dietary fiber. U.S. RDA: 164% vit. A, 13% vit. C, 24% thiamine, 33% riboflavin, 46% niacin, 30% calcium, 14% iron, 42% phosphorus.

BROWN 'N' SERVE CLOVERLEAVES

If your family is a twosome or threesome, wrap the rolls in small batches so you can thaw and bake a few at a time—

- ⅓ recipe Basic Yeast Dough (see recipe, page 144)
   Sesame seed, poppy seed, *or* dried fines herbes

Lightly grease 12 muffin cups or spray with nonstick spray coating.

On a lightly floured surface divide Basic Yeast Dough into 36 pieces. Shape each into a ball. Place *three* balls in *each* muffin cup. Brush with egg white mixture reserved from Crusty Oat Bread. Sprinkle with sesame seed, poppy seed, or fines herbes.

Cover and let rise in a warm place till rolls double (10 to 15 minutes).

Bake in a 325° oven for 10 minutes (rolls will not be brown). Remove rolls from muffin cups. Cool on a wire rack.

To wrap rolls for freezing, cut a piece of freezer wrap large enough to go around rolls 1½ times. Place rolls in center of wrap; bring opposite edges of wrap together. Fold edges down in series of locked folds (see photo I, page 143). Press wrap against rolls to press out air. Crease ends into points; fold up to center. Seal with freezer tape. Label and freeze up to 8 months.

To serve: Partially uncover rolls; let stand at room temperature for 15 minutes. Uncover; place on ungreased baking sheet. Bake in a 400° oven for 10 minutes or till brown. Serve warm. Makes 12 rolls.

Nutrition information per roll: 142 cal., 4 g pro., 20 g carbo., 5 g fat, 38 mg chol., 95 mg sodium, 1 g dietary fiber.

CHEESE TWIST

Shave time from your preparation by buying preshredded cheese—

- ⅓ recipe Basic Yeast Dough (see recipe, page 144)
- ½ cup shredded cheddar cheese

On a lightly floured surface roll Basic Yeast Dough into a 14x10-inch rectangle. Cut into two 14x5-inch rectangles. Sprinkle ¼ *cup* of the cheese lengthwise down the center of *each* rectangle (see photo E, page 143). Bring the long edges of each rectangle together over the cheese; pinch all edges together to seal. Place the ropes side by side, seam side down, on a greased baking sheet. Twist ropes together; secure ends. Cover and let rise in a warm place till double (20 to 25 minutes).

Brush with remaining egg white mixture from the Crusty Oat Bread. Bake in a 325° oven for 25 to 30 minutes or till golden. Remove from the baking sheet and cool completely on a wire rack. Wrap in moisture- and vaporproof wrap. Seal with freezer tape. Label and freeze up to 8 months.

To serve: Partially uncover frozen loaf and let stand at room temperature for several hours or till thawed. (Or, wrap frozen loaf in foil. Place in a 300° oven for 30 to 40 minutes or till warm.) Makes 1 loaf (16 servings).

Nutrition information per serving: 120 cal., 4 g pro., 15 g carbo., 5 g fat, 32 mg chol., 93 mg sodium, and 1 g dietary fiber.

NOVEMBER

THE MAGAZINE FOR AMERICAN FAMILIES

NOVEMBER 1987
$1.50

Better Homes
and Gardens

**Elegant-but-Easy
Thanksgiving Dinner**

• Simplified Recipes
• Step-by-Step How-To

**Good Cook's
Almanac**

**Home
Improvement
Contest
Winners**

CRANBERRIES!

NOW'S PRIME TIME TO ENJOY THESE TANGY, RUBY RED JEWELS IN NEW WAYS

By Barbara Greenwood

EASY FILLED-LADDER LOAF

Serve one loaf now, freeze the other for later. Just omit brushing milk and sugar over the loaf you plan to store—

- 1 **cup milk**
- 2 **tablespoons butter** *or* **margarine**
- 1 **16-ounce package hot roll mix**
- 1 **teaspoon apple pie spice**
- 1 **slightly beaten egg**

• • •

- 1 **cup Cranberry-Tangerine Conserve (recipe at right)**
- ½ **cup coconut**

Milk

Sugar

● **Grease two baking sheets;** set aside. In a small saucepan heat milk and butter or margarine, stirring constantly till warm (115° to 120°) and butter or margarine is almost melted; set aside.

● **In a large mixing bowl combine** flour mixture and yeast from roll mix with apple pie spice. Add milk mixture and egg. Mix till combined and dough pulls away from sides of bowl. Turn out onto a lightly floured surface; knead for 5 minutes or till smooth. Halve dough. Cover and let rest for 10 minutes.

● **On a floured surface, roll** *half* of the dough to a 12x10-inch rectangle. Transfer to a baking sheet. In a small mixing bowl combine Cranberry-Tangerine Conserve and coconut; spread *half* of the mixture lengthwise down center third of dough. Make 3-inch-long cuts at 1-inch intervals on both long sides. Fold strips diagonally over filling, overlapping strips. Brush dough strips with a little milk and lightly sprinkle with sugar. Repeat with remaining dough and conserve mixture for a second loaf. Cover; let rise till nearly double (30 to 45 minutes).

● **Bake loaves** in a 350° oven for 25 to 35 minutes or till done, covering with foil after 20 minutes to prevent over-browning. Makes 2 loaves, about 12 servings each.

Nutrition information per serving: *126 cal., 3 g pro., 23 g carbo., 3 g fat, 16 mg chol., 152 mg sodium.*

CRANBERRY-TANGERINE CONSERVE

A pretty spread that's just right for gift-giving. Personalize each jar with a label and ribbon-tied fabric over the lid. Tie the recipe for the bread to the jar—

- 3 **or 4 tangerines** *or* **tangelos**
- 2 **cups water**

• • •

- 1 **12-ounce package (3 cups) cranberries**

• • •

- 1 **1¾-ounce package powdered fruit pectin**
- 6½ **cups sugar**
- 1 **cup chopped walnuts**

● **Remove peels** from tangerines or tangelos; scrape off excess white membrane from inner peel with a sharp knife or vegetable peeler. Cut peels into very thin strips. Reserve ¾ *cup* peel strips; discard remaining. In a 6-quart kettle or Dutch oven combine peels and water. Bring to boiling; reduce heat. Cover and simmer for 10 minutes. *Do not drain.*

● **Meanwhile, remove** any white membrane from tangerine or tangelo fruit. Chop tangerines or tangelos, reserving juices; discard seeds. You should have 1⅓ *cups* chopped fruit. Add chopped fruit, reserved juices, and cranberries to the peel mixture. Return to boiling; reduce heat. Simmer, covered, for 10 minutes.

● **Uncover; stir in pectin.** Bring to boiling; stir in sugar. Bring to a full rolling boil; boil hard for 1 minute, stirring constantly. Stir in walnuts. Remove from heat; skim off foam.

● **Ladle** into hot, clean half-pint jars, leaving a ¼-inch headspace. Wipe jar rims; adjust lids. Process in a boiling water bath for 15 minutes (start this timing when the water boils). Makes 8 half pints of conserve.

Nutrition information per 2 teaspoons: *32 cal., 0 g pro., 7 g carbo., 0 g fat, 0 mg chol., 0 mg sodium.*

CRANBERRY-TANGERINE CONSERVE
A conserve is simply a jam with crunchy nuts added.

EASY FILLED-LADDER LOAF
Here's just one delightful way to savor this conserve.

AN ELEGANT THANKSGIVING
MADE EASY

By Lynn Hoppe

TERRIFIC TURKEY
THREE SCRUMPTIOUS STUFFING CHOICES

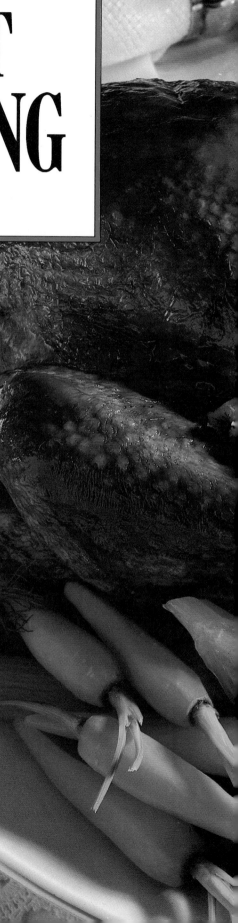

▲ **TURKEY WITH SAUSAGE-RICE STUFFING**

Apples, raisins, carrots, and Polish sausage accent this easy-fix stuffing.

TURKEY WITH CHESTNUT-FIG STUFFING

Treat yourself to seconds of this festive, chunky corn bread stuffing. It's loaded with figs, chestnuts, and mandarin oranges.

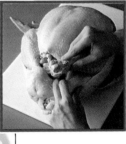

◄ TUCK IN DRUMSTICKS

Tuck the ends of the turkey drumsticks under the band of skin across the tail. No band of skin on your turkey? Tie the legs securely to the tail with string. This will help your bird hold its shape.

◄ TWIST WING TIPS UNDER

Pull the neck skin to the back of the bird. Then, twist the wing tips under the back to hold the neck skin in place. Now you're ready to roast your turkey to perfection.

◄ TURKEY WITH FENNEL-SEAFOOD STUFFING

Snip feathery fennel leaves to season the delectable crab and shrimp stuffing. Then, steam the licoricelike fennel bulb as a delicious vegetable side dish.

SIDE DISHES
MAKE THEM AHEAD FOR A NO-FUSS FEAST

▲ USE CABBAGE LEAVES AS LINERS

With a small sharp knife cut the core from a small head of cabbage. Remove eight of the large outer leaves to use as liners for the vegetable mixture.

▲ HARVEST VEGETABLES WITH EDAM CHEESE

So you can enjoy the good company when your guests arrive, get this creamy cabbage and potato side dish oven-ready on the eve of the feast.

▲ LINE THE MOLD

Sprinkle the sides, not the bottom, of greased molds with an almond-parsley mixture. Fill the molds with the pureed vegetables. Then, chill the vegetable mousses for up to 24 hours.

▲ CARROT-PARSNIP MOUSSE

These individual molds of hot pureed vegetables with a whisper of orange-nutmeg sweetness are a delightful accompaniment to baked ham.

▲ SHAPE BREAD BRAID

Shape the braided dough into a figure eight around balls of foil; tuck ends under in center. Let rise; bake, then freeze till needed.

▲ DRIZZLE SOUP WITH CREAM

Here's an elegant and easy dinner idea: Just before dinner, drizzle parallel lines of cream on individual servings of soup. Draw a knife through lines to make points.

◄ PUMPKIN-MUSHROOM SOUP; WILD RICE BRAID

Let the feast begin with this warm and rich, tradition steeped pumpkin soup. For a perfect complement to the creamy, savory soup, serve a knot of this classy, crisp-crusted bread speckled with wild rice and sweet chunks of apple.

GLORIOUS PIES
HOW TO ADD FESTIVE FLAIR

▲ **PIECE TOGETHER PHYLLO CUPS**

Layer and cut thawed phyllo dough into 18 strips. Cover the bottom of six greased custard cups with the strips of phyllo dough.

▲ APRICOT-APPLE TARTS

An ultraflaky crust made from frozen phyllo dough cradles the tangy fruit filling. Topped with ice cream, these pie cups are simple to make, hard to match.

▲ **SHIELD FOR PERFECT BROWNING**

For a just-right, golden-brown crust, cut an 8-inch circle from the center of a piece of foil. Drop foil over center of pie, covering edges with the foil.

▲ GINGERBERRY LATTICE PIE

Showcase this sweet-tart cranberry and pineapple pie in a herringbone variation on the lattice-topped pie. See how it's done on *page 156.*

▲ DECORATE EDGE WITH CUTOUTS
Use a miniature cutter or knife to cut shapes from rolled-out dough scraps. Brush pie edge with water. Arrange cutouts around edge.

▲ DRIZZLE CARAMELIZED SUGAR ATOP FLAN
Just before you bring the flan to the table, use a spoon to drizzle caramelized sugar back and forth over top of flan.

CHOCOLATE-PRALINE PIE; CARAMEL-PEAR FLAN

Give your family a delectable choice—the velvety custard flan with a caramel gossamer or the chunky, chocolaty pecan pie. Better yet, offer a sliver of each.

For pastry-making tips, see page 156.

PICTURE-PERFECT PASTRY

HOW-TO TIPS FROM AN EXPERT PIE BAKER

"I love making pies. It's the most fun and creative kind of baking there is."

"I've talked to a lot of people about pie baking and the problem they most often have is getting a dough that's neither too dry nor too wet for rolling out. My advice: Take a few minutes to practice. Get a feel for how much liquid (since most recipes give a range on liquid) you should add. If the dough doesn't seem right, I'd suggest that you just start over. After all, the ingredients for the crust are the least expensive part of the pie."

— Janet Herwig
Better Homes and Gardens
Food Stylist

For more pastry helps, see page 161.

QUICK LATTICE
Use a miniature cutter to make a cutout in center of dough. Repeat cuts in a regular pattern, working from center to edge.

ROPE-SHAPE EDGE
Pinch dough around edge of pie, pushing forward on slant with bent finger and pulling with thumb. Repeat around pie.

DOTTED PASTRY TOP
Use a toothpick or wooden skewer to prick a design in the top crust of a filled unbaked pie. Seal edge with tines of a fork.

SCALLOP FLUTE WITH VARIATIONS

BASIC SCALLOP
Place thumb flat against inside edge of a pie shell. Press dough around thumb using thumb and index finger of other hand.

RICKRACK VARIATION
Make a basic scallop, fluting as directed at left. Using your fingers, pinch the edge of each scallop to form a point.

FLOWER PETAL VARIATION
Make a scallop, fluting as directed at left. Press fork tines lightly in center of each scallop.

HERRINGBONE LATTICE

1. ROLL OUT DOUGH for top crust of a double-crust pie and use a fluted pastry wheel to cut into ½-inch strips. Arrange two strips in center of pie.

2. ARRANGE PASTRY STRIPS to form a small square in center of pie. Begin a second, larger square ½ inch from the first square.

3. CONTINUE PLACING STRIPS to form progressively larger squares. Trim pastry. Fold strips under bottom pastry to make a smooth raised edge. Flute.

Turkey and Stuffings

TURKEY WITH SAUSAGE-RICE STUFFING

    1 6-ounce package long grain and
       wild rice mix
    1 cup bulgur
    1 pound fully cooked Polish
       sausage *or* fully cooked
       boneless ham
    2 large apples, cored and coarsely
       chopped
  ¾   cup raisins
    5 green onions, sliced (½ cup)
    1 carrot, shredded (½ cup)
    2 tablespoons snipped fresh
       parsley
    1 14- to 16-pound turkey
Cooking oil
    1 recipe Pan Gravy for Roast
       Turkey (see recipe, *right*)
    1 recipe Acorn Squash Slices (see
       recipe, *below*) (optional)

In a 3-quart saucepan bring 4 cups *water* to boiling. Stir in rice mix, seasoning packet, and ½ teaspoon *salt*. Return to boiling. Reduce heat. Cover and simmer for 20 minutes. Add bulgur. Return to boiling. Reduce heat. Cover and simmer 5 to 10 minutes more or till bulgur is tender.

Halve sausage lengthwise. Cut into ¼-inch slices. (Or, cut ham into ½-inch pieces.) In a large mixing bowl toss together rice mixture, sausage, apples, raisins, onions, carrot, and parsley.

Stuff turkey as directed *at right*. Transfer remaining stuffing to a 1½-quart casserole; cover and chill.

Place turkey, breast side up, on a rack in a shallow roasting pan. Brush with oil. Insert a meat thermometer in the center of the inside thigh muscle, making sure the bulb does not touch the bone. Cover loosely with foil.

Roast in a 325° oven for 4½ to 5 hours or till thermometer registers 180° to 185°, basting occasionally with juices. Cut band of skin between legs after 3½ hours. Uncover turkey and add remaining stuffing in covered casserole to oven the last 45 minutes of roasting. Remove turkey from oven. Cover loosely with foil. Let stand 15 minutes before carving. Meanwhile, prepare gravy. Serve turkey with gravy and Acorn Squash Slices. Serves 20.

Acorn Squash Slices: Wash 4 *acorn squash;* cut in half crosswise. Remove seeds and strings. Cut each half into 4 or 5 slices. In a large saucepan cook squash in a small amount of boiling salted water for 5 to 7 minutes or till tender. Serve with turkey and stuffing.

Nutrition information per serving: 375 cal., 47 g pro., 16 g carbo., 12 g fat, 155 mg chol., 370 mg sodium, 2 g dietary fiber. U.S. RDA: 16% vit. A, 16% thiamine, 21% riboflavin, 48% niacin, 21% iron, 41% phosphorus.

TURKEY WITH CHESTNUT-FIG STUFFING

    1 pound dried light figs, snipped
Boiling water
    1 cup sliced leek *or* chopped onion
  ½   cup chopped green pepper
  ½   cup margarine *or* butter
    1 10-ounce jar whole chestnuts, *or*
       1¼ cups coarsely chopped
       pecans
    1 11-ounce can mandarin orange
       sections, drained
  ¼   cup snipped fresh parsley *or* 4
       teaspoons dried parsley flakes
    1 teaspoon dried thyme, crushed
  ¼   teaspoon ground red pepper
  4½ cups corn bread stuffing mix
  1½ to 2 cups chicken broth
    1 14- to 16-pound turkey
Cooking oil
    1 recipe Pan Gravy for Roast
       Turkey (see recipe, *right*)
       (optional)

Place figs in bowl; cover with boiling water. Let stand for 10 minutes. Drain well. In a medium skillet cook leek or onion, and green pepper in hot margarine or butter till leek is tender but not brown. Drain and chop chestnuts.

In a large bowl combine figs, leek mixture, chestnuts, orange sections, parsley, thyme, red pepper, and 1 teaspoon *salt*. Stir in stuffing mix. Toss with enough broth to moisten.

Stuff turkey as directed *at right*. Transfer remaining stuffing to a 1-quart casserole; cover and chill.

Place turkey, breast side up, on a rack in a shallow roasting pan. Brush with oil. Insert a meat thermometer in the center of the inside thigh muscle, making sure the bulb does not touch bone. Cover loosely with foil.

Roast in a 325° oven for 4½ to 5 hours or till thermometer registers 180° to 185°, basting occasionally with juices. Cut band of skin between legs after 3½ hours. Uncover turkey and add remaining stuffing in covered casserole to the oven the last 45 minutes of roasting. Remove turkey from oven. Cover loosely with foil. Let stand 15 minutes before carving. Meanwhile, prepare pan gravy. Pass with turkey. Makes 20 servings.

Nutrition information per serving: 486 cal., 48 g pro., 41 g carbo., 14 g fat, 140 mg chol., 756 mg sodium, 5 g dietary fiber. U.S. RDA: 12% vit. C, 18% thiamine, 26% riboflavin, 51% niacin, 11% calcium, 26% iron, 46% phosphorus.

PAN GRAVY FOR ROAST TURKEY

Hot drippings from roast turkey
  ¼   cup all-purpose flour
Water *or* chicken broth

Keep turkey warm while preparing gravy. Leaving crusty bits in the roasting pan, pour pan drippings into a large measuring cup. Skim off and reserve fat from drippings. (To skim the fat from the drippings, tilt the measuring cup and spoon off the oily liquid on the top.) Return *¼ cup* of the fat to the roasting pan. Discard remaining fat.

Stir flour into fat in pan. Cook and stir over medium heat till bubbly. Remove pan from heat. Add enough water or broth to drippings in measuring cup to equal *2 cups* total liquid. Add all at once to flour mixture in pan. Cook and stir till thickened and bubbly. Cook and stir 1 minute more. Season to taste with *salt* and *pepper*. Makes 2 cups.

Nutrition information per 2 tablespoons gravy: 37 cal., 0 g pro., 2 g carbo., 4 g fat, 0 mg chol., and 0 mg sodium.

Stuffing a Turkey

First, rinse off the turkey and pat it dry with paper towels. Sprinkle a little salt inside the turkey, if you like. Then, spoon some stuffing into the neck cavity. Skewer the neck skin to the back. Next, spoon some stuffing into the body cavity. Tuck the drumsticks under the tail skin (see photo, *page 151*). Twist the wing tips under (see photo, *page 151*).

TURKEY WITH FENNEL-SEAFOOD STUFFING

To prepare the light stuffing shown on the cover, use the frozen crab-meat-and-shrimp combination available in your grocer's freezer case. Or, use a 6-ounce package of frozen crab meat plus an 8-ounce package of frozen shrimp—

- 10 **cups French bread cubes (½-inch pieces)**
- 2 **6-ounce packages frozen crab meat with shrimp**
- 1 **large onion, chopped (1 cup)**
- 1 **medium red *or* green sweet pepper, chopped (¾ cup)**
- 3 **tablespoons margarine *or* butter**
- 3 **beaten eggs**
- 1 **10¾-ounce can condensed cream of shrimp soup**
- ¼ **to ½ cup milk**
- ½ **cup fresh snipped fennel leaves *or* ½ teaspoon fennel seed, crushed**
- ½ **teaspoon pepper**
- 1 **14- to 16-pound turkey**
- 1 **recipe Fennel Butter (see recipe, *right*) or cooking oil**
- 1 **recipe Pan Gravy for Roast Turkey (see recipe, *page 157*) (optional)**
- 1 **recipe Seasonal Vegetables (see recipe, *right*) (optional)**

Fresh sage *or* fennel leaves (optional)

Spread bread cubes in a shallow baking pan. Bake in a 300° oven for 10 to 15 minutes or till dry, stirring once. Meanwhile, place frozen crab meat with shrimp in a strainer. Run cool water over seafood to thaw.

In a medium skillet cook the onion and sweet pepper in hot margarine or butter till vegetables are tender. In a large mixing bowl stir together the thawed seafood, onion mixture, eggs, soup, ¼ cup of the milk, fennel, and pepper. Stir in the bread cubes till coated. (For a moister stuffing, stir in more of the milk.)

Stuff turkey as directed on *page 157*. Transfer the remaining stuffing to a 1½-quart casserole; cover and chill.

Place turkey, breast side up, on a rack in a shallow roasting pan. Brush with Fennel Butter or oil. Insert a meat thermometer in the center of the inside thigh muscle, making sure bulb does not touch bone. Cover loosely with foil.

Roast in a 325° oven for 4½ to 5 hours or till thermometer registers 180° to 185°, basting occasionally with juices. Cut band of skin between legs after 3½ hours. Uncover turkey and add remaining stuffing in a covered casserole to the oven the last 45 minutes of roasting. Remove turkey from oven. Cover loosely with foil. Let stand 15 minutes before carving.

Meanwhile, prepare the pan gravy. Serve turkey with stuffing, gravy, and Seasonal Vegetables. Garnish with sage or fennel leaves. Serves 20.

Fennel Butter: In a small mixing bowl combine ⅓ cup melted *margarine* or *butter*, 1 tablespoon snipped fresh *fennel leaves,* 1 tablespoon *lemon juice,* and ¾ teaspoon *pepper.*

Seasonal Vegetables: Cut 4 *fennel bulbs* into 4 to 6 wedges. In a large saucepan cook fennel and 1 pound *baby carrots,* covered, in a small amount of boiling water about 10 minutes or till crisp-tender. Serve vegetables with turkey and stuffing.

Nutrition information per serving: 363 cal., 49 g pro., 15 g carbo., 10 g fat, 210 mg chol., and 458 mg sodium. U.S. RDA: 17% vit. A, 16% vit. C, 14% thiamine, 24% riboflavin, 48% niacin, 22% iron, and 43% phosphorus.

HARVEST VEGETABLES WITH EDAM CHEESE

- 1 **small head cabbage (about 1 pound)**
- 1 **12-ounce package frozen loose-pack hash brown potatoes**
- 1 **red *or* green sweet pepper, chopped**
- ¼ **cup sliced green onion**
- ¼ **cup margarine *or* butter**
- ¼ **cup all-purpose flour**
- ¾ **teaspoon dried dillweed**
- ½ **teaspoon salt**
- ¼ **teaspoon pepper**
- 2½ **cups milk**
- ½ **cup shredded Edam cheese (2 ounces)**

Core the cabbage and remove 8 outer leaves (see photo, *page 152*). Wrap leaves in clear plastic wrap; chill. Coarsely chop the remaining cabbage.

In a large mixing bowl toss together the chopped cabbage and potatoes. In a large saucepan with a steamer basket cook *half* of the cabbage mixture, covered, over boiling water for 5 minutes. Remove cabbage and potatoes, and set aside. Repeat with the remaining cabbage mixture.

In a medium saucepan cook sweet pepper and onion in hot margarine or butter about 3 minutes or till vegetables are tender. Stir in flour, dillweed, salt, and pepper. Add milk all at once. Cook and stir over medium heat till thickened and bubbly. Remove from heat. Stir in cheese till melted. In a 2-quart casserole combine cabbage mixture and cheese mixture. Cover and chill up to 24 hours.

To serve, bake cabbage mixture, covered, in a 350° oven about 45 minutes or till potatoes are tender. Let stand 5 minutes.

Meanwhile, in a saucepan cook the reserved cabbage leaves in boiling salted water about 1 minute or till limp. Drain the cabbage leaves well. Arrange the cabbage leaves on individual plates or a serving platter. Spoon cabbage mixture into leaves. Makes 8 servings.

To serve immediately: Prepare vegetables as directed above. In a large saucepan prepare cheese mixture as directed above. Stir vegetables into cheese mixture; heat through. Serve in cabbage leaves as directed above.

Nutrition information per serving: 148 cal., 6 g pro., 11 g carbo., 9 g fat, 12 mg chol., 319 mg sodium, 2 g dietary fiber. U.S. RDA: 32% vit. A, 64% vit. C, 17% calcium, 13% phosphorus.

CARROT-PARSNIP MOUSSE

Pictured on page 147—

1 **pound carrots, thinly sliced**
1½ **cups coarsely chopped parsnips**
3 **eggs**
¼ **cup sour cream dip with chives**
1 **teaspoon finely shredded orange peel**
½ **teaspoon ground nutmeg**
¼ **teaspoon salt**
⅛ **teaspoon pepper**
3 **tablespoons finely chopped almonds**
3 **tablespoons snipped parsley**
Slivered almonds *or* shredded zucchini (optional)

In a large saucepan cook carrots and parsnips in a small amount of boiling water about 15 minutes or till very tender. (Or, in a 2-quart microwave-safe casserole cook carrots and parsnips in ¼ cup *water,* covered, on 100% power (high) for 14 to 16 minutes or till very tender, stirring twice.) Drain carrot-parsnip mixture. Remove *18* carrot slices; set aside.

In a blender container or food processor combine eggs, sour cream dip, orange peel, nutmeg, salt, and pepper. Add *half* of the carrot-parsnip mixture. Cover and blend till nearly smooth. Add remaining carrot-parsnip mixture. Cover and continue blending till smooth. Scrape sides as necessary.

Toss together the chopped almonds and parsley. Grease bottom and sides of six 6-ounce soufflé dishes or custard cups. (If you intend to micro-cook the carrot-parsnip mixture, prepare microwave-safe soufflé dishes or custard cups.) Coat sides with almond-parsley mixture (see photo, *page 152*). Use an hors d'oeuvre cutter to make decorative cutouts from reserved carrots. Arrange 3 cooked carrot slices on the bottom of *each* dish. Spoon carrot-parsnip mixture into prepared dishes. Smooth tops with a spatula. Cover and chill up to 24 hours.

To serve, bake in a 350° oven for 30 to 35 minutes or till a knife inserted near center comes out clean. (Or, arrange soufflé dishes or custard cups in a circle in the microwave oven. Micro-cook, uncovered, on 100% power (high) for 12 to 15 minutes or till a knife inserted near center comes out clean, rotating and rearranging dishes once during cooking.) Let stand 3 minutes. Run knife around edge. Unmold. Sprinkle slivered almonds on serving plate. (Or, arrange on a platter lined with shredded zucchini.) Makes 6 servings.

To serve immediately: Prepare as directed, *except* do not chill. Bake, uncovered, in a 350° oven for 20 to 25 minutes or till a knife inserted near center comes out clean. (Or, arrange soufflé dishes or custard cups in a circle in the microwave oven. Micro-cook, uncovered, on 100% power (high) for 5 to 7 minutes or till a knife inserted near center comes out clean, rotating and rearranging dishes once during cooking.) Let stand 3 minutes. Unmold and serve as directed above.

Nutrition information per serving: 147 cal., 5 g pro., 16 g carbo., 7 g fat, 142 mg chol., 160 mg sodium, 4 g dietary fiber. U.S. RDA: 431% vit. A, 18% vit. C, 11% riboflavin, 14% phosphorus.

QUICK CRANBERRY RELISH

Spruce up canned cranberry sauce with this easy five-ingredient recipe, as featured on page 147—

1 **16-ounce can whole cranberry sauce**
½ **cup chopped walnuts**
½ **cup light raisins**
¼ **teaspoon ground cinnamon**
⅛ **teaspoon ground cloves**
Chopped walnuts (optional)

In a small mixing bowl stir together cranberry sauce, the ½ cup chopped walnuts, raisins, cinnamon, and cloves.

Cover and chill cranberry mixture thoroughly in the refrigerator. Stir relish and sprinkle additional chopped walnuts over relish before serving, if desired. Makes 12 servings.

Nutrition information per ¼ cup: 108 cal., 1 g pro., 21 g carbo., 3 g fat, 0 mg chol., 13 mg sodium.

PUMPKIN-MUSHROOM SOUP

Dried mushrooms add heartiness to this soup pictured on page 147. Look for them in Oriental food shops—

⅓ **cup dried mushrooms (such as porcini, cepe, *or* shiitake)**
1 **cup water**
1 **medium onion, chopped (½ cup)**
1 **stalk celery, chopped (½ cup)**
2 **tablespoons margarine *or* butter**
1 **16-ounce can pumpkin**
1 **14½-ounce can chicken broth**
¼ **teaspoon ground mace**
½ **to ¾ cup light cream**

Rinse mushrooms well. To rehydrate, soak the mushrooms in water about 30 minutes or till rehydrated. Squeeze to drain, reserving water. Coarsely chop mushrooms, discarding stems.

In a large saucepan cook the onion and celery in hot margarine or butter till tender. Remove from heat. Stir in rehydrated mushrooms, reserved water from mushrooms, pumpkin, chicken broth, and mace. Pour mixture into a 1½-quart freezer container. Seal, label, and freeze up to 1 month.

To serve, in a large saucepan cook the pumpkin mixture, covered, over medium-low heat for 15 minutes. Increase heat to medium. Cook about 10 minutes more or till mixture is heated through, stirring often. Season to taste with *salt* and *pepper*. In a small saucepan cook and stir cream till heated through. *Do not boil.* Drizzle cream over individual servings of soup. Draw a knife through cream to make decorative pattern (see photo, *page 153*). Makes 8 servings.

To serve immediately: Prepare pumpkin mixture as directed, *except* do not freeze. In a large saucepan cook pumpkin mixture, covered, over medium heat for 6 to 8 minutes or till heated through, stirring often. Heat cream and serve as directed.

Microwave directions: Rehydrate and chop mushrooms as directed. In a 2-quart microwave-safe casserole micro-cook onion, celery, and margarine or butter on 100% power (high) for 3 to 5 minutes or till onion is tender. Stir in mushrooms, reserved liquid from mushrooms, pumpkin, chicken broth, and mace. Cook, covered, on high for 10 to 12 minutes or till heated through, stirring 2 or 3 times.

In a 2-cup measure cook cream, uncovered, on high for 1 to 2 minutes or till heated through, stirring once. *Do not boil.* Serve as directed.

Nutrition information per serving: 110 cal., 2 g pro., 8 g carbo., 8 g fat, 17 mg chol., 346 mg sodium, 2 g dietary fiber. U.S. RDA: 256% vit. A.

WILD RICE BRAID

Next time you cook wild rice for a side dish, cook extra to make Wild Rice Braid, as featured on page 147. Then, seal, label, and freeze the extra rice for three to six months—

1 **cup water**
⅓ **cup wild rice**
3¾ **to 4¼ cups all-purpose flour**
2 **packages active dry yeast**
¾ **cup milk**
¼ **cup margarine *or* butter**
¼ **cup honey**
1 **teaspoon salt**
1 **beaten egg**
2 **small tart apples, peeled and finely chopped (1 cup)**
1 **beaten egg yolk**
1 **tablespoon water**

In a small saucepan bring the water to boiling. Add the wild rice. Return to boiling. Reduce heat. Cover and simmer for 40 to 50 minutes or till the wild rice is tender. Let cool.

In a large mixer bowl stir together *1½ cups* of the flour and yeast. In a saucepan heat milk, margarine or butter, honey, and salt just till warm (120° to 130°) and the margarine is melted, stirring constantly.

Add milk mixture to flour mixture. Add egg. Beat with an electric mixer on low speed for ½ minute, scraping the sides of the bowl as necessary. Beat on high speed for 3 minutes. Stir in the rice and chopped apples. Using a spoon, stir in as much of the remaining flour as you can.

Turn out the dough onto a lightly floured surface. Knead in enough of the remaining flour to make a moderately stiff dough that is smooth and elastic (about 6 to 8 minutes total). Shape the dough into a ball. Place the dough in a greased mixing bowl. Turn the dough once to grease the surface. Cover bowl. Let rise in a warm place till double (about 1 hour).

Punch dough down. Turn out onto a long counter that is lightly floured. Divide the dough in half. Divide each half into thirds. Cover dough. Let rest for 10 minutes.

Roll each portion into a 26-inch rope. Lightly grease 2 baking sheets. Place 3 ropes, side by side, on a baking sheet (dough ropes will extend beyond edge of baking sheets). Braid ropes loosely starting at the center and working toward the ends. Shape the braid into a figure eight around balls of foil. Tuck the ends of the braid under the center of loaf (see photo, *page 153*). Repeat with remaining 3 ropes of dough. Cover and let rise in a warm place till nearly double (about 40 minutes).

Bake in a 375° oven for 5 minutes. Cover with foil; bake 25 minutes more or till done. Test by tapping the top with your finger. A hollow sound means the loaf is done. Transfer loaves to wire racks. In a custard cup combine egg yolk and water. Brush on the hot loaves. Cool completely. Wrap in moisture- and vaporproof wrap; seal, label, and freeze.

To serve, thaw the loaves, loosely covered, at room temperature for 2 hours. Unwrap loaves completely. Place the loaves on an ungreased baking sheet. Bake in a 375° oven about 10 minutes or till warm. Makes 2 loaves, 24 servings total.

To serve immediately: Prepare the dough and let rise as directed. Brush the dough with yolk mixture before baking. Bake the loaves in a 375° oven for 25 to 30 minutes or till done, covering loaves with foil after 15 to 20 minutes to prevent overbrowning. Test by tapping the top with your finger. A hollow sound means the loaf is done.

Nutrition information per serving: 126 cal., 3 g pro., 21 g carbo., 3 g fat, 35 mg chol., 120 mg sodium, 1 g dietary fiber. U.S. RDA: 10% thiamine.

GLORIOUS PIES

Common Pastry Problems

Perplexed by less-than-perfect pastry? Here are some common pastry problems and their causes:

The problem	The cause
Tough	Not enough fat
	Too much water
	Overmixing
	Too much flour added when rolling out
Crumbly	Not enough water
	Too much fat
Doesn't brown	Rolled too thick
	Underbaked
	Overmixed
Shrinks	Stretched when put in pan
	Overhandled
	Rolled too thin
Blistered	Not pricked enough
	Baked at too low a temperature

APRICOT-APPLE TARTS

- 6 sheets frozen phyllo dough (18x14-inch rectangles), thawed
- ¼ cup margarine *or* butter, melted
- 1 6-ounce package dried apricots, snipped
- 1 cup water
- ½ cup light raisins
- ½ cup sugar
- ½ cup brandy
- 1 tablespoon lemon juice
- 1½ cups chopped, peeled tart apples (2 medium)
- 1 tablespoon water
- 1 tablespoon cornstarch
- Vanilla ice cream (optional)

Brush *one* sheet of phyllo dough with some of the melted margarine or butter. Top with another phyllo dough sheet. Repeat brushing and layering with remaining margarine or butter, and phyllo. Cut phyllo stack lengthwise into 6 strips. Cut strips crosswise into thirds, forming 18 rectangles. Press 3 rectangles into *each* of 6 greased 6-ounce custard cups so entire cup is covered (see photo, *page 154*). Bake in a 350° oven for 15 to 20 minutes or till golden. Remove from custard cups and cool completely on a wire rack.

In saucepan combine apricots, the 1 cup water, raisins, sugar, brandy, and lemon juice. Bring to boiling. Reduce heat. Simmer, uncovered, for 5 minutes. Add apples. Cook 5 minutes more or till apples are tender, stirring occasionally. Stir the 1 tablespoon water into cornstarch. Stir into apricot mixture. Cook and stir till thickened and bubbly. Cook and stir 2 minutes more. Spoon warm apricot mixture into shells. Top with ice cream. Serves 6.

Microwave directions: Bake the phyllo cups conventionally. In a 2-quart microwave-safe casserole combine apricots, the 1 cup water, raisins, sugar, ¼ *cup* brandy, and lemon juice. Micro-cook, covered, on 100% power (high) for 5½ to 7½ minutes or till the mixture boils, stirring once. Stir in apples. Cook, covered, on high for 2 to 4 minutes more or till apples are tender, stirring once. Stir the 1 tablespoon water into cornstarch. Stir into the apricot mixture. Cook, uncovered, on high for 1 to 2 minutes or till thickened and bubbly, stirring after every 30 seconds. Cook, uncovered, on high for 1 minute more. Serve as directed.

Nutrition information per tart: 332 cal., 2 g pro., 55 g carbo., 8 g fat, 0 mg chol., 149 mg sodium, 5 g dietary fiber. U.S. RDA: 48% vit. A, 10% iron.

GINGERBERRY LATTICE PIE

- 1 15¼-ounce can crushed pineapple (juice pack)
- 4 cups cranberries (1 pound)
- 1¾ cups sugar
- ¼ cup cornstarch
- 1 to 2 tablespoons finely chopped crystallized ginger *or*
- ½ teaspoon ground ginger
- 1 recipe Pastry for Double-Crust Pie (see recipe, *right*)
- Milk
- Sugar
- 1 recipe Orange Cream (see recipe, *right*)

Drain pineapple, reserving *1 cup* juice. (Add *water* if necessary to make 1 cup.) In a medium saucepan cook cranberries in reserved juice over medium-high heat for 5 to 8 minutes or till cranberries begin to pop. (Or, in a 2-quart microwave-safe casserole micro-cook reserved juice and cranberries, covered, on 100% power (high) for 7 to 9 minutes or till the cranberries begin to pop.)

Combine sugar and cornstarch. Stir into hot cranberry mixture. Cook and stir till thickened and bubbly. (Or, micro-cook, uncovered, on 100% power (high) for 4 to 6 minutes or till thickened and bubbly, stirring after every minute.) Remove from heat. Stir in the pineapple and ginger. Set aside to cool.

Prepare the pastry. On a lightly floured surface flatten 1 ball of dough. Roll dough from center to edge, forming a 12-inch circle. Ease pastry into a 9-inch pie plate. Trim crust to ½ inch beyond edge of pie plate. Roll out remaining pastry. Using a pastry wheel or sharp knife, cut dough into ½- to ¾-inch strips.

Pour cranberry mixture into pastry-lined pie plate. To make herringbone-lattice top, arrange *four* strips of pastry in center of pie to make a small square (see photos 1 and 2, *page 156*). Working from center to edges, continue placing strips to make progressively larger squares (see photo 3, *page 156*). Trim strips even with bottom crust. Fold strips under bottom pastry. Seal and flute edge.

Brush pastry with milk. Sprinkle with sugar. Cover edge of pie with foil (see photo, *page 154*). Bake in a 375° oven for 25 minutes. Remove foil. Bake 20 to 25 minutes more or till golden. Cool on wire rack. Serve with Orange Cream. Makes 8 servings.

Pastry for Double-Crust Pie: In medium mixing bowl stir together 2 cups *all-purpose flour* and ½ teaspoon *salt*. Cut in ⅔ cup *shortening* till pieces are the size of small peas. Sprinkle 1 tablespoon cold *water* over part of mixture; gently toss with a fork. Push to the side of the bowl. Repeat till all is moistened (6 to 7 tablespoons total). Divide dough in half, forming into 2 balls.

Orange Cream: In a small medium mixer bowl beat 1 cup *whipping cream* and 2 tablespoons *sugar* with an electric mixer on low speed till soft peaks form. Fold in 1 teaspoon finely shredded *orange peel.* Serve immediately.

Nutrition information per serving: 618 cal., 4 g pro., 91 g carbo., 28 g fat, 41 mg chol., 149 mg sodium, 4 g dietary fiber. U.S. RDA: 10% vit. A, 22% vit. C, 18% thiamine, 10% riboflavin.

CHOCOLATE-PRALINE PIE

To eliminate spills, place the pastry shell on the rack of the oven, then pour the filling into the shell—

  1 **recipe Pastry for Single-Crust Pie (see recipe, *right*)**
Semisweet chocolate pieces
  3 **eggs**
  1 **cup light corn syrup**
  ½ **cup sugar**
  ⅓ **cup margarine *or* butter, melted**
  2 **tablespoons praline liqueur *or* Amaretto**
  1 **cup pecan halves**
  ½ **cup semisweet chocolate pieces**

Prepare the pastry. On lightly floured surface flatten the dough with hands. Roll the dough from the center to the edge, forming a circle about 12 inches in diameter. Ease the pastry into a 9-inch pie plate, being careful to avoid stretching the pastry. Trim the crust even with the edge of the pie plate.

Reroll the dough scraps. Use an hors d'oeuvre cutter to make cutouts from scraps. Brush the edge of pastry with *water*. Arrange cutouts and chocolate pieces around the edge (see photo, *page 155*). *Do not* prick the pastry.

For filling, in a mixing bowl beat the eggs slightly with a rotary beater or a fork. Stir in the corn syrup. Add the sugar, margarine or butter, and praline liqueur or Amaretto, stirring till sugar is dissolved. Stir in the pecans and the ½ cup chocolate pieces.

Place the pastry-lined pie plate on oven rack. Pour the filling into the plate. To prevent the pastry from over-browning, cover the edge of the pie with a piece of foil (see photo, *page 154*).

Bake pie in a 350° oven for 25 minutes. Remove the foil. Bake for 20 to 25 minutes more or till a knife inserted near the center of the pie comes out clean. Cool pie thoroughly on a wire rack before serving. Cover the pie. Chill in the refrigerator to store. Serves 8.

Pastry for Single-Crust Pie: In a medium mixing bowl stir together 1¼ cups *all-purpose flour* and ½ teaspoon *salt*. Cut in ⅓ cup *shortening* till the pieces are the size of small peas. Sprinkle 1 tablespoon cold *water* over part of the flour and shortening mixture. Gently toss with a fork. Push mixture to the side of the bowl. Repeat till all is moistened (3 to 4 tablespoons water total). Form dough into a ball.

Nutrition information per serving: 574 cal., 6 g pro., 70 g carbo., 32 g fat, 103 mg chol., 280 mg sodium, 1 g dietary fiber. U.S. RDA: 18% thiamine, 20% iron, 12% phosphorus.

CARAMEL-PEAR FLAN

The caramel topping is prettiest just after you drizzle it onto the flan, as featured on page 147. For leftover flan, however, just cover and chill the flan—

  1 **recipe Sweet Pastry for 10-inch Flan Pan (see recipe, *right*)**
  2 **eggs**
  1 **8-ounce carton dairy sour cream**
1½ **teaspoons finely shredded orange peel**
  ¾ **cup orange juice**
  ¼ **cup sugar**
  1 **tablespoon lemon juice**
1¼ **cups water**
  3 **tablespoons lemon juice**
  2 **tablespoons sugar**
  3 **or 4 pears, peeled, cored, and sliced (4 cups)**
  ⅓ **cup sugar**
  ¼ **teaspoon water**

Prepare the sweet pastry. Press the prepared dough evenly over the bottom and up the sides of a 10-inch flan pan or a 10-inch pie plate. *Do not* prick pastry.

Bake pastry in a 375° oven about 15 minutes or till the pastry is golden. Cool the pastry thoroughly in the pan on a wire rack. Reduce the oven temperature to 350°.

For the custard, in a mixing bowl beat eggs with a rotary beater till frothy. Stir in the sour cream, finely shredded orange peel, orange juice, the ¼ cup sugar, and the 1 tablespoon lemon juice till smooth.

Place the flan pan with prebaked crust on a baking sheet on oven rack. Pour custard into the flan pan. Bake in a 350° oven for 35 to 40 minutes or till custard is set. Cool completely on a wire rack. Chill flan.

Meanwhile, in a skillet combine the 1¼ cups water, the 3 tablespoons lemon juice, and the 2 tablespoons sugar. Add the pear slices. Bring to a gentle boil. Reduce heat. Cover and simmer for 3 to 5 minutes or till just tender. (Or, in a 2-quart microwave-safe casserole micro-cook the 1¼ cups water, the 3 tablespoons lemon juice, the 2 tablespoons sugar, and pears, covered, on 100% power (high) for 3½ to 4½ minutes or till the pears are just tender, stirring once.) Let the pears stand, covered, in the cooking liquid.

Up to 30 minutes before serving the flan, drain the pears well. Arrange pears over top of the flan. In a small heavy saucepan heat the ⅓ cup sugar over medium heat. When the sugar starts to melt, stir constantly till the mixture is a medium caramel color. (The syrup will continue to darken after it's removed from the heat.) Stir in the ¼ teaspoon water. Drizzle syrup over pears, turning the flan as you work (see photo, *page 155*). Serves 10.

Sweet Pastry for 10-inch Flan Pan: In a medium mixing bowl stir together 1½ cups *all-purpose flour*, 2 tablespoons *sugar*, and ⅛ teaspoon *salt*. Cut in ¼ cup *margarine* or *butter* till pieces are the size of small peas. Combine 1 beaten *egg*, 2 tablespoons *cooking oil*, and 4 teaspoons cold *water*. Make a well in the center of the flour mixture. Add egg mixture. Stir till combined. Work mixture with hands till well blended. Form into a ball.

Nutrition information per serving: 318 cal., 5 g pro., 44 g carbo., 14 g fat, 96 mg chol., 114 mg sodium, 2 g dietary fiber. U.S. RDA: 13% vitamin C, 11% thiamine, 11% riboflavin.

DECEMBER

THE MAGAZINE FOR AMERICAN FAMILIES

DECEMBER 1987
$1.50

Better Homes and Gardens.

Happy Holidays!

FABULOUS HOLIDAY FOOD FOR BUSY, BUSY FAMILIES

EASY, FESTIVE RECIPES TO MAKE AHEAD OR FIX FAST

By Barbara Greenwood

ANYTIME APPETIZERS
SURPRISINGLY SIMPLE, YET UNDENIABLY ELEGANT

1. YOGURT DILL BREAD
Bake ahead, then freeze
A tender, tangy batter bread based on quick-rising yeast. Come serving time, simply thaw bread and set on a ring of cheese slices.

2. PEPPED-UP CHEESE BAKE
Assemble in five minutes
Only five ingredients plus toppers—all the keep-on-hand type. Micro-cook a mere five minutes for an irresistible, creamy dip.

3. HOLIDAY APPLE FLING
Mix and store
Steep cinnamon in both apple and cranberry juice for an always-ready whistle wetter. Just add champagne or ginger ale to serve.

4,5.PARMESAN PUFFS HAM-ONION BITES

Use one cheese dough to make both appetizers
Mound the Parmesan dough and bake 20 minutes for melt-in-your mouth puffs. Or, pipe the dough around a tasty filling for Ham-Onion Bites.

6.SALMON ON CORN CAKES

Cook ahead to freeze
Posh, elegant, and would you believe simple, too? Warm the flapjacks in your oven before adding the classy toppings.

4

6

5

READY-TO-SERVE SWEETS

SPEND LESS TIME BAKING, MORE TIME MAKING MERRY

1. HOLIDAY SPIRAL LOAF

Fix and serve in 50 minutes
Roll up cashews and candied cherries in a convenient refrigerated bread dough. It's a nut- and fruit-lover's paradise—a busy cook's dream come true.

2. MINCEMEAT BREAD WREATH

Bake ahead and freeze
Wow! Spicy mincemeat and applesauce really jazz up easy-to-make bread mix. Apple cutouts make a festive garnish.

3. SPICED EGGNOG COCOA

Mix up to have on hand
Spike cocoa mix with tantalizing spices. Heat with eggnog, and top with cream and grenadine or liqueur to enjoy.

> **READY-TO-SERVE SWEETS RECIPES BEGIN ON PAGE 173.**

4. PEPPERMINT ICE CREAM TORTE
Fill, frost, and freeze
Nestle a scrumptious layer of peppermint ice cream betwixt tender cake and fluffy frosting. Simply decorate with candy to enjoy in a jiff!

5. AMBROSIA SPREAD
Stir up in 10 minutes
Combine a few easy-to-keep-on-hand ingredients to create one incredible spread. It's chock-full of pineapple, oranges, coconut, and nuts. Spread on cutout fruit breads.

6, 7, 8. ALMOND TWISTS, ANISE BELLS, REFRIGERATOR COTTAGE COOKIES
Chill or freeze now; bake later
Perfect cookies for ringing in the holidays! Bake a few whenever the fancy strikes.

167

MAKE-AHEAD BRUNCH

BAKE BOTH MAIN DISH AND MUFFINS WHILE YOU CELEBRATE!

MENU

*Prosciutto Soufflé Roll
in Parsley Sauce
Grenadine Fruit Mélange
Sugar-Top Muffins
Citrus Eye-Opener*

1. PROSCIUTTO SOUFFLÉ ROLL IN PARSLEY SAUCE

Tuck a fabulous prosciutto and provolone filling inside a stunning jelly-roll soufflé. Chill it all overnight, then simply oven-warm the next day.

2. GRENADINE FRUIT MÉLANGE

Marinate this brilliant fruit menagerie in grenadine and sugar syrup overnight. Stir in kiwi fruit to serve.

3. SUGAR-TOP MUFFINS

You can mix, cover, and chill the oat-walnut batter up to a week ahead. Just before you bake, dust each muffin-cupful of batter with cinnamon sugar for attractive tops.

4. CITRUS EYE-OPENER

Early morning risers will perk up when they taste this tangy juice combo: sweet orange and tart lemon.

FAST-TO-FIX DINNER

A SPECIAL 65-MINUTES-FROM-START-TO-FINISH CHRISTMAS FEAST

─ MENU ─

Sweet 'n' Sour Beet Soup
Veal Loin with Mushroom Au Jus
Long grain and wild rice pilaf
Greens and Papaya Salad; Rolls
Grasshopper Cheesecake

1. SWEET 'N' SOUR BEET SOUP

Tongue-tingling and creamy, this soup conveniently starts with canned vegetables. What's more, it's made in a single whir of your blender.

2. VEAL LOIN WITH MUSHROOM AU JUS

Take just five minutes to add smoked flavor to a veal roast by shingling bacon strips on top. Serve juicy, roasted veal au jus made with wild mushrooms and dry red wine.

3.GREENS AND PAPAYA SALAD

A high-falutin' salad based on four main ingredients—Bibb lettuce, Belgian endive, papaya, and grapefruit. Jazz up a bottled dressing with poppy seed to pour atop.

4.GRASSHOPPER CHEESECAKE

Frozen cheesecake never looked so classy nor tasted so ambrosial. Chocolate topping and chocolate-mint wafers add the festive finishing touch.

MENU
INSTRUCTIONS BEGIN
ON PAGE 172.

FAST-TO-FIX DINNER
65-MINUTE TIMETABLE

0:00: Begin by preheating your oven to 425°, then roll up your sleeves!

Set the cheesecake out on your counter to thaw.

Place the meat on the rack in the roasting pan and lay on the bacon (see photo A). Insert the thermometer into the meat. Slide it all into your oven and move on!

A: Shingle the bacon slices on top of the roast to flavor the meat and keep it moist as it roasts.

0:05: For the juice, soak the dried mushrooms in warm water.

Meanwhile, work on the salad. Add the poppy seed to the salad dressing bottle; shake up and chill. Rinse all your greens; pat 'em dry. Peel, seed, and slice the papaya (see photo B). Arrange greens, fruit, and nuts on a platter; chill. Salad is done!

B: Peel the papaya, then use a spoon to scoop out and discard the seeds.

0:25: Take the cheesecake out of its container. Score into 8 pieces, and drizzle the fudge topping onto each piece (see photo C).

0:35: Drain the mushrooms you've been soaking. Cut off the stems and slice the remaining caps. Simmer all of

C: Using a back-and-forth motion, gently squeeze the fudge ice-cream topping onto each cheesecake wedge.

the juice ingredients as the recipe directs. Remove from the heat; cover and let stand till you serve.

While the juice simmers, in Dutch oven bring 6 cups hot water to boiling. You'll use this to cook the rice.

For the dessert, carefully halve *four* of the chocolate-mint wafers diagonally. With the vegetable peeler, carve curls from the remaining wafers. Use to decorate the cheesecake. Chill till serving time.

0:45: Cook the rice mix according to the package directions. Place on a serving platter; cover to keep warm.

Meanwhile, for the soup, in the blender combine and blend all the ingredients. Pour into a medium saucepan and heat through. Cut garnishes from the reserved beet slices (see photo D).

D: With an hors d'oeuvre cutter, cut decorative shapes from the reserved beet slices. Use these to garnish the soup.

1:05: Remove the roast from the oven; cover and let stand while you enjoy your soup. Dinner is served!

SHOPPING LIST

MEAT ....
- 1 2½- to 3-pound boneless veal sirloin roast or beef tenderloin
- 8 slices bacon (about ½ pound)

PRODUCE ....
- 2 heads Bibb or Boston lettuce
- 1 head Belgian endive
- 1 papaya
- ½ of a small onion
- ½ cup dried mushrooms (porcini, cepe, or shiitake)

Chives*
Enoki mushrooms*
Fresh basil*
Fresh marjoram*
Fresh sage*

PACKAGED AND CANNED GOODS ....
- 1 14½-ounce can beef broth
- 1 8½-ounce can whole white potatoes
- 1 8¼-ounce can sliced beets
- 1 8-ounce can grapefruit sections (water pack)
- 1 8-ounce bottle coleslaw salad dressing
- 8 bakery dinner rolls
- ⅓ cup sliced almonds
- 6 layered chocolate-mint wafers

Fudge ice-cream topping in squeeze bottle

DAIRY ....
- ½ cup light cream or milk

FROZEN FOODS ....
- 2 10-ounce packages frozen long grain and wild rice
- 1 6-inch-round frozen plain cream cheesecake

STAPLES ....
Fines herbes
Pepper, salt, and sugar
Poppy seed
Vinegar

ALCOHOL ....
- ½ cup crème de menthe
- ⅓ cup dry red wine

WINE SUGGESTIONS TO ACCOMPANY VEAL .....
Chardonnay, Chenin Blanc, Pinot Blanc, Sauvignon Blanc, or Riesling

*For garnish

UTENSIL LIST

blender
shallow roasting pan with rack
4-quart Dutch oven
medium saucepan
small saucepan with lid
small bowl
cutting board
chef's knife
paring knife
vegetable peeler
wooden spoon
spoon
meat thermometer
hors d'oeuvre cutter

Fast-to-Fix Dinner recipes begin on page 179.

YOGURT DILL BREAD

If you're a real dill lover, spring for the larger amount of the herb—

2¼ cups all-purpose flour
1 package quick-rising active dry yeast
2 to 3 teaspoons dried dillweed
1 8-ounce carton plain yogurt
¼ cup sugar
¼ cup water
¼ cup margarine *or* butter
1 egg
Cheddar and Monterey Jack cheese slices (optional)
Plain yogurt (optional)
Fresh dill (optional)

Grease an 8-inch fluted tube pan or a 9-inch tube pan. Set aside.

In a large mixer bowl stir together *1 cup* of the flour, yeast, and dillweed.

In a medium saucepan heat yogurt, sugar, water, margarine or butter, and ½ teaspoon *salt* just till warm (125° to 130°), stirring constantly. Add to flour mixture along with egg. Beat with an electric mixer on low speed for ½ minute, scraping bowl. Beat on high speed for 3 minutes. Stir in remaining flour. (Batter will be sticky.)

Cover and let rise in a warm place till double (20 to 25 minutes).

Stir down dough. Spoon into prepared pan. Cover and let rise till nearly double (15 to 20 minutes). Bake in a 375° oven about 30 minutes or till golden. Remove from pan; cool on a rack.

To freeze, wrap bread in moisture- and vaporproof wrap. Seal, label, and freeze up to 6 months. To thaw, let bread stand, loosely covered, several hours at room temperature.

Serve slices of bread with cheeses and yogurt, if desired. Garnish with fresh dill, if desired. Serves 12.

Nutrition information per serving: 156 cal., 4 g pro., 24 g carbo., 5 g fat, 24 mg chol., 154 mg sodium, 91 mg potassium, 1 g dietary fiber. U.S. RDA: 12% thiamine, 10% riboflavin.

HOLIDAY APPLE FLING

1 14-ounce jar spiced apple rings
1 32-ounce bottle (4 cups) apple juice
1 32-ounce bottle (4 cups) cranberry juice cocktail
1 cup water
4 to 5 inches stick cinnamon
Peel from 1 orange
1 750-milliliter bottle champagne *or* one 28-ounce bottle ginger ale
Cinnamon sticks (optional)
Orange peel stars (optional)

Drain the spiced apple rings, reserving syrup. In a 3-quart container stir together the reserved syrup, *2 cups* of the apple juice, the cranberry juice cocktail, water, and the 4 to 5 inches stick cinnamon. Cover and chill for 24 hours. Remove the cinnamon sticks. Cover and chill up to 2 weeks.

In a 4-cup ring mold freeze a little of the remaining apple juice just till slushy (about 30 to 45 minutes). Using an hors d'oeuvre cutter, cut the orange peel into stars.

Press the stars into the slushy apple juice in mold. Center the spiced apple rings over stars. Freeze till firm. Add remaining apple juice to mold. Freeze up to 2 weeks.

To serve, unmold ice ring and place in a large punch bowl. Add syrup mixture. Slowly stir in champagne or gingerale. Serve immediately with cinnamon stick stirrers and additional orange peel stars, if desired. Makes about 24 (4-ounce) servings.

Nutrition information per serving: 73 cal., 0 g pro., 14 g carbo., 0 g fat, 0 mg chol., 3 mg sodium, 66 mg potassium. U.S. RDA: 29% vit. C.

PEPPED-UP CHEESE BAKE

To make the corkscrewlike olive garnish, carve a pitted ripe olive into a spiral, cutting just to, but not through, the center—

1 8-ounce carton dairy sour cream
½ cup mayonnaise *or* salad dressing
2 tablespoons all-purpose flour
½ to 1 teaspoon bottled minced garlic
1½ cups shredded Monterey Jack cheese with jalapeño peppers (6 ounces) *or* one 6-ounce package shredded Monterey Jack cheese (1½ cups)
1 2-ounce can sliced pimiento, drained
¼ cup sunflower nuts
1 green onion, sliced
Assorted crackers (optional)

In a large mixing bowl stir together sour cream, mayonnaise or salad dressing, flour, and garlic. Stir in shredded cheese. Tranfer to a 7-inch microwave-safe quiche dish.

Micro-cook, uncovered, on 70% power (medium-high) for 4 to 6 minutes or till heated through, stirring twice.

Place pimiento in center and sunflower nuts around edge of dish. Sprinkle a ring of onion between pimiento and nuts. Serve warm with crackers. Makes about 2 cups.

Conventional directions: Prepare Pepped-Up Cheese Bake as directed above, *except* place cheese mixture in a 7-inch quiche dish or pie plate, and add toppings as directed *before* baking. Bake in a 350° oven for 30 to 35 minutes or till mixture is heated through.

Nutrition information per 2 tablespoons dip: 131 cal., 4 g pro., 2 g carbo., 12 g fat, 20 mg chol., 104 mg sodium, 49 mg potassium. U.S. RDA: 10% calcium.

PARMESAN PUFF DOUGH

½ cup margarine *or* butter
1 cup water
1 cup all-purpose flour
¼ teaspoon ground red pepper
    (optional)
4 eggs
⅓ cup grated Parmesan cheese

In a medium saucepan melt margarine or butter. Stir in water. Bring to boiling. Add flour and red pepper all at once. Stir vigorously.

Cook and stir till mixture forms a ball that doesn't separate. Remove from heat. Let stand about 5 minutes or till slightly cooled.

Add eggs, one at a time, stirring vigorously with a wooden spoon after each addition for 1 to 2 minutes or till smooth. Stir in Parmesan cheese.

Use dough immediately or cover and chill up to 2 days. Use to make Parmesan Puffs or Ham-Onion Bites.

PARMESAN PUFFS

**Parmesan Puff Dough
    (see recipe, above)
Grated Parmesan cheese**

Place Parmesan Puff Dough in a pastry bag fitted with a ⅝-inch-wide plain tip.

On a greased baking sheet pipe the dough into 32 mounds, each about 1¾ inches in diameter. Sprinkle with the Parmesan cheese.

Bake in a 400° oven for 20 to 25 minutes or till puffy and golden. Serve warm. Makes 32.

Nutrition information per puff: 59 cal., 2 g pro., 3 g carbo., 4 g fat, 36 mg chol., 80 mg sodium, 16 mg potassium.

SALMON ON CORN CAKES

1 cup packaged pancake mix
⅓ cup cornmeal
¼ to ½ teaspoon garlic powder
1 beaten egg
1½ cups buttermilk
1 tablespoon cooking oil
½ cup dairy sour cream
1 to 2 tablespoons buttermilk *or*
    milk
½ pound sliced smoked red salmon
    (lox)
**Lemon wedges
Carrot tops
Caviar**

For batter, in a medium mixing bowl stir together the pancake mix, cornmeal, and garlic powder.

In a small mixing bowl stir together the beaten egg, the 1½ cups buttermilk, and oil. Add all at once to dry ingredients, stirring till combined but still slightly lumpy.

For *each* cake, pour *1 tablespoon* of the batter onto a hot, lightly greased griddle or heavy skillet. Cook till golden brown, turning to cook other side when pancakes have a bubbly surface and slightly dry edges. Cool.

Stack, with waxed paper between each cake, in a moisture- and vaporproof freezer container. Seal, label, and freeze up to 8 months.

To serve, let stand, covered, at room temperature for 30 minutes. Separate cakes and place on an ungreased baking sheet. Cover cakes with foil. Bake in a 350° oven about 15 minutes or till cakes are heated through.

Stir together sour cream and the 1 to 2 tablespoons buttermilk or milk. Top corn cakes with a rolled-up salmon slice and a dollop of buttermilk mixture. Garnish with lemon wedges, carrot tops, and caviar. Makes 32 cakes.

Microwave reheating: Prepare and freeze corn cakes as directed. Let frozen cakes stand, covered, at room temperature for 30 minutes. Separate cakes and place 10 to 12 on a 12-inch glass pizza plate or other microwave-safe plate. Cover with waxed paper.

Micro-cook on medium (50%) power for 2½ to 3 minutes or till heated through, turning dish once.

Nutrition information per appetizer: 50 cal., 3 g pro., 5 g carbo., 2 g fat, 13 mg chol., 511 mg sodium, 46 mg potassium.

HAM-ONION BITES

Bake these golden bites ahead. Come party time, simply reheat to serve—

2 cups finely chopped celery
4 green onions, finely chopped
¼ cup water
½ cup finely chopped fully cooked
    turkey ham
⅓ cup fine dry seasoned bread
    crumbs
¼ teaspoon ground nutmeg
1 egg
**Parmesan Puff Dough (see
    recipe, far left)**

For filling, in a medium saucepan combine chopped celery, chopped green onions, and water. Bring to boiling. Reduce heat. Cover and simmer for 6 to 8 minutes. Drain well.

Stir in turkey ham, bread crumbs, and nutmeg. Cool slightly. Beat in egg.

Line baking sheets with foil and grease the foil. Drop the filling by rounded teaspoonfuls 2 inches apart onto prepared baking sheets, mounding the filling slightly.

Place Parmesan Puff Dough in a pastry bag fitted with a ⅜-inch-wide star tip. Pipe dough around filling mounds in concentric circles, starting at base and working toward top, leaving peaks uncovered.

Bake in a 400° oven for 16 to 18 minutes or till golden brown. Serve immediately. *Or,* transfer to wire racks to cool. Place in moisture- and vaporproof freezer containers. Seal, label, and freeze up to 1 month.

To reheat, place frozen appetizers on a greased baking sheet. Bake in a 350° oven about 10 minutes or till heated through. Makes about 60.

Nutrition information per appetizer: 36 cal., 1 g pro., 2 g carbo., 2 g fat, 24 mg chol., 57 mg sodium, 26 mg potassium.

HOLIDAY SPIRAL LOAF

1 egg white
¼ cup packed brown sugar
⅓ cup chopped cashews
¼ cup candied red cherries, finely chopped
¼ cup candied green cherries, finely chopped
1 10-ounce package refrigerated white bread dough
Powdered Sugar Icing
Candied cherry halves
Cashews

In a small mixing bowl beat egg white slightly. Stir in brown sugar. Stir in the chopped cashews. Divide mixture in half. Stir chopped red cherries into one half. Stir chopped green cherries into remaining half. Set aside.

On a greased baking sheet unroll bread dough. Pinch slashes together to make a solid sheet of dough. Spread red cherry mixture crosswise over half of the dough to within ½ inch of edges. Spread green cherry mixture over remaining half of dough to within ½ inch of edges.

Roll up the red-cherry-topped dough from the short side, just to center of the dough rectangle. Repeat with the green-cherry-topped dough, ending at center when it meets the red cherry portion. Pinch the two rolls together at the top where they meet.

Bake in a 350° oven about 35 minutes or till loaf sounds hollow when tapped. Cover with foil the last 5 to 10 minutes to prevent overbrowning. Cool slightly on a wire rack. Drizzle Powdered Sugar Icing over loaf. Top with cherry halves and cashews. Serve warm. Serves 12 to 16.

Powdered Sugar Icing: In a small mixing bowl stir together 1 cup sifted *powdered sugar*, ¼ teaspoon *vanilla*, and enough *milk* (1 to 2 tablespoons) to make of drizzling consistency.

Nutrition information per serving:
169 cal., 3 g pro., 32 g carbo., 3 g fat, 2 mg chol., 139 mg sodium, 76 mg potassium, 1 g dietary fiber.

MINCEMEAT BREAD WREATH

To make the simple apple garnish, use hors d'oeuvre cutters to cut two small flower shapes from a slice of apple. Dip in lemon juice to prevent darkening—

1 16-ounce can applesauce
1 9-ounce package instant condensed mincemeat
1 cup apple juice
2 tablespoons margarine *or* butter
1 16-ounce package hot roll mix
1 slightly beaten egg
Milk
Pearl sugar
Walnut halves
Apple cutouts (optional)
Lemon leaves (optional)

In a medium saucepan stir together applesauce and mincemeat. Bring to boiling. Reduce heat and simmer, uncovered, for 8 to 10 minutes or till thick, stirring occasionally. Cool to room temperature.

Grease a baking sheet. Set aside. In a small saucepan heat apple juice and margarine or butter, stirring constantly, till warm (120° to 130°) and margarine or butter is almost melted.

In a large mixing bowl combine flour mixture and yeast from roll mix. Add apple juice mixture and egg. Stir till combined and dough pulls away from sides of bowl. Turn out onto a floured surface. Knead 5 minutes or till smooth. Cover; let rest 10 minutes.

On a floured surface, roll dough into a 15x10-inch rectangle. Spread mincemeat mixture over dough to

within 1 inch of edges. Roll up from one of the long sides. Press edges to seal.

On prepared baking sheet bring ends together to form a ring. Seal ends. With sharp kitchen shears, make 10 vertical cuts at 1½-inch intervals around outside edge of ring, cutting to within ½ inch of inside of ring. Twist outside edge of cut pieces to the left, exposing filling (see photo, above).

Cover and let rise till nearly double (30 to 45 minutes). Brush with a little milk. Sprinkle with pearl sugar. Bake in a 350° oven about 30 minutes or till the bread sounds hollow when tapped, covering with foil after 20 minutes of baking to prevent overbrowning. Cool completely on a wire rack.

To freeze, wrap bread in moisture- and vaporproof wrap. Seal, label, and freeze up to 6 months. To thaw, let stand, loosely covered, at room temperature several hours or till thawed.

To serve, top with walnuts. Secure apple cutouts and lemon leaves to bread with a toothpick, if desired. Serves 12 to 16.

Nutrition information per serving:
249 cal., 5 g pro., 49 g carbo., 3 g fat, 23 mg chol., 299 mg sodium, 107 mg potassium, 2 g dietary fiber. U.S. RDA: 17% thiamine, 15% riboflavin, 12% niacin, 11% iron.

SPICED EGGNOG COCOA

Rich and spicy, it'll warm you from the inside out—

- 1 **16-ounce can instant cocoa mix**
- ½ **teaspoon ground mace**
- ¼ **teaspoon ground allspice**
- ¼ **teaspoon ground nutmeg**
- 8 **cups water**
- 1 **quart dairy eggnog, one 32-ounce can eggnog, or three 12-ounce cans (4½ cups total) evaporated milk**
Pressurized whipped dessert topping
Green crème de menthe or grenadine syrup

In a 1-quart airtight container combine cocoa mix, mace, allspice, and nutmeg. Cover and store at room temperature.

To serve, in a 4½-quart Dutch oven, bring water to boiling. Stir in cocoa mixture, and eggnog or evaporated milk. Heat through. Top each serving with dessert topping and drizzle with crème de menthe or grenadine. Makes 16 to 18 (6-ounce) servings.

For individual servings: For each serving, in a saucepan bring ½ cup *water* to boiling. Stir in ¼ cup cocoa mixture and ¼ cup *dairy or canned eggnog or evaporated milk.* Heat through. Serve as above.

Nutrition information per serving: 210 cal., 5 g pro., 30 g carbo., 9 g fat, 42 mg chol., 149 mg sodium, 284 mg potassium. U.S. RDA: 14% riboflavin, 17% calcium.

PEPPERMINT ICE CREAM TORTE

You'll get two tortes from this recipe—

- 1 **10¾-ounce frozen loaf pound cake**
- 1 **½-gallon carton brick-style peppermint, cherry, or chocolate ice cream**
- 2 **3-ounce packages cream cheese**
- ¼ **cup margarine or butter**
- 1 **teaspoon vanilla**
- 3 **cups sifted powdered sugar**
Crushed red-striped round peppermint candies or candy canes
Red- and green-striped round peppermint candies

For tortes, with a serrated knife, slice cake horizontally into fourths. Halve ice cream lengthwise. Freeze one half for another use. Cut remaining ice cream lengthwise into two 1-inch-thick slices. Place *two* of the cake slices on a baking sheet. Top *each* cake slice with *one* of the ice-cream slices. Top with remaining cake slices. Place in freezer.

In a small mixer bowl beat cream cheese, margarine or butter, and vanilla with an electric mixer on medium speed for 30 seconds or till fluffy. Gradually add powdered sugar, beating till smooth. Pipe or spread over tops and sides of tortes. Freeze till firm.

Place tortes in moisture- and vaporproof containers. Seal, label, and freeze up to 6 months.

To serve, let tortes stand, covered, at room temperature for 10 minutes. Unwrap and place on a serving platter. Sprinkle with crushed candies. Surround with whole candies. Makes 2 tortes, 8 servings each.

Nutrition information per serving: 749 cal., 9 g pro., 99 g carbo., 36 g fat, 167 mg chol., 422 mg sodium, 252 mg potassium. U.S. RDA: 29% vit. A, 23% riboflavin, 17% calcium.

ALMOND TWISTS

How easy! Add a three-ingredient filling to frozen puff pastry—

- ½ **of a 17½-ounce package (1 sheet) frozen puff pastry**
- ½ **cup almond paste**
- 1 **egg**
- ¼ **cup packed brown sugar**
Powdered Sugar Icing (see recipe, page 175)
Coarsely chopped sliced almonds (optional)

Let pastry stand at room temperature for 20 minutes or till easy to roll. Unfold onto a floured surface. Roll pastry into a 14-inch square. Halve with a fluted pastry wheel.

In a small mixer bowl crumble almond paste. Add egg and brown sugar. Beat with an electric mixer on medium speed till combined. Spread over *one* of the pastry halves. Position remaining pastry half over filling. Using a fluted pastry wheel, cut dough into seven 14x1-inch strips. Cut each strip crosswise into quarters (you should have 28). Twist each piece twice. Place twists on an ungreased baking sheet.

Bake in a 400° oven for 12 to 15 minutes or till golden. Cool slightly on a wire rack. Drizzle with Powdered Sugar Icing. Top with almonds. Serve warm. Makes 28.

Freezing directions: Place unbaked twists in a moisture- and vaporproof freezer container. Seal, label, and freeze up to 6 months. To bake, place frozen twists on an ungreased baking sheet. Bake, top, and serve as directed.

Nutrition information per twist: 66 cal., 1 g pro., 9 g carbo., 3 g fat, 10 mg chol., 25 mg sodium, 42 mg potassium.

AMBROSIA SPREAD

- 1 11-ounce can mandarin orange sections, chilled and drained
- 1 8-ounce container soft-style cream cheese with pineapple
- ¼ cup toasted coconut
- ¼ cup toasted chopped almonds
- Whole almonds
- Banana bread and canned date-nut roll

Reserve several orange sections for garnish. Chop remaining sections.

In a medium bowl stir together chopped orange sections, cream cheese, coconut, and chopped almonds.

Spoon into a serving dish. Surround with the whole almonds. Top with the reserved orange sections. Slice banana bread and date-nut roll. Use a cookie cutter to cut banana bread into star shapes. Serve Ambrosia Spread with bread. Makes 2 cups.

Nutrition information per tablespoon: 34 cal., 1 g pro., 2 g carbo., 3 g fat, 0 mg chol., 19 mg sodium, 27 mg potassium.

ANISE BELLS

Crisp, sugar-edged cookies with colorful candy clappers—

- ¾ cup margarine *or* butter
- ¼ teaspoon salt
- ⅔ cup sugar
- 1 egg
- ¼ teaspoon anise extract *or* coconut flavoring
- 1¾ cups all-purpose flour
- Red *or* green colored sugar
- Red and green candy-coated milk chocolate pieces

In a large mixer bowl beat margarine or butter and salt with an electric mixer on medium speed for 30 seconds. Add sugar and beat till fluffy. Add egg and anise extract or coconut flavoring; beat well. Add flour and beat till well combined. Cover and chill about 30 minutes or till easy to handle.

Divide dough in half. Shape dough into two 6-inch rolls. Roll each half in colored sugar. Wrap in moisture- and vaporproof wrap. Freeze dough till firm (4 to 6 hours). *Or,* seal, label, and freeze up to 6 months.

To bake, let dough rolls stand at room temperature for 5 minutes. Cut into ¼-inch-thick slices. Let stand 10 minutes to soften. Place on an ungreased cookie sheet.

Place a milk chocolate piece on the bottom half of each slice for bell clapper. Fold in sides; overlap at top and slightly cover candy (see photo, above).

Bake in a 350° oven for 10 to 12 minutes or till edges and bottoms are very lightly browned. Remove and cool on a wire rack.

To freeze, place in a moisture- and vaporproof freezer container. Seal, label, and freeze up to 12 months. Makes about 48 bells.

Nutrition information per cookie: 59 cal., 1 g pro., 7 g carbo., 3 g fat, 6 mg chol., 46 mg sodium, 7 mg potassium.

REFRIGERATOR COTTAGE COOKIES

Cottage cheese is the secret ingredient that makes these cookies doubly moist and cakelike—

- ¾ cup diced mixed candied fruits and peels
- ½ cup chopped candied pineapple
- ¼ cup brandy
- 1½ cups all-purpose flour
- ½ teaspoon baking powder
- ¼ teaspoon baking soda
- ½ cup margarine *or* butter
- ⅔ cup sugar
- ½ teaspoon vanilla
- 1 egg
- ½ cup cream-style cottage cheese
- Pecan *or* walnut halves
- Diced mixed candied fruits and peels

In a small bowl combine the ¾ cup fruits and peels, pineapple, and brandy. Cover and chill overnight.

Meanwhile, in a small mixing bowl combine flour, baking powder, and baking soda. Set aside.

For batter, in a large mixer bowl beat margarine or butter with an electric mixer on medium speed for 30 seconds. Add sugar and vanilla and beat till fluffy. Add egg and cottage cheese and beat till well combined. Beat in dry ingredients. Cover and chill overnight.

Stir fruit mixture into the batter. Bake immediately. *Or,* cover and chill batter up to 3 weeks.

To bake, drop from a level measuring tablespoon onto an ungreased baking sheet. Press a nut half and additional fruits and peels into top of each dough mound.

Bake in a 375° oven for 9 to 11 minutes or till the bottoms are lightly browned and the tops spring back when lightly touched. Serve warm.

Or, cool completely on a wire rack. Place in a moisture- and vaporproof freezer container. Seal, label, and freeze up to 12 months. To serve, let stand, covered, at room temperature till thawed. Makes about 54.

Nutrition information per cookie: 55 cal., 1 g pro., 8 g carbo., 2 g fat, 5 mg chol., 38 mg sodium, 23 mg potassium.

PROSCIUTTO SOUFFLÉ ROLL IN PARSLEY SAUCE

For rose garnish, tightly roll a narrow strip of very thinly sliced prosciutto—

- ¼ **cup margarine *or* butter**
- ½ **cup all-purpose flour**
- ⅛ **teaspoon ground white pepper**
- 2 **cups milk**
- 6 **beaten egg yolks**
- 6 **egg whites**
- ¼ **teaspoon cream of tartar**
- 6 **ounces thinly sliced prosciutto *or* ham**
- 6 **ounces thinly sliced provolone cheese**

Parsley Sauce
Prosciutto roses (optional)
Parsley sprigs (optional)

Line a 15x10x1-inch baking pan with foil, extending foil 1 inch beyond edges of pan. Grease and lightly flour the foil. Set pan aside.

For soufflé, in a 2-quart saucepan melt margarine or butter. Stir in flour and pepper. Add milk all at once. Cook and stir till mixture is thickened and bubbly. Remove from heat.

In a medium mixing bowl *slowly* stir milk mixture into egg yolks.

In a large mixer bowl beat the egg whites and cream of tartar till stiff peaks form (tips stand straight). Fold a little of the beaten whites into the yolk mixture. Fold the yolk mixture into the remaining beaten egg whites. Spread in the prepared pan.

Bake in a 375° oven about 20 minutes or till puffed and slightly set.

Immediately loosen soufflé from the pan. Turn out onto another large piece of foil. (Remove and discard foil that lines pan.) Place prosciutto or ham and provolone cheese in a thin layer on top of soufflé.

Use foil to roll up soufflé from one of the short sides. Lightly grease the 15x10x1-inch baking pan. Return roll to pan. Cover; chill up to 24 hours.

To serve, heat roll, covered, in a 375° oven about 40 minutes or till heated through. Loosen the ends of the roll where the cheese has melted onto the foil. Using large spatulas transfer the roll to a platter.

Slice the roll with a serrated knife. Serve the slices atop Parsley Sauce. Garnish with prosciutto roses and parsley, if desired. Makes 8 servings.

Parsley Sauce: In a blender container or food processor bowl combine 1 cup *parsley leaves,* 2 cut-up *shallots,* and 2 teaspoons *dried basil or oregano,* crushed. Cover and blend or process till finely chopped.

Add 1½ cups *whipping cream,* 1 tablespoon *cornstarch,* and 1 tablespoon *Dijon-style mustard.* Cover and blend or process till nearly smooth. (*Do not* overblend.) Transfer to a screw-top jar. Cover and chill up to 3 days.

To serve, shake mixture in jar. Transfer to a 1½-quart saucepan. Cook and stir over medium heat till thickened and bubbly. Cook and stir for 1 minute more. Makes 2 cups sauce.

Nutrition information per serving with ¼ cup Parsley Sauce: 439 cal., 19 g pro., 13 g carbo., 35 g fat, 295 mg chol., 657 mg sodium, 336 mg potassium. U.S. RDA: 37% vit. A, 15% vit. C, 19% thiamine, 25% riboflavin, 31% calcium, 12% iron.

GRENADINE FRUIT MÉLANGE

Remember to stir in the kiwi fruit just before serving to keep its bright color—

- 1 **cup cranberries (4 ounces)**
- ½ **cup water**
- ⅓ **cup sugar**
- ¼ **cup currants**
- 1 **teaspoon lemon juice**
- 1 **teaspoon grenadine syrup**
- 4 **plums (about 1 pound), pitted and cut into thin wedges (about 3 cups)**
- 6 **kiwi fruit (about 1½ pounds), peeled, sliced, and slices halved (about 3 cups)**

Fresh mint sprigs (optional)

In a small saucepan stir together the cranberries, water, sugar, currants, lemon juice, and grenadine syrup.

Cook and stir over medium heat for 5 to 7 minutes or till the cranberry mixture reaches the consistency of a thin syrup. Cool slightly.

In a large bowl stir together the cranberry mixture and the plum wedges. Mix well.

Cover bowl and marinate fruit mixture in the refrigerator overnight, stirring occasionally.

To serve, gently stir the kiwi fruit into the fruit mixture. Transfer to a serving bowl.

Garnish with fresh mint sprigs, if desired. Makes 8 servings.

Nutrition information per serving: 107 cal., 1 g pro., 26 g carbo., 1 g fat, 0 mg chol., 4 mg sodium, 302 mg potassium, 3 g dietary fiber. U.S. RDA: 96% vit. C.

SUGAR-TOP MUFFINS

You also can bake these oatmeal muffins right after mixing up the batter—

    1 cup all-purpose flour
    1 cup quick-cooking rolled oats
   ¾ cup packed brown sugar
   ¾ teaspoon baking powder
   ¾ teaspoon baking soda
    1 beaten egg
   ¾ cup milk
   ⅓ cup cooking oil
   ½ cup chopped walnuts
Cinnamon sugar

In a medium mixing bowl stir together the all-purpose flour, quick-cooking rolled oats, brown sugar, baking powder, and baking soda.

In a small mixing bowl stir together the beaten egg, milk, and cooking oil. Add the egg mixture to the flour mixture, stirring just till moistened. Stir in the chopped walnuts. Store muffin batter, tightly covered, in the refrigerator for up to 1 week.

To bake, stir the batter. Grease muffin pans or line with paper bake cups. Fill ⅔ full with batter. Sprinkle the tops of the batter with the cinnamon sugar.

Bake in a 375° oven for 18 to 20 minutes or till muffins are golden. Cool slightly on a wire rack. Serve warm. Makes 12 muffins.

Microwave directions: Prepare and chill batter as directed above.

To serve, stir batter. Line 6-ounce glass custard cups or a microwave-safe muffin pan with paper bake cups. Fill each cup ⅔ full with batter. Sprinkle tops with cinnamon sugar. If using custard cups, arrange in a ring on a microwave-safe plate.

Micro-cook, uncovered, on 100% power (high) for 30 to 60 seconds for 1 muffin, 1 to 2 minutes for 2 muffins, 1½ to 2½ minutes for 4 muffins, or 2½ to 3½ minutes for 6 muffins or till done, giving plate or pan a half-turn after every minute.

To test for doneness, scratch the slightly wet surface with a wooden toothpick. Muffins should be cooked underneath. If using custard cups, remove each cup as muffin is done.

Nutrition information per muffin: 224 cal., 4 g pro., 30 g carbo., 10 g fat, 24 mg chol., 106 mg sodium, 137 mg potassium, 1 g dietary fiber.

CITRUS EYE-OPENER

For ridged orange wedges, use a fruit zester to carve strips from the orange peel before cutting the orange into wedges—

    1 12-ounce can (1½ cups) frozen
       orange juice concentrate
    1 6-ounce can (¾ cup) frozen
       lemonade concentrate
    1 cup water
    1 2-liter bottle carbonated water
       (67.6 ounces)
    1 orange, cut into wedges

In a 1-gallon container stir together the orange juice concentrate, lemonade concentrate, and the 1 cup water. Cover the container and chill in the refrigerator till serving time.

Just before serving, slowly add carbonated water to the container. Stir gently to mix.

Serve citrus mixture over ice. Hook orange wedges on side of glasses or float wedges in punch. Makes about 8 (10-ounce) servings.

Nutrition information per serving: 144 cal., 1 g pro., 36 g carbo., 0 g fat, 0 mg chol., 2 mg sodium, and 296 mg potassium. U.S. RDA: 150% vit. C and 11% thiamine.

GREENS AND PAPAYA SALAD

Mix this dressing right in the bottle!

   1½ teaspoons poppy seed
    1 8-ounce bottle coleslaw salad
       dressing
    1 papaya
    2 heads Bibb *or* Boston lettuce
    1 head Belgian endive
    1 8-ounce can grapefruit sections
       (water pack), drained
   ⅓ cup sliced almonds

Carefully add poppy seed to salad dressing bottle. Cover and shake well. Chill.

Peel, seed, and slice papaya (see photo B, page 172). Line a large platter with Bibb or Boston lettuce leaves. Fan papaya slices to one side of platter. Fan endive to the other side of the platter.

Spoon grapefruit sections down the center of the platter. Sprinkle with nuts. Cover and chill till serving time.

Before serving, shake salad dressing. Drizzle salad dressing over salad. Makes 8 servings.

Nutrition information per serving: 184 cal., 2 g pro., 13 g carbo., 15 g fat, 14 mg chol., 17 mg sodium, 355 mg potassium, 2 g dietary fiber. U.S. RDA: 33% vit. A, 58% vit. C.

VEAL LOIN WITH MUSHROOM AU JUS

1   2½- to 3-pound boneless veal
    sirloin roast *or* beef tenderloin
8   slices bacon (about ½ pound)
½   cup dried mushrooms (such as
    porcini, cepe, *or* shiitake)
¾   cup beef broth
⅓   cup dry red wine
¾   teaspoon fines herbes, crushed
Dash pepper
6   cups water
2   10-ounce packages frozen long
    grain and wild rice mix
Fresh sage, marjoram, and basil
    leaves (optional)

Place meat on a rack in a shallow roasting pan. Lay bacon slices over top of roast, overlapping edges (see photo A, page 172). Insert a meat thermometer into the center of the meat.

Roast in a 425° oven for 45 to 60 minutes or till the thermometer registers 150° (medium). Cover and let stand about 10 minutes before serving.

Meanwhile, soak the dried mushrooms in warm water for 25 minutes. Squeeze water out. Remove and discard stems. Halve or slice mushrooms.

In a small saucepan stir together the mushrooms, beef broth, red wine, fines herbes, and pepper. Bring mixture to boiling. Reduce heat and simmer, covered, for 2 minutes. Remove saucepan from heat. Let stand, covered, till serving time.

In a 4-quart Dutch oven bring the 6 cups water to boiling. Cook frozen rice mix in its pouch in the boiling water according to package directions. Serve rice with meat. Garnish with fresh herbs, if desired. Pass mushroom mixture. Makes 8 servings.

Nutrition information per serving: 280 cal., 37 g pro., 17 g carbo., 11 g fat, 77 mg chol., 607 mg sodium, 458 mg potassium, 2 g dietary fiber. U.S. RDA: 23% thiamine, 21% riboflavin, 44% niacin, 24% iron.

SWEET 'N' SOUR BEET SOUP

1   8¼-ounce can sliced beets
1   8½-ounce can whole white
    potatoes, drained
1   cup beef broth
½   cup light cream *or* milk
½   of a small onion, cut up
2   tablespoons sugar
2   tablespoons vinegar
¼   teaspoon salt
¼   teaspoon pepper
Decorative beet shapes (optional)
Chives and enoki mushrooms

Reserve *four* beet slices. Set the beet slices aside.

In a blender container combine remaining *undrained* beets, whole potatoes, beef broth, light cream or milk, onion, sugar, vinegar, salt, and pepper. Cover and blend till pureed.

Transfer the pureed beet mixture from the blender to a medium saucepan. Cook till heated through, stirring occasionally. *Do not boil.*

Meanwhile, use an hors d'oeuvre cutter to cut 8 decorative shapes from reserved beet slices (see photo D, page 172). Float beet shapes atop individual servings of soup, if desired. Garnish with chives and enoki mushrooms. Makes 8 appetizer servings.

Nutrition information per serving: 67 cal., 1 g pro., 9 g carbo., 3 g fat, 10 mg chol., 293 mg sodium, 138 mg potassium, 1 g dietary fiber.

GRASSHOPPER CHEESECAKE

If your frozen cheesecake has a less-than-beautiful top, drape all of it in fudge topping. Then, add the wafers—

1   6-inch-round frozen plain cream
    cheesecake
6   layered chocolate-mint wafers
Fudge ice-cream topping in squeeze
    bottle
½   cup green crème de menthe

Let cheesecake and wafers stand at room temperature for 25 minutes.

Remove the cheesecake from its container. Score the top into 8 wedges. Using a back-and-forth motion, squeeze the fudge ice-cream topping over *each* wedge (see photo C, page 172).

Cut *four* of the chocolate-mint wafers in half diagonally. Arrange wafers in spoke fashion around the outside edge of the cheesecake, standing the wafers on the cut edge.

To make curls, carefully draw a vegetable peeler across the edge of remaining wafers. Pile the wafer curls around the bottom edge of the cheesecake. Chill till serving time.

Before serving, drizzle green crème de menthe over each serving. Makes 8 servings.

Nutrition information per serving: 318 cal., 5 g pro., 44 g carbo., 11 g fat, 4 mg chol., 140 mg sodium, 127 mg potassium. U.S. RDA: 11% riboflavin.

HAPPY HANUKKAH

FROM THE BORESOW FAMILY

By Joy Taylor

Jewish families everywhere agree: Hanukkah is full of tradition. Don and Harriet Boresow and their 14 children cherish many holiday activities including games and candle lighting. They also share traditions created within their own home. Come join their celebration!

▲ **ALL TOGETHER**
Don and Harriet Boresow with their children, daughter-in-law, and Granny Boresow.

◄ **GLOWING MOMENT**
Danny, the youngest Boresow, lights the menorah while his big brother, Michael, looks on.

HANUKKAH

Michael Boresow lives in Dallas. Dennis lives in St. Louis. Four more Boresow children live away at college. But at Hanukkah, all of the Boresow children, ranging in age from 11 to 29, will be together in Kansas. They'll

● A banner decorates the Boresow home at Hanukkah.

attend a service at Temple B'nai Jehudah in Kansas City, Missouri, share some laughter and games, and feast on their favorite holiday foods.

"With everyone coming and going, we need a special time like Hanukkah to get us all together," says their father Don, a mail carrier.

Prior to out-of-town arrivals, the younger Boresow children eagerly go to work. There's a paper chain to cut and staple, decorations to hang in the family room, and cookies to frost. Once everyone is together, gifts are exchanged—the favorite holiday activity for Danny, aged 11.

"Of course, all the children look forward to opening gifts during Hanukkah, but it's not the most important part of the holiday," explains Harriet. "We instill the idea that being together, caring, sharing, and the love of the family is the greatest gift of all."

● Granny Boresow passes crackers with Chopped Liver to Dennis, 25, and Susan, 27.

▲ GRANNY'S SPECIALTY
Leah Boresow, aged 84, is well-known for her good cooking. Her recipe for chopped liver is a "must" food for Hanukkah and other special family gatherings. "The grandchildren count on me to make their favorite foods," says Granny.

▶ A FAMILY CHAIN
The Boresows' Hanukkah chain was first made when Michael was in kindergarten. He made one out of blue and white paper, the traditional Hanukkah colors. Since then, the paper chain has been remade every year. "It's just not Hanukkah without the chain," says Lori, aged 20.

● Fun work: Amy and Danny make the Hanukkah chain.

● Traditional Hanukkah dishes fill the Boresows' table: Potato Latkes, Cheese Blintzes, and Sweet Noodle Kugel.

"Hanukkah is a real fun time in our house, because we make the decorations and all kinds of food. Mom does most of the cooking, but we all help."

—Amy, aged 12

▲ THE FEAST

Harriet admits that it takes her up to two weeks to plan, shop, and cook for a holiday dinner. But with help from her daughters, the potatoes are fried into latkes, the blintzes are rolled, and the kugel baked. Organization, cooperation, and a large kitchen are the key!

▶ COOKIES TOO!

It takes dozens and dozens of cookies to satisfy the Boresow kids and friends. They make extras because Harriet annually visits the children's grade school to share the Hanukkah story—and cookies!

● Sarah, aged 14, and Harriet frost Hanukkah Cookies.

CHOPPED LIVER

- 3 pounds kosher beef liver, cut ½ inch thick
- 3 large onions, chopped (3 cups)
- 1 bay leaf
- 2 tablespoons cooking oil
- 12 hard-cooked eggs
- 2 tablespoons mayonnaise *or* salad dressing
- ½ teaspoon salt
- ¼ teaspoon pepper
- Lettuce leaves
- Halved cherry tomatoes (optional)
- Sieved hard-cooked egg yolk (optional)
- Snipped chives (optional)
- Assorted crackers

Place *half* of the liver on the unheated rack of a broiler pan. Broil 4 inches from heat about 3 minutes per side or till center is just pink. Repeat with remaining liver. Remove membranes from liver, if present.

In a large saucepan cook the onions and bay leaf in hot oil till onions are tender. Discard bay leaf.

Using the coarse blade of a food grinder, grind the liver, onions, and hard-cooked eggs. Grind again using the fine blade. (*Or*, using the steel blade in a food processor bowl process the mixture, *one-third* at a time, till of desired consistency.)

In a large bowl stir together the liver mixture, mayonnaise or salad dressing, salt, and pepper. Cover the bowl and chill thoroughly.

To serve, mound liver mixture onto a large lettuce-lined plate. Garnish with tomatoes, egg yolk, and chives, if desired. Serve with crackers. Makes 8 cups.

Note: This recipe easily divides in half.

Nutrition information per tablespoon: 27 cal., 3 g pro., 1 g carbo., 1 g fat, 58 mg chol., 31 mg sodium, 40 mg potassium, U.S. RDA: 90% vit. A and 20% riboflavin.

CHEESE BLINTZES

These cheese pillows are a welcome addition to any Hanukkah celebration—

- 1 cup all-purpose flour
- 1½ cups cold water
- 3 eggs
- Cooking oil
- 16 ounces dry-curd farmer cheese *or* dry-curd cottage cheese
- 2 tablespoons margarine, melted
- 1 beaten egg
- 1 tablespoon sugar
- Margarine
- Strawberry preserves
- Dairy sour cream

For batter, in a large mixing bowl combine the flour and ½ teaspoon *salt*. Gradually add cold water, stirring till smooth. Add the 3 eggs, one at a time, beating 1 minute after each addition.

Heat a greased 6-inch skillet over medium heat. Spoon in *2 tablespoons* batter. Lift and tilt skillet to spread batter evenly and coat the bottom of the pan. Return pan to heat. Brown on one side only or till pancake pulls away from side of pan. Invert pan over a paper towel and remove pancake. Cover prepared pancakes with paper towels. Repeat with remaining batter, adding oil as needed.

For filling, in a medium mixing bowl stir together farmer cheese or cottage cheese, the 2 tablespoons margarine, the 1 beaten egg, sugar, and ¼ teaspoon *salt*.

To assemble, place a rounded *tablespoon* of the filling in the center of *each* pancake. Overlap two opposite sides atop filling, then overlap ends to form a pillow shape.

Fry blintzes, *half* at a time, in hot margarine for 4 to 5 minutes per side or till golden brown, adding more margarine as needed to prevent sticking. Transfer to a serving platter. Cover and keep blintzes warm.

Serve immediately with preserves and sour cream. Makes about 20.

To make ahead: Freeze fried blintzes on a baking sheet till firm. Wrap in moisture- and vaporproof wrap. Seal, label, and freeze. To serve, unwrap blintzes and place on an ungreased baking sheet. Bake, uncovered, in a 350° oven for 15 to 20 minutes or till heated through. Serve blintzes as directed.

Nutrition information per blintz: 90 cal., 6 g pro., 6 g carbo., 5 g fat, 58 mg chol., 125 mg sodium, 25 mg potassium.

Bake, covered, in a 350° oven for 30 minutes. Uncover and bake 15 minutes more or till apples are tender.

Nutrition information per serving: 367 cal., 13 g pro., 67 g carbo., 6 g fat, 45 mg chol., 256 mg sodium, 286 mg potassium, 4 g dietary fiber. U.S. RDA: 15% thiamine, 10% riboflavin.

HANUKKAH COOKIES

For extra-bright frostings, use paste food colorings. They won't thin the frosting—

- 2 **cups all-purpose flour**
- 1½ **teaspoons baking powder**
- ⅔ **cup shortening**
- ¾ **cup sugar**
- 1 **egg**
- 1 **tablespoon milk**
- ½ **teaspoon vanilla**
  Almond Icing

In a medium mixing bowl combine flour, baking powder, and ¼ teaspoon *salt*. Set aside.

In a large mixing bowl beat shortening with an electric mixer on medium speed for 30 seconds or till softened. Add sugar; beat till fluffy. Add egg, milk, and vanilla; beat well. Add dry ingredients, beating till well combined. Cover; chill at least 1 hour or overnight.

Divide dough into thirds. On a lightly floured surface, roll each third of the dough ¼ inch thick. (Keep remaining dough chilled.)

Cut with cookie cutters in Hanukkah shapes or use other shape cutters. Dip cookie cutter into flour between cuts. Place on greased cookie sheets.

Bake in a 350° oven for 8 to 10 minutes or till lightly browned. Remove; cool completely on wire racks.

Frost cookies with white or colored Almond Icing. On dreidel-shape cookies, add Hebrew letter in contrasting color, if desired. Makes 60 cookies.

Almond Icing: In a small mixer bowl beat ½ cup *margarine* with an electric mixer on medium speed for 30 seconds or till softened; gradually add 4 cups sifted *powdered sugar*, beating till smooth. Add 4 to 5 tablespoons *milk* and ¼ teaspoon *almond extract* to make of spreading consistency. Divide white icing into small bowls; add a different food color to icing in each bowl.

Nutrition information per cookie: 90 cal., 1 g pro., 12 g carbo., 4 g fat, 5 mg chol., 36 mg sodium, 8 mg potassium.

POTATO LATKES

- 4 **medium potatoes (about 1¼ pounds)**
- 1 **slightly beaten egg**
- 1 **small onion, finely chopped**
- 2 **tablespoons all-purpose flour**
- ½ **teaspoon salt**
- ¼ **teaspoon pepper**
  Cooking oil
  Applesauce (optional)

Peel and coarsely shred potatoes. (Place potatoes in cold water as you work to prevent darkening.) Drain potatoes well. Pat dry with paper towels.

In a large mixing bowl combine shredded potatoes, egg, onion, flour, salt, and pepper. Mix well.

In a 12-inch skillet heat *1 tablespoon* oil over medium-high heat. For each latke, drop potato mixture by tablespoon into hot oil. Fry for 2 to 3 minutes or till edges are crisp. Turn and cook for 2 to 3 minutes more or till golden. Drain on paper towels. Cover and keep warm. Repeat, adding oil as necessary. Serve with applesauce. Makes 20.

To make latkes ahead: Cook and drain as directed above. Cover and chill. To reheat, arrange on an ungreased baking sheet. Bake, uncovered, in a 400° oven for 10 to 12 minutes, turning once.

Nutrition information per latke: 54 cal., 1 g pro., 6 g carbo., 3 g fat, 14 mg chol., 58 mg sodium, 160 mg potassium, 1 g dietary fiber.

SWEET NOODLE KUGEL

- 1 **24-ounce carton cream-style cottage cheese**
- 3 **apples, peeled, cored, and sliced (about 2¾ cups)**
- 1¼ **cups raisins**
- 1 **8-ounce can crushed pineapple**
- 1 **cup sugar**
- 1 **tablespoon ground cinnamon**
- 2 **tablespoons margarine, melted**
- 1 **16-ounce package wide egg noodles, cooked and drained**
  Sliced apples

In a large mixing bowl combine the cottage cheese, the 2¾ cups sliced apples, raisins, and *undrained* pineapple. In a small mixing bowl combine the sugar and cinnamon.

In a greased 13x9x2-inch baking dish place *one-third* of the cooked and drained noodles. Top with *half* of the cottage cheese mixture and *one-third* of the sugar-cinnamon mixture. Place another one-third of the noodles atop, the remaining cottage cheese mixture, and sprinkle with another third of the cinnamon-sugar. End layering with the last of the noodles. Brush noodles with margarine. Sprinkle remaining sugar-cinnamon mixture over all. Arrange additional sliced apples in the middle of the baking dish.

Bake, covered, in a 325° oven about 1 hour or till hot and apples are tender. Serve kugel immediately, spooning juices in bottom of dish over each serving. Makes 12 to 15 servings.

Note: This recipe divides easily in half. Layer noodles, cottage cheese mixture, and cinnamon-sugar as directed above in an 8x8x2-inch baking pan.

MEXICAN FIESTA!
40 MINUTES FROM START TO FEAST
By Barbara Greenwood

Rush-hour cooking for busy families.

..... F I E S T A .....
MENU
STACKS OF CHILI
Chili, hominy, olives, and cheese in tortilla layers.
AVOCADO ORANGE SALAD
A cool contrast to the chili stacks.
LEMONADE
Or, margaritas if you like!

STACKS OF CHILI

Substitute a can of corn for the hominy, if you like—

- 1 24-ounce can chili with beans
- 1 16-ounce can hominy, drained
- 2 to 3 tablespoons jalapeño pepper relish *or* canned chopped jalapeño peppers
- 6 7-inch flour tortillas
- ½ of a 4-ounce package shredded cheddar cheese (½ cup)
- 1 2¼-ounce can sliced pitted ripe olives, drained
- 1 large tomato, cut into thin wedges

Dairy sour cream *or* salsa (optional)
Sliced green onion

● **Preheat the oven to 375°.** In a 2-quart saucepan stir together the chili, hominy, and jalapeño pepper relish or jalapeño peppers; cook and stir till heated through.

● **Meanwhile,** on a lightly greased large baking sheet place 2 of the tortillas side by side. Spoon ⅔ *cup* of the chili mixture onto *each* tortilla. Sprinkle *each* tortilla with about *1 tablespoon* of the cheese and a few olives. Repeat layers twice.

● **Cover baking sheet loosely** with foil. Bake in a 375° oven about 25 minutes or till hot. Cut into wedges; top with tomato, sour cream or salsa, and onion. Makes 2 stacks, 4 servings.

Nutrition information per serving: 443 cal., 20 g pro., 51 g carbo., 18 g fat, 44 mg chol., 1,207 mg sodium, and 5 g dietary fiber. U.S. RDA: 14% vit. A, 14% riboflavin, 17% niacin, 26% calcium, 29% iron, 37% phosphorus.

AVOCADO ORANGE SALAD

Fan thin wedges from 2 chilled *avocados* and sections from 2 chilled *oranges* over *lettuce* leaves. Top with halved *lime* slices. Makes 4 servings.

Nutrition information per serving: 193 cal., 3 g pro., 15 g carbo., 16 g fat, 0 mg chol., 10 mg sodium.

SUPER SANDWICHES
TO BANISH LUNCH-BOX BLAHS

Ensure that your kids eat right when away from home by packing these too-good-to-swap sandwich treats.

By Lynn Hoppe

Make Nutty Cheese Sandwich and Chicken Salad Roll-Ups ahead. In the morning, just pack 'em up and move 'em out.

CHICKEN SALAD ROLL-UPS

Break the routine with a a snazzy version of a chicken salad sandwich that takes on a new shape in a rolled flour tortilla—

- 1 5- *or* 5½-ounce can chunk-style chicken, drained
- ¼ cup sunflower nuts
- ¼ cup mixed dried fruit bits
- ¼ cup thinly sliced celery
  • • •
- ¼ cup mayonnaise *or* salad dressing
- 3 tablespoons lemon yogurt
- 4 6-inch flour tortillas

In a small mixing bowl stir together the chicken, sunflower nuts, dried fruit bits, and sliced celery. Set chicken mixture aside.

For dressing, in a small mixing bowl stir together mayonnaise or salad dressing and lemon yogurt. Add to chicken mixture; toss to coat.

Spread ⅓ cup of the chicken mixture over *each* tortilla to within ½ inch of edge. Roll up tightly; wrap rolled tortilla in clear plastic wrap. Place in a freezer bag or container. Seal, label, and freeze tortillas for up to 1 month.

For *each* serving, pack a frozen filled tortilla in a lunch box or brown bag with a frozen ice pack or a carton of frozen fruit juice. Eat tortilla within 4 hours. Makes 4 servings.

Nutrition information per sandwich: 309 cal., 12 g pro., 26 g carbo., 18 g fat, 31 mg chol., 279 mg sodium. U.S. RDA: 11% thiamine, 14% niacin, 11% calcium, 13% iron, 15% phosphorus.

HOW TO AVOID THE LUNCH-BOX BLUES

▲ The secret to keeping your packed sandwiches safe and fresh is keeping them cold till lunchtime. Add a frozen ice pack designed for coolers and your lunch will remain cold for up to six hours.

▲ These blue plastic ice packs are relatively inexpensive, and you can buy them almost anywhere. Look for this type of ice pack in discount stores, hardware stores, and large grocery stores.

▲ Put your ice pack into the freezer the night before so that it's frozen solid when you add it to your lunch box the next morning.

▲ For a one-way-trip ice pack, a frozen carton of fruit juice is a good alternative. Just place a carton in the freezer the night before and add it to your lunch box in the morning. The juice keeps your sandwich cool and provides a delicious drink, too.

NUTTY CHEESE SANDWICH

This slightly sweet apple-carrot-peanut sandwich spread keeps on call up to one week for kid and adult brown-baggers. Just store it in an airtight container in the refrigerator—

- 1 3-ounce package cream cheese, softened
- ½ cup shredded cheddar *or* colby cheese (2 ounces)
- ½ cup finely shredded carrot *or* zucchini
- 2 teaspoons honey
- 1 small apple *or* pear, cored and coarsely chopped
- ¼ cup chopped peanuts *or* pecans

Whole wheat bread slices

In a medium mixing bowl stir together the softened cream cheese, the shredded cheddar or colby cheese, shredded carrot or zucchini, honey, apple or pear, and peanuts or pecans. Cover and chill the cream cheese mixture up to 1 week.

For *each* cheese sandwich, spread about ¼ *cup* of the cream cheese mixture on *1* slice of whole wheat bread. Top cream cheese mixture with another bread slice.

Pack the individual cheese sandwiches in a lunch box or a brown paper bag with a frozen ice pack. Eat the sandwich within 4 hours of packing. Makes 5 servings.

Nutrition information per sandwich: 232 cal., 9 g pro., 20 g carbo., 14 g fat, 31 mg chol., and 287 mg sodium. U.S. RDA: 69% vit. A, 10% niacin, 13% calcium, and 17% phosphorus.

INDEX

A–B

Acorn Squash Slices, 157
Almond Icing, 185
Almond Twists, 176
Ambrosia Spread, 177
Anise Bells, 177
Antipasto-Style Omelet, 93
Appetizers
  Artichoke-Chili Dip, 123
  Cheese and Spinach Puffs, 123
  Chicken Ham Pinwheels, 124
  Chopped Liver, 184
  Festive Onion Crackers, 13
  Garlic-Spinach Dip, 13
  Ham-Onion Bites, 174
  Melon-Prosciutto Kabobs, 111
  Nut and Raisin Spread, 124
  Parmesan Puff Dough, 174
  Parmesan Puffs, 174
  Pepped-Up Cheese Bake, 173
  Salmon on Corn Cakes, 174
  Salmon-Stuffed Mushrooms, 62
  Shrimp Artichoke Bites, 62
  Tuna-Cucumber Spread, 112
  Wonton Chips, 110
Apple Chicken with Pilaf, 86
Apple-Cinnamon Swirl Loaf, 135
Apricot-Apple Tarts, 161
Apricot-Bran Muffins, 60
Artichoke-Chili Dip, 123
Avocado Orange Salad, 186
Bacon-Cheese Potato Slices, 62
Baked Beans Supreme, 59
Baked Potatoes with Chef's Cheese
  Sauce, 129
Banana Split Cake, 132
Barbecued Pork Ribs, 127
Basic Soup Stock, 144
Basic Yeast Dough, 144
Beef
  Beef Stir-Fry with Blue Cheese, 42
  Better Burgers, 71
  Cincinnati Chili, 16
  Crockery Beef Stew, 27
  Five-Spice Beef in Oyster Sauce, 48
  Green Chili Roundups, 11

Beef *(continued)*
  Hawaiian Chili, 16
  Lasagna in a Bun, 124
  Light 'n' Spicy Tostada Cups, 71
  Meat-Loaf Burrito to Go, 75
  Mozzarella-Stuffed Meat Loaf, 30
  Orange 'n' Spice Pot Roast, 125
  Outside-In-Burgers, 110
  Pepper Steak Salad, 126
  Potato Shell Taco-Pie, 127
  Pot Roast with Spring
    Vegetables, 58
  Reuben Submarine, 27
  Sirloin with Apple-Yogurt
    Sauce, 71
  Skirt Steak with Cream Gravy, 28
  Southern-Style Beef and Slaw
    Special, 75
  Stuffed Manicotti, 10
  Texas Chili, 16
  Texas Ribs, 83
Beggers' Pockets, 91
Better Burgers, 71
Beverages
  Citrus-Eye Opener, 179
  Claret Punch, 123
  Fresh-Fruit Alexanders, 99
  Holiday Apple Fling, 173
  Sparkling Peaches and Cream, 123
  Spiced Eggnog Cocoa, 176
Blackened Fish, 84
Blueberry-Apple Crisp, 30
Bok Choy Relish, 46
Breads
  Apple-Cinnamon Swirl Loaf, 135
  Apricot-Bran Muffins, 60
  Basic Yeast Dough, 144
  Brown 'n' Serve Cloverleaves, 146
  Butterhorns, 135
  Cheese Twist, 146
  Confetti Corn Bread, 60
  Corn-Rye Biscuits, 135
  Croissants with Cheese, 88
  Crusty Oat Bread, 145
  French Mustard Slices, 123
  Holiday Spiral Loaf, 175
  Hot Cross Buns, 59
  Mincemeat Bread Wreath, 175
  Molasses Corn Bread, 136
  Raspberry Bran Muffins, 136
  Raspberry-Cream Cheese Coffee
    Cake, 136

Breads *(continued)*
  Rosettes, 135
  Shortcut Cloverleafs, 135
  Sugar-Top Muffins, 179
  Whole Wheat and Cottage Cheese
    Roll, 135
  Wild Rice Braid, 160
  Yogurt Dill Bread, 173
Broccoli and Wild Rice Bake, 130
Brownie Fruit Torte, 46
Brown 'n' Serve Cloverleaves, 146
Bulgur-Raisin Pilaf, 29
Burnt-Sugar Chiffon Cake, 133
Burnt-Sugar Frosting, 133
Butterhorns, 135

C

Cajun-Style Seafood Stew, 11
Cakes
  Banana Split Cake, 132
  Burnt-Sugar Chiffon Cake, 133
  Carrot Cake with Pineapple, 60
  Carrot-Coconut Cake, 110
  Pumpkin Cake Roll, 132
  Raspberry-Glazed Pound Cake, 112
  Swiss Nut Torte, 133
Camembert Soufflé, 127
Caramel-Banana Cups, 112
Caramel-Pear Flan, 162
Caramel Pecan Brownies, 134
Carrots
  Carrot Cake with Pineapple, 60
  Carrot-Coconut Cake, 110
  Carrot-Parsnip Mousse, 159
Cheese
  Cheese and Spinach Puffs, 123
  Cheese and Vegetable Pizza, 139
  Cheese Blintzes, 184
  Cheese Twist, 146
Cherry-Chocolate Smiles, 111
Chicken
  Apple Chicken with Pilaf, 86
  Five-Spice Game Hens, 86
  Chicken à la Maria, 124
  Chicken and Creamy
    Mushrooms, 57
  Chicken Ham Pinwheels, 124
  Chicken Salad Roll-Ups, 187

Chicken *(continued)*
  Chicken Spaetzle Chowder, 146
  Chicken with Sweet Potato Pilaf, 43
  Curried Chicken Croissant, 75
  Hawaiian Chicken Stir-Fry, 49
  Indian Chicken and Rice, 94
  Italian Artichokes and Chicken, 95
  Orange-Sauced Chicken, 29
  Plum Delicious Chicken, 95
  Sesame Chicken and Rice
    Salad, 111
Chinese Noodle Skillet, 33
Chocolate
  Cherry-Chocolate Smiles, 111
  Chocolate and Vanilla Tarts, 132
  Chocolate-Covered Cherry
    Cookies, 133
  Chocolate-Praline Pie, 162
  Fudge Brownie Pie, 25
  Ice-Cream with Hot Fudge
    Sauce, 61
Chopped Liver, 184
Cincinnati Chili, 16
Citrus Eye-Opener, 179
Claret Punch, 123
Coleslaw Soufflé Salad, 131
Common Pastry Problems, 161
Confetti Corn Bread, 60
Cookies
  Anise Bells, 177
  Caramel Pecan Brownies, 134
  Chocolate-Covered Cherry
    Cookies, 133
  Hanukkah Cookies, 185
  Oatmeal Caramel Bars, 61
  Refrigerator Cottage Cookies, 177
Cordon Bleu Casserole, 103
Corn-Rye Biscuits, 135
Creamed Seafood and Pasta, 33
Creamy Celery-Zucchini Soup, 129
Creamy Turkey Sauté, 93
Crockery Beef Stew, 27
Croissants with Cheese, 88
Crusty Oat Bread, 145
Cumin-Spiked Acorn Squash, 12
Curried Chicken Croissant, 75
Curry Slices, 130

D–F

Desserts (see also Cakes and Pies)
  Almond Twists, 176
  Apricot-Apple Tarts, 161
  Banana Split Cake, 132
  Blueberry-Apple Crisp, 30
  Brownie Fruit Torte, 46
  Burnt-Sugar Chiffon Cake, 133
  Camembert Soufflé, 127
  Caramel-Banana Cups, 112
  Caramel-Pear Flan, 162
  Caramel Pecan Brownies, 134
  Carrot-Coconut Cake, 110
  Cheese Blintzes, 184
  Cherry-Chocolate Smiles, 111
  Chocolate and Vanilla Tarts, 132
  Chocolate-Praline Pie, 162
  Frosty Strawberry Squares, 134
  Fudge Brownie Pie, 25
  Grasshopper Cheesecake, 180
  Ice Cream with Hot-Fudge
    Sauce, 61
  Lemon-Nut Ice Cream, 131
  Marble Cheesecake, 131
  Melon Cream with Berries, 99
  Peach-Almond Kuchen, 99
  Pear-Date Pie, 42
  Peppermint Ice Cream Torte, 176
  Pumpkin Cake Roll, 132
  Raisin Puffs with Orange
    Sauce, 134
  Raspberry-Glazed Pound Cake, 112
  Rhubarb Pie, 61
  Strawberry Pie Deluxe, 131
  Sweet Cherry-Nut Tart, 100
  Sweet Noodle Kugel, 185
  Swiss Nut Torte, 133
Deviled Crab Lobster Tails, 84
Dips and Spread
  Ambrosia Spread, 177
  Artichoke-Chili Dip, 123
  Garlic-Spinach Dip, 13
  Nut and Raisin Spread, 124
  Tuna-Cucumber Spread, 112
Fennel Butter, 158
Festive Onion Crackers, 13
Fish and Seafood
  Blackened Fish, 84
  Cajun-Style Seafood Stew, 11
  Creamed Seafood and Pasta, 33
  Deviled Crab Lobster Tails, 84

Fish and Seafood *(continued)*
  Horseradish-Dill Trout, 85
  Lemon Shrimp Oriental, 126
  Lime-Seasoned Salmon, 85
  Linguine with White Clam
    Sauce, 58
  Red Snapper Veracruz, 126
  Salmon on Corn Cakes, 174
  Salmon-Stuffed Mushrooms, 62
  Seafood Gumbo, 145
  Sesame Fish with Bok Choy
    Relish, 46
  Shrimp Artichoke Bites, 62
  Shrimp-Zucchini Pizza, 43
  Speedy Salmon Fillet, 88
  Stuffed Flounder Florentine, 103
  Super Salmon Burgers, 28
  Tuna Cucumber Spread, 112
Five-Fruit Salad with Peanut
  Butter, 132
Five Spice Beef in Oyster Sauce, 48
Five-Spice Game Hens, 86
French Mustard Slices, 123
Fresh-Fruit Alexanders, 99
Frosty Strawberry Squares, 134
Fruited Spare Ribs, 84
Fruits
  Apple-Cinnamon Swirl Loaf, 135
  Apricot-Apple Tarts, 161
  Brownie Fruit Torte, 46
  Caramel-Pear Flan, 162
  Five-Fruit Salad with Peanut
    Butter, 132
  Fresh-Fruit Alexanders, 99
  Frosty Strawberry Squares, 134
  Fruited Spare Ribs, 84
  Gingerberry Lattice Pie, 161
  Grenadine Fruit Mélange, 178
  Lemon Fresh Waldorf Salad, 111
  Melon Cream with Berries, 99
  Melon-Prosciutto Kabobs, 111
  Peach-Almond Kuchen, 99
  Pear-Date Pie, 42
  Plum Delicious Chicken, 95
  Quick Cranberry Relish, 159
  Rainbow Fruit Bowl, 109
  Raspberry Bran Muffins, 136
  Raspberry Cream-Cheese Coffee
    Cake, 136
  Raspberry Glazed Pound Cake, 112
  Rhubarb Pie, 61
  Sparkling Peaches and Cream, 123

Index

Fruits *(continued)*
  Strawberry Pie Deluxe, 131
  Summer Sampler with Custard, 100
  Sweet Cherry-Nut Tart, 100
  Tossed Turkey, Greens, and
    Berries, 65
Fudge Brownie Pie, 25

G–L

Garlic-Spinach Dip, 13
Gingerberry Lattice Pie, 161
Gingered Turkey Stir-Fry, 12
Grasshopper Cheesecake, 180
Green Chili Roundups, 11
Green Pea Guacamole, 45
Greens and Papaya Salad, 179
Grenadine Fruit Mélange, 178
Hanukkah Cookies, 185
Ham
  Chicken à la Maria, 124
  Chicken Ham Pinwheels, 124
  Chinese Noodle Skillet, 33
  Ham-Onion Bites, 174
  Ham with Orange-Raisin Sauce, 57
  Home-Style Ham 'n' Bean Soup, 27
  Moroccan Salad Express, 65
  Pepper Ham, 95
  Prosciutto Soufflé Roll in
    Parsley Sauce, 178
  Stuffed to the Rim Vegetable
    Roll, 74
Ham-Onion Bites, 174
Ham with Orange-Raisin Sauce, 57
Harvest Vegetables with Edam
  Cheese, 158
Hawaiian Baked Beans, 109
Hawaiian-Chicken Stir Fry, 49
Hawaiian Chili, 16
Hazelnut-Pesto Turkey Breast, 85
Hearty Bean Stew, 44

Hock 'n' Bean Soup, 145
Holiday Apple Fling, 173
Holiday Spiral Loaf, 175
Home-Style Ham 'n' Bean Soup, 27
Homemade Cajun Seasoning, 11
Homemade Chili Powder, 11
Homemade Curry Powder, 11
Homemade Garam Masala, 11
Honey Sauterne Jelly, 128
Horseradish-Dill Trout, 85
Hot Cross Buns, 59
Ice Cream with Hot-Fudge Sauce, 61
Iced Almonds, 123
Idaho Chili, 16
Indian Chicken and Rice, 94
Italian Artichokes and Chicken, 95
Lasagna in a Bun, 124
Lasagna Pie, 44
Lemons
  Lemon-Fresh Waldorf Salad, 111
  Lemon-Nut Ice Cream, 131
  Lemon Shrimp Oriental, 126
Light 'n' Spicy Tostada Cups, 71
Lime-Seasoned Salmon, 85
Linguine with White Clam Sauce, 58

M–O

Marble Cheesecake, 131
Marinated Mushrooms and
  Vegetables, 128
Marshmallow-Pecan Squash, 130
Meat-Loaf Burrito to Go, 75
Melon Cream with Berries, 99
Melon-Prosciutto Kabobs, 111
Microwave Recipes
  Apricot Apple Tarts, 161
  Apricot-Bran Muffins, 60
  Artichoke Chili Dip, 123
  Bacon-Cheese Potato Slices, 62
  Baked Beans Supreme, 59
  Basic Yeast Dough, 144
  Beef Stir-Fry with Blue Cheese, 42
  Blueberry-Apple Crisp, 30
  Brownie Fruit Torte, 46
  Caramel Pear Flan, 162
  Carrot Cake with Pineapple, 60
  Carrot-Parsnip Mousse, 159
  Chicken and Creamy
    Mushrooms, 57
  Chicken Spaetzle Chowder, 146
  Chicken with Sweet Potato Pilaf, 43
  Confetti Corn Bread, 60
  Cordon Bleu Casserole, 103
  Cumin-Spiked Acorn Squash, 12
  Gingerberry Lattice Pie, 161
  Gingered Turkey Stir-Fry, 12

Microwave Recipes *(continued)*
  Ham with Orange-Raisin Sauce, 57
  Hawaiian Baked Beans, 109
  Hock 'n' Bean Soup, 145
  Home Style Ham 'n' Bean Soup, 27
  Hot Cross Buns, 59
  Ice Cream Hot Fudge Sauce, 61
  Lasagna Pie, 44
  Mozzarella-Stuffed Meat Loaf, 30
  Oatmeal Caramel Bars, 61
  Orange-Sauced Chicken, 29
  Parmesan Potato Salad, 109
  Pepped-Up Cheese Bake, 173
  Pork Chop and Vegetable
    Skillet, 26
  Pork Chops with Sweet-Sour
    Cabbage, 45
  Pork Tenderloin with Gingered
    Fruit Sauce, 72
  Pot Roast with Spring
    Vegetables, 58
  Pumpkin-Mushroom Soup, 160
  Rainbow Fruit Bowl, 109
  Rhubarb Pie, 61
  Salmon on Corn Cakes, 174
  Salmon Stuffed Mushrooms, 62
  Saucy Meatball Sandwich, 57
  Sausage-Spinach Loaf, 25
  Seafood Gumbo, 145
  Sesame Fish with Bok Choy
    Relish, 46
  Shrimp Artichoke Bites, 62
  Skirt Steak with Cream Gravy, 28
  Stuffed Flounder Florentine, 103
  Sugar-Top Muffins, 179
  Texas Ribs, 83
  Vegetables Hollandaise, 58
Mincemeat Bread Wreath, 175
Molasses Corn Bread, 136
Moroccan Salad Express, 65
Mozzarella-Stuffed Meat Loaf, 30
Mustard-Glazed Pork Chops, 12
Nut and Raisin Spread, 124
Nutty Cheese Sandwich, 187
Oatmeal Caramel Bars, 61
Onion Knockwursts, 94
Oranges
  Orange Cream, 161
  Orange Custard Sauce, 100
  Orange 'n' Spice Pot Roast, 125

Oranges *(continued)*
  Orange Sauce, 134
  Orange-Sauced Chicken, 29
Oriental-Style Pork Steaks, 125
Outside-In-Burgers, 110

P–R

Pan Gravy for Roast Turkey, 157
Parmesan Potato Salad, 109
Parmesan Puff Dough, 174
Parmesan Puffs, 174
Parsley Sauce, 178
Pasta
  Creamed Seafood and Pasta, 33
  Chinese Noodle Skillet, 33
  Lemon-Fresh Waldorf Salad, 111
  Linguine with White Clam
    Sauce, 58
  Spaghetti Ring Florentine, 130
  Spinach Pasta Salad, 109
  Sweet Noodle Kugel, 185
Pastry for Double-Crust Pie, 161
Pastry for Single-Crust Pie, 162
Peach-Almond Kuchen, 99
Peanut-Sauced Ribs, 83
Pear-Date Pie, 42
Pepped-Up Cheese Bake, 173
Pepper Cheese Vegetables, 110
Peppered Meatballs in Tomato
  Sauce, 71
Pepper Ham, 95
Peppermint Ice Cream Torte, 176
Pepper Salad, 88
Pepper Steak Salad, 126
Pick-a-Cheese Pita Pocket, 75
Pies
  Chocolate-Praline Pie, 162
  Gingerberry Lattice Pie, 161
  Pear-Date Pie, 42
  Rhubarb Pie, 61
Pineapple Frosting, 60
Pizza Turnovers, 138
Plum Delicious Chicken, 95
Pork (see also Ham)
  Barbecued Pork Ribs, 127
  Fruited Spare Ribs, 84
  Hawaiian Chili, 16

Pork *(continued)*
  Mustard-Glazed Pork Chops, 12
  Oriental-Style Pork Steaks, 125
  Peanut-Sauced Ribs, 83
  Peppered Meatballs in Tomato
    Sauce, 71
  Pork Chop and Vegetable
    Skillet, 26
  Pork Chops with Sweet-Sour
    Cabbage, 45
  Pork Tenderloin with Gingered
    Fruit Sauce, 72
  Pork with Pineapple, 91
  Pork with Spring Rhubarb
    Sauce, 72
  Saucy Meatball Sandwich, 57
  Sausage-Spinach Loaf, 25
  Stuffed Crown of Ribs, 83
  Szechwan Pork Roast, 13
  Vegetable and Pork Stir-Fry, 72
Potato Latkes, 185
Potato-Shell Taco Pie, 127
Pot Roast with Spring Vegetables, 58
Powder Sugar Icing, 175
Prosciutto Soufflé Roll in Parsley
  Sauce, 178
Pumpkin Cake Roll, 132
Pumpkin-Mushroom Soup, 160
Quick Cranberry Relish, 159
Rainbow Fruit Bowl, 109
Raisin Puffs with Orange Sauce, 134
Raspberries
  Raspberry Bran Muffins, 136
  Raspberry-Cream Cheese Coffee
    Cake, 136
  Raspberry-Glazed Pound Cake, 112
Red Chili Oil, 13
Red-Pepper Two-Grain Salad, 13
Red Snapper Veracruz, 126
Refrigerator Cottage Cookies, 177
Reuben Submarine, 27
Rhubarb Pie, 61
Rice
  Broccoli and Wild Rice Bake, 130
  Indian Chicken and Rice, 94
  Sesame Chicken and Rice
    Salad, 111
Rosettes, 135

S

Salads
  Avocado Orange Salad, 186
  Coleslaw Soufflé Salad, 131
  Five-Fruit Salad with Peanut
    Butter, 132
  Greens and Papaya Salad, 179
  Lemon-Fresh Waldorf Salad, 111
  Moroccan Salad Express, 65
  Parmesan Potato Salad, 109
  Pepper Salad, 88
  Pepper Steak Salad, 126
  Rainbow Fruit Bowl, 109
  Red-Pepper Two-Grain Salad, 13
  Sarah's Salad, 129
  Sesame Chicken and Rice
    Salad, 111
  Spinach Pasta Salad, 109
  Tossed Turkey, Greens, and
    Berries, 65
  Wilted Savory Salad, 92
Salmon on Corn Cakes, 174
Salmon-Stuffed Mushrooms, 62
Sandwiches
  Better Burgers, 71
  Lasagna in a Bun, 124
  Onion Knockwursts, 94
  Outside-In-Burgers, 110
  Reuben Submarine, 27
  Saucy Meatball Sandwich, 57
  Super Salmon Burgers, 28
Sarah's Salad, 129
Saucy Meatball Sandwich, 57
Sausage
  Onion Knockwursts, 94
  Sausage-Spinach Loaf, 25
  Savory Sausage Stew, 128
  Turkey with Sausage-Rice Stuffing,
    157
Seafood Gumbo, 145
Seasonal Vegetables, 158
Sesame Chicken and Rice Salad, 111
Sesame Fish with Bok Choy
  Relish, 46
Shortcut Cloverleafs, 135
Shrimp Artichoke Bites, 62

Index

Shrimp-Zucchini Pizza, 43
Sirloin with Apple-Yogurt Sauce, 71
Skirt Steak with Cream Gravy, 28
Soups
  Basic Soup Stock, 144
  Cajun-Style Seafood Stew, 11
  Chicken Spaetzle Chowder, 146
  Cincinnati Chili, 16
  Creamy Celery-Zucchini Soup, 129
  Crockery Beef Stew, 27
  Hawaiian Chili, 16
  Hearty Bean Stew, 44
  Hock 'n' Bean Soup, 145
  Home-Style Ham 'n' Bean Soup, 27
  Idaho Chili, 16
  Pumpkin-Mushroom Soup, 160
  Savory Sausage Stew, 128
  Seafood Gumbo, 145
  Sweet 'n' Sour Beet Soup, 180
  Texas Chili, 16
Southern-Style Beef and Slaw
  Special, 75
Southern Tostadas, 92
Spaghetti Ring Florentine, 130
Sparkling Peaches and Cream, 123
Speedy Salmon Fillet, 88
Spiced Cheese Sauce, 10
Spiced Eggnog Cocoa, 176
Spices
  Homemade Cajun Seasoning, 11
  Homemade Chili Powder, 11
  Homemade Curry Powder, 11
  Homemade Garam Masala, 11
  Red Chili Oil, 13
Spinach and Potato Pie, 94
Spinach Pasta Salad, 109
Stacks of Chili, 186
Strawberry Pie Deluxe, 131
Stuffed Crown of Ribs, 83
Stuffed Flounder Florentine, 103
Stuffed Manicotti, 10
Stuffed-to-the-Rim Vegetable Roll, 74
Stuffing a Turkey, 157
Sugar-Top Muffins, 179
Summer Sampler with Custard, 100
Super Salmon Burgers, 28
Sweet Cherry-Nut Tart, 100
Sweet Noodle Kugel, 185
Sweet 'n' Sour Beet Soup, 180
Sweet Pastry for 10-inch Flan
  Pan, 162
Swiss Nut Torte, 133
Szechwan Pork Roast, 13

T–Z

Texas Chili, 16
Texas Pinto Beans, 16
Texas Ribs, 83
Tomato and Broccoli Bake, 129
Tossed Turkey, Greens, and
  Berries, 65
Tuna-Cucumber Spread, 112
Turkey
  Creamy Turkey Sauté, 93
  Gingered Turkey Stir-Fry, 12
  Hazelnut-Pesto Turkey Breast, 85
  Lasagna Pie, 44
  Tossed Turkey, Greens and
    Berries, 65
  Turkey Fajitas with Green Pea
    Guacamole, 45
  Turkey with Chestnut-Fig
    Stuffing, 157
  Turkey with Curry Sauce, 125
  Turkey with Fennel-Seafood
    Stuffing, 158
  Turkey with Sausage-Rice
    Stuffing, 157
Veal Loin with Mushroom Au
  Jus, 180
Vegetable and Pork Stir-Fry, 72
Vegetables
  Acorn Squash Slices, 157
  Bacon-Cheese Potato Slices, 62
  Baked Beans Supreme, 59
  Baked Potatoes with Chef's Cheese
    Sauce, 129
  Broccoli and Wild Rice Bake, 130
  Carrot-Parsnip Mousse, 159
  Chinese Noodle Skillet, 33
  Coleslaw Soufflé Salad, 131
  Creamy Celery-Zucchini Soup, 129
  Cumin-Spiked Acorn Squash, 12
  Curry Slices, 130
  Harvest Vegetables with Edam
    Cheese, 158
  Hawaiian Baked Beans, 109
  Hearty Bean Stew, 44
  Idaho Chili, 16
  Marinated Mushrooms and
    Vegetables, 128
  Marshmallow-Pecan Squash, 130
  Parmesan Potato Salad, 109
  Pepper Cheese Vegetables, 110
  Pepper Steak Salad, 126
  Potato Latkes, 185
  Spinach and Potato Pie, 94
  Spinach Pasta Salad, 109
  Tomato and Broccoli Bake, 129
  Vegetable and Pork Stir-Fry, 72
  Vegetables Hollandaise, 58
Wheat Germ Topping, 60
Whole Wheat and Cottage Cheese
  Rolls, 135
Wild Rice Braid, 160
Wilted Savory Salad, 92
Wonton Chips, 110
Yogurt Dill Bread, 173

Microwave Wattage

All microwave recipes were tested in countertop microwave ovens that provide 600 to 700 watts of cooking power. The cooking times are approximate because microwave ovens vary by manufacturer.

Nutrition Analysis

Some nutrient information is given by gram weight per serving. The United States Recommended Daily Allowances (U.S. RDAs) for selected vitamins and minerals are given in the recipes when the value exceeds 10 percent. The U.S. RDAs tell the amounts of certain nutrients necessary to meet the dietary needs of most healthy people.

To obtain the nutrition analysis of each recipe, the following guidelines were used:
● When ingredient options appear in a recipe, the analysis was calculated using the first ingredient choice.
● Optional ingredients were omitted in the analyses.
● The nutrition analyses for recipes calling for fresh ingredients were calculated using the measurements for raw fruits, vegetables, and meats.
● If a recipe gives optional serving sizes (such as "Makes 6 to 8 servings"), the nutrition analyses was calculated using the first choice.